THE GATHERING DARKNESS

The Fourth Awakening Series

Be careful what you wish for. A year earlier, with the help of enigmatic industrialist Michael Walker, all of Penelope Drayton Spence's dreams had come true. Now, as one of the country's top journalists, she has discovered what she thought would make her happy was only making her busy.

After months of avoiding her, Michael Walker burst back into her life with an outlandish plan to launch his controversial "Hermes" satellite into space. But she soon learns someone just as resourceful and well-financed is willing to go to any lengths to stop the launch.

After the Hermes Project's facility in Jackson Hole is attacked, Penelope gets a ringside seat as two of the world's most powerful men go toe-to-toe in a battle of wills that could change the course of humanity.

FROM THE PUBLISHER

THE FIRST BOOK in this series, "The Fourth Awakening" focused on the science and history of the previous awakenings. "The Gathering Darkness" explores what all this means on a more personal level. Penelope, like so many before her, has started down the path toward enlightenment but has lost her way.

Throughout this fast-paced thriller are gentle clues and suggestions that readers can use to advance their personal growth. By presenting this science in a Joseph Campbell "myth" format, the authors are striving to capture the timeless "around the campfire" storytelling that will resonate on multiple levels.

ABOUT THE AUTHORS

ROD PENNINGTON HAS seven previous novels, including his recent dark comedy entitled "A Family Reunion." It is a continuing series about a dysfunctional family of four of the world's best assassins working as the enforcement arm for a shadowy Zen cabal that has been around for thousands of years.

JEFFERY A. MARTIN, PhD, is a Harvard-trained scholar specializing in higher states of consciousness. He is the author, co-author, or contributor to over twenty books in addition to numerous other scholarly and non-scholarly publications, videos, audio, and other media. The methods and science in the Fourth Awakening series that can have an immediate impact on most readers' lives can be found in his recent book, "The God Formula: A simple scientifically proven blueprint that has transformed millions of lives."

THE GATHERING DARKNESS

The Fourth Awakening Series

ROD PENNINGTON
&
JEFFERY A. MARTIN

Integration Press, LLC
Charleston, SC

CHAPTER ONE

A LIGHT TAPPING ON the door brought a smile to Penelope Drayton Spence's face. As usual, Michael Walker was right on time. Penelope paused at the door and closed her eyes. Even though, before last night, they had only briefly seen each other once in the past three months, just being in the same room had seemed to rekindle something. Having been out of the dating game for more years than she cared to admit, Penelope wasn't exactly sure what she felt but was hopeful a quiet breakfast together would bring some clarity to the matter.

She drew in a deep cleansing breath but it didn't do much to help her relax. Her heart was racing like a school girl's on prom night. After checking her hair in the mirror, she turned the knob. Her heart jumped into her throat when suddenly five men in suits and sunglasses burst unceremoniously past her and entered the room. Her shoulders relaxed, a bit, when she saw Michael Walker's personal bodyguard, Lucas Haley, cross the threshold.

"Good Lord, not again," Penelope shook her head and muttered. The first man to enter the room had already sprinted across it and pulled the curtains shut, blotting out the view of Central Park. The others fanned out and began inspecting the rest of her suite.

For a variety of reasons, some she understood and some he never fully explained, Michael Walker occasionally felt the need to provide her with one or more of his testosterone troopers. Knowing the intrusions always rankled her, Walker usually sent a familiar face along to calm the waters. This wasn't Haley's first dramatic entrance and, knowing Michael Walker, it probably wouldn't be his last.

Once again Penelope slowly drew in a breath and tried to calm herself, but she wasn't having any success. Six months earlier she could have easily released this unexpected jolt. She frowned when she realized that her many excuses for dodging yoga in the past year were finally catching up with her. Lately when it came to controlling these types of pesky emotions, she was definitely out of practice, and luck. She could still easily handle the small bumps in the road of life but when she hit an unexpected pothole like this it was another matter entirely. She sighed. Who was she kidding? Recently even the small bumps had become a challenge.

The five men with Haley were different from the beef brigade he usually surrounded her with; they were all compact in build with short military style haircuts and deep tans. They looked like they would be more comfortable poolside than in their current attire of dark designer suits and ties. "What's going on, Lucas?" Penelope snapped, more annoyed with herself than Haley.

Before she could get an answer, there were three soft raps on the door. Out of nowhere, four of the five men accompanying Haley had automatic weapons in their hands. She had always assumed that Haley and his playmates were armed, but this was the first time she had actually seen physical proof. The sight of the guns was unnerving enough, but what sent a chill up her spine was that Haley didn't instantly order them put back in their holsters.

Something was obviously very different today.

Penelope felt a hand on her elbow and the only bodyguard without a weapon in his hand began directing her toward the bedroom. As they reached the door, she heard a familiar voice behind her. "Have you lost your mind?"

"Sally?" Spence shouted as she tried to slow her momentum down without much success. "Is that you?"

"Yes," answered Sally Winters, VP of Public Relations for Walker Industries. "Put those things away."

"Stand down," Haley said in a serious, deep baritone that perfectly matched his height and weight, as he motioned for the men to put away their weapons.

"What were you thinking?" Winters demanded as she glared up at Lucas Haley; the top of her head barely clearing his chin.

Haley shrugged. "The boss said 'Code Red' and these guys happened to be with me." A broad smile that seemed to be permanently affixed on his face didn't flicker. "You got a problem, take it up with him."

"What's going on?" Penelope asked as she squeezed past the undersized bodyguard who was still partially blocking her way. "Where's Michael?"

"He already left," Winters answered. "We need to get you out of here."

"Why?"

"The Wyoming compound was attacked," Winters said as she hit the speed dial on one of her multiple cell phones.

"What happened? Was anybody hurt?"

Sally Winters held up a finger. "We have her." She dropped the phone back in her oversized purse. "Let's go. Leave your stuff. We'll have someone get it for you."

"Go? Why do I have to go?"

"You may be the next target."

CHAPTER TWO

"DAMN IT, MICHAEL. That's just crazy!" The man in a business suit said as he slammed his fist on the arm of his chair.

Penelope Spence hesitated in the doorway of the Gulfstream G550 with a Walker Industries logo on the tailfin, unsure if she should enter or not. Michael Walker, CEO of Walker Industries, was deep in conversation around a small conference table near the rear of the jet. Crammed in across the table, in a space designed for two, were three men in dark blue suits. Hovering over Walker's shoulder was his personal aide, Timothy Ellison.

Walker and Ellison were both dressed casually in Dockers, and each wore a deep violet-colored golf shirt with the company logo embroidered over the left breast. Walker was tanned and incredibly fit for a man his age; he radiated vitality and confidence. Next to his boss, Timothy Ellison was like a remake of a favorite song two decades later. While the newer version wasn't an exact copy of the original, it was close enough that you could comfortably hum along. Walker caught a glimpse of Penelope and his intense blue gray eyes locked on her. He acknowledged the new arrivals with a small, barely perceptible nod before turning his full attention back to the grim-faced men across the table from him. Ellison, who had followed his boss's eyes to the front of the plane, excused himself from the meeting and joined Penelope and the other new arrivals.

"They're just about to wrap this up," Ellison said softly.

"Looks serious," Penelope said as she glanced past Ellison toward the men, listening silently as Michael Walker addressed them. "Is it about the attack on the compound?"

"No," Ellison answered, pulling back as if surprised by the question. "It's corporate stuff."

When it was clear no additional information about the conference was going to be shared, Penelope smiled warmly at the handsome young man. Not only was he Walker's personal assistant, he had been dating

Penelope's eldest daughter, Carrie, off and on for almost a year. With Carrie now living in Boston and Ellison seldom more than an arm's length from Walker's side, they had challenged the limits of long distance dating. Still, twelve months for her high energy little darling was approaching a lifetime best for a long-term commitment. "I haven't heard a peep out of Carrie for over a week. With her," Penelope said with a weak smile, "I always assume no news is good news."

Ellison pursed his lips and avoided Penelope's eyes. "I talked to her earlier today," he answered and left it at that.

"*Oh boy*," Penelope thought to herself. She had seen that look from Carrie's suitors before. There was trouble in paradise. Since the wound appeared fresh, she decided not to press the issue. Still, this was another recent example of her mother radar malfunctioning. Usually when one of her three children was in distress she would sense it long before the tearful call arrived. Lately, swept up in the new complexity of her own life, Penelope hadn't been hearing any of the faint early warning bells. These days if it wasn't about her or her career, it took seventy-six trombones or a fog horn to penetrate the shell she had allowed to form around her.

The sound of Michael Walker's voice shook her back to reality.

"Gentlemen, this isn't a discussion." Walker, as usual, was calm and relaxed; Penelope had never met anyone as comfortable in his own skin as he was. While he had a smile on his face, his voice had an edge Penelope had never heard before. "You have your instructions. Draw up the papers." The three men on the other side of the conference table exchanged concerned glances, but none was willing to pursue the issue further.

"We're done here." Walker stood up and shook hands with each of the men. "I want these documents prepared by someone you trust. Make sure there are no leaks. I don't need to remind you of the implications if any of this gets out." The three men nodded their heads, packed up their briefcases and left. As soon as the last man had exited the plane, the steps were retracted and the twin Rolls Royce turbo fan engines started to rev.

Walker joined the others and fell heavily into the oversized leather chair closest to the cockpit. He motioned for Penelope to take the seat across the aisle from him. With Penelope and Walker claiming the front row, Haley and Winters claimed the next with Ellison and the man who had tried to move her into her bedroom at the hotel in the third row.

The other four men who had escorted her to Teterboro Airport had long since peeled off and headed toward the main terminal.

Penelope pivoted in her seat and studied the laconic man in the back row. He appeared to be around the same age as her son William and seemed completely unremarkable. He could vanish in a crowded room, possibly an empty one as well. Why was he still with them while the others were being left behind? This little epiphany caused Penelope's internal warning system to click on. In the year plus that she had known Michael James Walker, she had never seen him do anything without a reason. Penelope made a mental note to keep an eye on this new addition.

As would be expected of the CEO from a Fortune 50 multi-national corporation, Walker was usually surrounded by staff. In fact, Penelope could count on one hand the number of times they had been alone together for more than a few minutes since their cross country trip a year earlier. Sitting across the aisle from each other was as close to a private one-on-one moment as they'd had in months.

"I'm not used to seeing you with people in suits," Penelope said.

"Unavoidable from time to time," Walker said with a laugh. "Casual Friday is a concept that tends to escape corporate lawyers. Especially when they're meeting with the CEO," Walker answered.

"What kind of papers are you having them draw up for you?"

"The kind that could get all of us in trouble with the Securities and Exchange Commission if we talked about them," Walker answered, immediately changing the subject. "Last night was fun. I had nearly forgotten how much I enjoyed your company."

"Same here," she answered with a smile. "You disappeared early."

"It was your party and it was tough to get within ten feet of you," Walker answered. His eyes locked on hers and he smiled broadly. "Plus, you seemed to be having an especially good time."

Penelope closed her eyes and rubbed her forehead. "I might have had a bit more champagne than necessary." Realizing her mouth was dry, she was about to ask for some water when the mysterious man from the hotel appeared at her side with her favorite brand of sparkling water. "Thank you," she mumbled as she accepted the bottle.

"Who's your new playmate?" Penelope asked as the young man returned to his seat.

"That's Ian," Walker answered.

"Does his sudden appearance have anything to do with the attack on the Wyoming compound?"

"Not really. He's been in the works for a while." Walker studied her closely; she could almost feel his eyes probing her. "Have you been making time for your meditation?" They both knew the answer. While nothing in Walker's words or tone was judgmental, they still raised her hackles. She pulled back and straightened up, allowing her hands to drop back into her lap.

"Not as much as I would like," she answered stiffly as she leaned back into her seat and closed her eyes again. Her headache continued to build. It was annoying that she was so transparent. Before she could muster a pithy response, she felt the jet starting to rumble down the runway for its takeoff. While she loved to fly, especially on a private jet, that brief transition from land to air and back again always put a knot in her stomach. Involuntarily she tightly gripped the armrest until she felt the wheels leave the ground. Her body relaxed as the jet nosed upward. For the record, she didn't need Walker to tell her she had been back-sliding on her personal growth. She'd been aware of it for some time now and had been cutting with the old "I'm too busy" saw for so long it had lost its edge even for her.

Now it was Penelope's turn to want to change the subject. "Tell me what happened at the compound?"

Walker smiled. "Someone was sending us a message."

"What does that mean?" Penelope asked.

"Remember when I told you there were others who were trying to develop technology similar to the Hermes Project?"

"Yes. It scared me half to death."

"Remember the electro-magnetic burst we hit your friend Mark with while he was in the cube?"

Penelope had an involuntary shiver. "It's hard to forget," Penelope answered. A year earlier, to demonstrate the potential dark side of the Hermes Project to the senior management of *The Washington Post*, managing editor Mark Hatchet had volunteered to be a human guinea pig. He was hit with an EM burst that temporarily made him a raving paranoid. While the process was quickly reversed and Mark was fine, it was easily one of the most terrifying moments in her life. "It's hard to forget," Penelope answered.

"Someone shot a similar beam at the Jackson Hole compound."

Penelope's hand flew to her mouth. "My God! Was anyone hurt?"

Walker waved it off. "It wasn't that powerful, and besides everything is shielded at the compound. There were a few people caught in the open, but since we had been expecting the attack, we were prepared."

"What do you mean? You had been expecting the attack?"

"No comment."

Penelope sighed. "How about we pretend I'm just a concerned friend and not a reporter?"

Walker shook his head. "As a reporter you get nothing. As a friend I wouldn't put you at risk."

"Ha!"

"Ha what?" Walker asked.

"You already think I'm at risk or you wouldn't have sent Lucas and his posse to bring me here. Considering that was far and away the largest and most impressive group of bodyguards you have ever sent in my direction, the only question is how nervous should I be?" Penelope's eyes narrowed. "And if you say I'm not ready to understand your answer, I may slug you."

For the first three days that Penelope had known Michael Walker, which included a prison break, having her house burn to the ground, and a wild sprint cross country with Homeland Security nipping at their heels, his stock response to her every question was that she was not ready to understand his answers. Having been raised in the South, she'd had her fill of condescending men telling her to "not worry her pretty little head" about something best left to the menfolk. If he hadn't been the key to a big story, she would have left him filleted on the berm like so many other arrogant, chauvinistic males that had crossed her path. While traveling with Walker, she had bitten her tongue so often it had started to resemble a new puppy's chew toy.

"We wanted to get you out of New York quickly and all of those men just happened to be meeting with Lucas at the time."

"So they weren't there just for me?"

"No," Walker said with a laugh. "I had planned to introduce Ian to you later today. You're going to be seeing a lot of him for the next few days."

Penelope pivoted in her seat. The young man she had first laid eyes on in the hotel earlier was in the back row totally engrossed in a portable electronic game. She wasn't sure but she thought she heard him giggling.

She shook her head and turned back to Walker. "Why do I need him?"

"We've reached the endgame and things could get very interesting. He has a role to play."

"Are we talking Pulitzer Prize interesting?

"Maybe."

"You always did know how to sweet talk me." Sensing that no more information would be forthcoming about Ian, Penelope continued, "Can I ask about the job you have planned for those other bodyguards?"

"Sure, you can ask all you want as long as you won't get upset if you don't get an answer."

Penelope sighed and shook her head. Michael Walker could either be the most charming or most exasperating man she had ever met. Last night he had been Dr. Jekyll and today he had reverted to his annoying alter ego, Mr. Hyde.

"They certainly didn't look like the bodyguards you usually send my way."

"How so?" Walker asked.

"They looked like you borrowed them from the set of *Beach Blanket Bingo*." Walker shook his head to indicate that he didn't follow. "Frankie Avalon, Annette Funicello? You remember," Penelope said, "all the beach and surf movies from the 1960s."

"Sorry," Walker answered, "never saw them. The beach part is right though; they are all old friends of Lucas from his Navy SEAL days."

"Why do you need a bunch of Navy SEALs?"

Walker shrugged. "It will be clear in the fullness of time."

"Something is full of it today and it's not time," Penelope half muttered to herself.

"Excuse me?"

"Forget it." From past experience, Penelope knew she was on a hopeless quest. While she enjoyed their banter, Walker had spent his entire adult life dealing with the press. It was nearly impossible to get anything out of him that he didn't want her to know. She decided to try a different line of attack. "Who else has the story about the attack on your compound?"

"No one but you; not that it means much," Walker said.

"Why do you say that?"

"Your newspaper wouldn't touch the story with a ten foot pole."

"Michael," Penelope said leaning closer, "an attack on the Hermes Project is big news."

"I seriously doubt it."

As if on cue, Sally Winters reached over the seat and handed Penelope one of the airplane's telephones. "Mark wants to talk to you."

Penelope did a double take. In addition to being her friend for over three decades, Mark Hatchet was also her boss at the *The Post*. Hatchet was the one who had both revitalized her career and turned her life around by hiring her for the Hermes story. In less than a year she had gone from an empty nest divorcee to an "A" list celebrity entirely because of Michael Walker and the Hermes Project. None of it would have happened without Mark.

A puzzled expression covered her face as she accepted the phone. "Mark?"

"Nellie!" Penelope nearly dropped the phone when she heard her editor's voice booming from the conference call speaker embedded in the handset instead of the lower volume earpiece. "What's going on? Your little diva exit from the Ritz-Carlton has the rumor mill churning overtime."

"I am with Michael Walker..."

"Gee, no kidding. I got that much from Sally."

"The Jackson Hole compound was attacked."

"Really," Hatchet said with little enthusiasm. "Why hasn't it made the wire?"

"Mark, Michael Walker here. This morning someone shot an EM blast at the compound. A blast similar to the one you experienced."

"Do you have any proof?"

Penelope started to speak but Walker's hand on her arm stopped her short. "What kind of proof do you need?" Walker asked as he shot Penelope a Cheshire cat grin.

"Independent confirmation. A few bloody people in the ER would be nice."

"Sorry," Walker answered. "All we have are firsthand accounts from the people who took the blast, but no concrete proof."

"Are they all Walker Industry people?"

"Yes."

There was another long silence before Hatchet finally spoke again. "Pass," he said with a sigh.

"What?" Penelope demanded as she started to rise from her seat but was jerked back into place by her seatbelt. "How can you possibly not be interested in this story?"

"If," Hatchet answered, "all we've got is Michael Walker and his people's word that an attack took place, then without independent confirmation I'll have to pass."

Penelope was stunned. "Why?"

"No offense Michael, but right now your word doesn't carry much weight."

"None taken," Walker answered calmly.

"After that little melt-down on cable TV, I won't put the newspaper's reputation at further risk."

"Further risk?" Penelope rolled the words over in her mind for a moment then repeated them to be sure she had heard them correctly. "Further risk!? What further risk are you talking about?" Penelope demanded.

"People are saying *The Post* is too close to Walker and the Hermes Project and that we've lost our objectivity."

Penelope felt her cheeks darken. She knew exactly what Mark had really meant but was too polite to say in front of a prized source. *The Post* wasn't too close to Walker and the Hermes Project, she was. All she had was Walker's word and nothing else. Why hadn't she asked for confirmation the same way Mark had? Had she gotten so swept up in the concept of being a "celebrity journalist" she had forgotten the basics of being a reporter?

Hatchet continued. "If this turns out to be a publicity stunt and it blows up in our faces, we'll get laughed out of town. Sorry, but unless you get me a whole lot more than this, we're going to pass."

"Thanks, Mark," Walker said while shooting Penelope an 'I told you so' look.

As he started to hand the phone back to Sally Winters, Hatchet's voice boomed again. "Nellie, if you want to get paid this week, I need that contract signed and on my desk by Friday noon. I mean it."

"Okay," Penelope answered as the line went dead.

"I figured you needed to hear it from him in person," Walker said.

Penelope sat sulking in her seat trying to decide who she should direct her fury toward but kept coming back to herself.

After a few moments a voice came over the intercom. "We should be at Reagan International within fifteen minutes, Mr. Walker."

Michael pushed a button Penelope hadn't noticed on the arm rest of his chair. "Thank you, Alex."

"Reagan?" Penelope asked. "I didn't think they let private planes like this land at Reagan anymore."

"They let in a few as long as you have an air marshal or someone from Homeland Security onboard."

"Is there someone I'm missing in the cockpit?"

"Just our normal flight crew."

Penelope pivoted in her seat and only counted five other people on board. Her eyes locked on the mysterious new bodyguard she'd met that morning. His attention was still focused on the Nintendo DS in his lap but somehow he felt her eyes on him. Looking up, he smiled and waved. With a forced smile, Penelope returned the wave. Leaning further across the aisle, she said softly, "That's a great disguise for an air marshal."

Walker shook his head. "Who said he was an air marshal?"

Penelope's eyes grew wide. "You're kidding."

Walker pointed his thumb toward the rear of the jet. "He's one of Noah Shepherd's men."

"Homeland Security?" Penelope shook her head. "Correction. Noah Shepherd at Homeland Security? The man whose career you very nearly ended less than a year ago has lent you one of his men?"

"Not me," Walker answered calmly.

"What does that mean?" Penelope demanded.

"He's been assigned to you."

CHAPTER THREE

"WHAT?" PENELOPE WAS stunned. The first time she had met Michael Walker he was handcuffed to an interrogation table in the U.S. Naval Consolidated Brig in Charleston, South Carolina. Walker's reservation had been booked compliments of Noah Shepherd, the Director of Homeland Security's Emerging Technology Division. Other guests sharing the accommodations in the high security wing included some of the world's best known terrorists. The list included a guy who couldn't decide if boxers were superior to briefs when it came to smuggling explosives on an airplane and another who was similarly torn between Nike and Reeboks for his shoe bomb.

"Noah and I decided..."

"Noah? Noah!" Penelope pulled back in shock. "Since when are you on a first name basis with Noah Shepherd?"

"We've been working closely for the past few months."

Penelope shook her head in disbelief. "He's the one who tried to use your technology to create some kind of super spies and instead fried their brains."

"True," Walker answered, "but thanks to you we were able to fix that."

"Yeah," Penelope said with a snarl, "I never did thank you properly for nearly turning me into one of them."

Walker shrugged, "Because of what happened with you, we were able to figure out how to pull the others back."

Penelope closed her eyes and started a mental ten count. "After the incident he cut off funding to the Hermes Project."

"Which," Walker said, "if you remember correctly, worked out great since we got Hermes away from Homeland Security and under the direct control of Walker Industries."

"And," Penelope continued, "when he tried to get it back and you refused, he had you arrested three times."

"Four, if you count the Salt Lake City Airport," Walker corrected.

"Sorry," Penelope said as she rubbed her forehead again. "Four times."

"Right."

"He tried to get all of your government contracts cancelled."

"Right."

"He did everything within his considerable power to discredit and humiliate you."

Walker smiled. "We will be landing in a few minutes. Can we just stipulate that in the past Noah, ah, I mean, Director Shepherd and I have had our differences and move on?"

Penelope resisted the urge to roll her eyes and instead turned her attention to her new bodyguard. "So what's the deal with the guy back in the rumble seat?"

Penelope leaned out into the aisle and again studied the young man strapped into one of the seats in the back row of the jet. He appeared totally oblivious to the activity swirling around him. With his fingers racing across the buttons of his Nintendo and his baby face, he looked more like a tuned out teenager who had been forced to attend a boring family event than the guy you would want covering your back if trouble broke out.

"I have shoes older than him," Penelope muttered.

Walker shrugged. "He was top ten in his class at Georgetown, IQ off the charts, plus he's been with the Hermes Project since almost the beginning."

Penelope searched her memory. While names would occasionally elude her, she was excellent with faces. Unless he'd had extensive cosmetic surgery, she was pretty sure this was one face she had never seen before. "If he's been involved with Hermes for so long, how come I don't recognize him?"

Walker shrugged again. "Just trust me on this one. He's the man you want watching over you."

"If you say so." Penelope shook her head. Michael Walker was on the short list of people who were able to flummox her at will. Others included her mother, brother and, on increasingly rarer occasions, her ex-husband. Walker seemed to take special delight in dropping tantalizing bread crumbs in front of Penelope and then watching her peck at them.

If being annoyed wasn't enough, Penelope could feel herself coming down from the adrenalin rush of being whisked out of New York by a group of heavily armed men. Combined with a night of too much dancing and champagne that ended well past her usual bedtime, she knew she was headed for a crash. And soon. The lack of food wasn't helping. She leaned forward slightly in an attempt to stop her stomach from growling but it was too late.

At that moment Ian appeared at her side bearing orange juice and a pair of foil wrapped granola bars. "How did he know I was hungry?" Penelope muttered to herself.

"Pardon?" Walker asked.

"You owe me breakfast."

"Bon Appetite!" Walker said with a laugh as he pointed to the granola bars.

"I was thinking more in terms of linen tablecloths at the Ritz. Celebratory eggs Benedict and maybe a Mimosa."

"Sorry," Walker said. "Let me make it up to you. We have a business dinner tomorrow evening you might find interesting."

"Business?" She shook her head and sighed. "You are the last of the romantics."

"Is that a yes or a no?"

"It's an 'I'll think about it.'"

"You look tired," Walker said as he studied her face.

"I am," Penelope said as she tried to roll the stiffness out of her neck. "I haven't been sleeping well lately."

"Any particular reason?"

"Have you ever had one of those periods where it seems everything in your life starts to head south?"

"What do you mean?" Walker asked.

"My cell phone won't hold a charge. I got a virus on my laptop. I was at a White House dinner and the heel on my shoe broke. It has just been one little thing after another."

"How have you been dealing with these little setbacks?"

"I ignore them and just try to move on."

"Excellent."

Penelope sighed. "I just knew you were going to say something like that. Pray tell. Why are the Perils of Penelope so excellent?"

"You're being tested."

"Tested?"

Walker shrugged.

"Whenever you're in one of your 'let's keep Penelope in the dark and guessing' moods, you can be quite annoying."

Walker laughed. "You're not being tested by me. It's something a bit bigger than that and the timing couldn't be any better for you."

"Okay. I'll bite. Why is the timing so good?"

Walker motioned over his shoulder with his thumb toward the back of the jet where her freshly minted Homeland Security issued bodyguard was sitting. "You've got Ian."

"Be still my heart," Penelope said as she opened her orange juice. Clearly he was no intimidating physical specimen. She wondered what other super powers he had, other than, of course, the ability to read her mind.

Penelope sighed as she unwrapped one of the granola bars and took a bite. As the food hit her system, it calmed her appetite but did nothing for her fatigue. She closed her eyes and felt her body relaxing into the comfortable chair as the day's tension drained away. The steady hum of the jet's engines had the calming effect of a mantra and her mind began to wander. "This just keeps getting stranger and stranger," she said softly, more to herself than to Walker. "Between my new playmate, Haley's dramatic entrance this morning, and that completely off the wall cable news interview you gave..." She stopped mid-sentence and her eyes flew open. Michael Walker shot Penelope one of his famous grins as she finally got up to speed. "OH! MY! GOD!" Penelope shook a finger in Walker's direction. "You're running another one of your little plans aren't you?!" She folded her arms across her chest and focused her eyes straight ahead. "This is the Fourth Awakening and Hermes Project all over again. Listen, Buster. I am not going to be led around by my nose like you did last time."

"Actually," Walker said with a laugh, "this is part of the same plan. The ultimate goal was to always get the Hermes satellite in place before the bad guys."

She glanced up at Walker and discovered him looking at her with a lopsided grin she had seen before. "Your little performance on cable was entirely staged, wasn't it?"

"Let's just say we were hoping it would have the desired effect. The jury is still out on that. We'll know in a few hours if it convinced the right people that Michael Walker has gone completely nuts."

"You've got my vote. Why did you do it?"

"The charade on cable was designed to influence a decision that was critical to our plan."

"So, let me get this straight," Penelope said. "You went on national television and made a complete ass of yourself in the hope that it would make some unknown party tip their hand and attack you?"

"The attack had nothing to do with my plan, it was just a welcome addition," Walker said with a smirk.

Penelope felt her headache building again. "Nothing is ever simple with you, is it?"

Walker started laughing. It was a booming laugh; the kind that can fill a room and make others want to join in. "You, of all people, should understand the importance of what we're doing. I have certainly paid a price to deliver my message."

"What does that mean?"

"Sometimes you have to invest a few dollars to get the results you're seeking."

"Gee," Penelope said while shaking her head. "Exactly how much is the going rate for making an ass of yourself on national television these days?"

"A lot more than you probably think."

"If it's more than a mocha latte then it's more than I think."

Walker glanced over his shoulder toward Timothy Ellison. "How much has the value of my holdings in Walker Industries decreased since the cable show?"

"I haven't checked yet today, but as of the market close yesterday," Ellison answered, "you're down eight hundred and sixty-four million, give or take a few hundred thousand."

Penelope blinked a few times and had to force her mouth to stay closed as she tried to absorb the magnitude of a number that large. "Isn't Homeland Security or one of the government spy agencies going to try to stop you from launching your own personal Star Wars satellite?"

As usual Walker was calm and relaxed. "I sincerely doubt it since they helped us design and build it."

CHAPTER FOUR

"**T**HEY DID WHAT?" Penelope asked as she recoiled in disbelief.

"We're not the only ones worried about the Hermes technology falling into the wrong hands," Michael Walker said. "Having seen it in action, Homeland Security doesn't want this to happen either."

Penelope blinked her eyes a few times as the new reality set in. "So, you're telling me you're in bed with the same people who threw you in jail, cut off funding to the Hermes Project, and belittled your theory on the Fourth Awakening?"

"Yes," Walker answered with a mischievous twinkle in his eyes. "If memory serves, they didn't have a monopoly in the belittlement department. You held up your end quite nicely."

"You know," Penelope said as she ignored the verbal jab aimed in her direction, leaned back into her seat and shook her head, "just when I start to think you can't surprise me anymore. After everything that happened, I can't believe Homeland Security would ever want to see you again."

"You have a very limited perspective of Walker Industries' relationship with Homeland Security," he said with a laugh. "They are not always trying to throw us in jail. Before the Hermes dustup we had a great working relationship with Shepherd and the Emerging Technologies Division. Granted there were a few bruised feelings about what happened, but they're adults and got past it. We were, and still are, their number one subcontractor for ultra high-end technical work."

"So, working in conjunction with Homeland Security, you have a satellite version of Hermes technology built and ready to launch?"

"Yes."

"You've been a busy boy."

"I was well motivated. If Hermes can get into space first, we might be able to avoid the bloodshed that has accompanied all of the previous Awakenings." Walker said seriously. "But, of course, I don't need to tell you about the violence that can accompany an Awakening, you wrote about it brilliantly in your book."

While initially skeptical of the concept of an "Awakening" where the world and all of the people in it fall through an evolutionary trapdoor to a new reality, Penelope had to admit the historical evidence was compelling. One of the key elements of *The Fourth Awakening* involved those with positions of power feeling threatened and fighting the changes with any and all of the weapons they had at hand. A device able to calm or incite entire nations would be the tool those clinging to power and wealth would be unable to resist.

A puzzled expression crossed Penelope's face. "How are you getting your new toy into space to do all of these wonderful things?"

"We'll know the answer to that before the end of the day. We're meeting with NASA right after we get back to Washington and will learn if they'll let us launch it from one of their civilian flights."

"Can I tag along?" Penelope asked.

"Sure."

"On the record?"

"Absolutely," Walker answered as he noticed the smile on Penelope's face. "Don't get too excited," Walker said with a laugh, "we have a four o'clock press conference already scheduled."

Penelope was disappointed when she learned she wasn't going to have a scoop, but at least she might have an inside angle no other reporter would have. "What happens if NASA turns you down?"

"Then we go to plan 'B,'" Walker answered firmly.

This wasn't Penelope Drayton Spence's first rodeo with Michael Walker. She had been a firsthand witness as he had exasperated a powerful US Senator, done an end run around the Department of Homeland Security, and completely manipulated everyone around him - including her. She knew he was resourceful and usually six steps ahead of everyone else. When he had a plan in motion, heck even when he was standing still, she had to run just to keep up...something she couldn't say about anyone else she'd ever met.

"What exactly does plan "B" look like?" Penelope asked.

"Now that we're close to figuring out the other players in this little melodrama," Walker answered, "that eliminates variables and we can narrow our focus." Walker sighed. "Still, the sooner we can get Hermes into space the better."

"Why?

"That's one of those good news, bad news things."

"What's the good news?" Penelope asked.

"If you had evil intent, would you waste your money and best scientists on a weapon that was already obsolete and could be instantly neutralized by a superior system that was already in place?"

"No. What's the bad news?"

Walker smiled at her and waited. That was his way of saying she already had all of the pieces in front of her and there was just some assembly required. She leaned back against the soft leather of the seat, and her eyes danced from side to side. She slapped herself in the middle of the forehead. "The Hermes satellite is not in place yet. Whoever these mysterious people are, they are going to do everything within their power to try and stop you."

Walker touched the end of his nose.

"Who is your mystery rival?"

"We have a pretty good candidate," Walker answered, "but we're still not one hundred percent certain who we're up against."

"Isn't being so public about all this just adding risk?" Penelope asked. "Wouldn't it have been better to quietly launch the satellite and announce it after it was safely in space?"

"That was the initial plan," Walker answered, "but we had to make a quick adjustment."

"I'm guessing you're not ready to share what caused this change in plans?"

Walker shook his head. "Not yet, but soon."

"Define soon."

"Four, maybe five days."

"Really? That's hard to believe."

"Why?" Walker asked.

"If NASA turns you down, won't you be a sitting duck until you can get an alternative satellite launch?"

"We have factored that in as well," Walker answered. "If NASA refuses, then our next choice will be Boeing Sea Launch."

"Boeing does space launches? I had no idea."

"They have two facilities. One in Central Asia and the one we normally use which is on the equator due south from Los Angeles," Walker said. "In fact we have a replacement communications satellite which left the Boeing assembly facility in Long Beach three days ago and should arrive at the equator sometime tomorrow. It has a launch date of early next week."

A puzzled expression covered Penelope's face. "Why don't you use this launch to get Hermes in place?"

"It's not like changing shoes. The satellite still has to be encapsulated and placed into the rocket. That takes several weeks or even months. If you have about an hour, I can give you all the details."

"I'll pass." Penelope pulled back and made a face

"There is a launch window open in ten weeks. And since we have a contract for up to three launches per year we'll be able to bump..."

"Three!" Penelope interrupted. "How many satellites do you have?"

"We have twenty-seven communication satellites in orbit, but this scheduled launch is to replace one of our major units which is currently offline."

"What happened to Hermes being your main concern?"

"Even if we could get Hermes ready in time, the satellite we're replacing was our golden goose. It handled nearly a third of all of our traffic. While short term we can afford to lease other satellites while this one is offline, during the time it has been unavailable the cash flow in the Telecom division has taken a major hit. It would be crazy to not do everything we could to restore the lost capacity."

"Ahh," she said playfully. "So there is still a decadent capitalist left in there somewhere?"

"Without those golden eggs there wouldn't even be a Hermes satellite..."

Timothy Ellison interrupted them and handed Penelope and Walker each another bottle of water as he took away the trash from Penelope's breakfast. He glanced sideways at Spence then focused his attention on his boss. "The papers you wanted should be waiting when we land."

"Excellent," Walker said as he accepted his water.

Timothy Ellison avoided eye contact with Penelope, turned and returned to his seat. "I assume this is another part of your master plan?"

"Join me for dinner tomorrow night and see for yourself."

"We're back to your little business dinner again? What's so special about it?"

Walker just shrugged.

They sat in silence for a few moments. One of the things Penelope liked most about Walker was that he never felt the need to fill an awkward silence with mindless chatter. Another was he had never once pulled the 'you owe me one' card out of the deck. He had to know, with everything he had done for her, if he insisted she show up at his little business dinner she would be there with bells on. It was nice that it was still an invitation and not a summons.

Glancing over at Walker, out of the corner of her eye she suddenly saw it again for the first time in ages. Like a shimmering translucent suit of armor, Walker was encased in white light. She had seen this before on a lonely stretch of highway in West Virginia. She tried to keep herself from gasping but was only partially successful.

Michael Walker looked up from the document he was reading and softly asked, "What?"

"I just saw your aura again."

"Excellent," Walker answered

"What does it mean?"

Walker shrugged. "What it means is pretty much up to you."

Penelope closed her eyes and began rubbing her forehead. "Just once I would like to get a straight answer from you." Penelope leaned in closer and talked more softly. "Can I ask you something?"

"Of course," Walker answered.

"It's personal." Walker shrugged and indicated with a nod she should continue. "When we spent the time together going from Charleston to Jackson Hole last year, I thought we connected." Walker nodded his agreement but remained mute. Penelope lowered her eyes as she tried to compose her thoughts. Walker didn't intrude by speaking. Penelope drew in a breath, she lifted her head, and her eyes locked on Walker's. "You already know what I'm going to ask you, don't you?"

Walker nodded.

"You're going to make me say it, aren't you?"

He nodded again but still didn't speak.

Penelope folded her arms across her chest and leaned back in her seat. "You know, you're not being very helpful here."

A mischievous grin was on his face and his eyes twinkled. After nearly a minute of silent head scratching and fidgeting by Penelope, Walker finally spoke. "I know exactly what you want to know but you have to hear yourself ask the question."

"Why?"

"Let's just say you need to for your own good and leave it at that."

Penelope's eyes narrowed as she glared at Walker. "You didn't suffer some kind of unfortunate battlefield injury I should know about?" He shook his head. "Are you gay?" He shook his head. "Do you find me hideous to look at?" He shook his head. "Then why the heck haven't you tried to have sex with me?"

CHAPTER FIVE

WALKER'S EXPRESSION NEVER wavered. "Two reasons. The first one will mildly annoy you and the second one will send you through the roof."

"Okay, I'll bite. What's behind door number one?"

"Your personal safety."

"You're joking." Penelope pulled her hands out from under Walker's. "I'm sitting home alone on Saturday night because you're worried about my personal safety?" Penelope motioned to the back of the jet. "What about Lucas and Chuckles."

"His name is Ian," Walker said shaking his head. "Remember, you arrived in the middle of a high risk multi-year operation which was and still is in process. With the final act unfinished, my concern is that if someone thinks we're close, they may try to get to me through..."

Penelope cut him off in mid-sentence as her eyes flashed with anger. "You arrogant twit," she said loudly enough to turn heads in the rear of the Gulfstream. Haley, Winters and Ellison exchanged glances and without a word reached a unanimous decision: for the duration of the brief flight they would all stay as far away from Walker and Spence as the confines of the business class jet would allow. "You actually think if we go out on a few real dates someone might kidnap me just to get to you?"

Walker, with a calm that Penelope usually found reassuring but which was starting to get annoying, answered, "We're approaching the endgame, Penelope. We're up against people who would stop at nothing, including mass murder, to keep the Hermes satellite from getting into space. I refuse to put a bull's-eye on your back."

"I don't believe it. What an ego!" She glared at Walker. "Half the time you have me surrounded with a larger security detail than the President and the other half you completely ignore me."

"Exactly."

"Exactly? Exactly!" Penelope's eyes narrowed.

"When I'm ignoring you," Michael Walker answered, "you don't need security. When I'm paying attention to you, you do."

Penelope closed her eyes and rubbed her forehead again. "Unbelievable. Remind me. Is that the reason that was going to annoy me or drive me out of my mind?"

"That was the annoying one," Walker answered.

"Mission accomplished. I can't wait to hear the next one."

"I'll tell you, but only on one condition."

"Which is?"

"No matter how mad you get at me, you'll still take me as your date to *The Washington Post's* reception at the Mitchell's house on Saturday."

Penelope's eyes narrowed as she glared at Walker. She waited a full count of ten before speaking. "What exactly is your definition of a date these days? I know what normal healthy people think, but I would love to hear your take." Penelope folded her arms across her chest. "I mean would I be allowed to stand next to you or would that put me too close to the line of fire? Should I be looking for a Kevlar evening dress?"

"Penelope, please."

"You self-centered, arrogant..." Penelope caught herself and fought to regain a measure of self-control. Blinking her eyes a few times, she forced herself to lower both the volume and rapidity of her words. "All I know is when I asked you to go with me you gave me the big song and dance about how much you hated stuff like that. You made me feel as if you were doing me some BIG favor. Now you want to go? Obviously it's not my irresistible charms. Why the sudden interest in Josephine's party?" Penelope pointed a warning finger in Walker's direction. "And you might want to take a moment before you answer."

"Why?"

"According to Mark, you and the Hermes Project's fifteen minutes of fame are up. Without the potential of a big story and with our personal relationship obviously going nowhere, you don't have a lot of leverage. You either start giving me straight answers to direct questions or as soon as we're on the ground in Washington, we'll have seen the last of each other."

"You don't mean that?"

"Try me."

Walker studied Penelope for a moment and concluded she was serious. Penelope's body language and facial expression convinced Michael Walker that if he didn't give her a name, he would be scrambling for another date on Saturday night. He also knew, since the party was a function of *The Washington Post* and was being held at her best friend's house, that with one phone call from Penelope it wouldn't matter if he found another date or not. He would never get past the first layer of security. Walker struggled to keep the smile off of his face. For the first time since they had met, he now needed her more than she needed him. More importantly, for the first time since they had met, she was willing to release him. "I want to chat with someone who is going to be there."

"Who?"

"Have you ever heard of a man named Viktor Kursolov?"

Penelope ran Kursolov's name through her personal internal memory bank. "Isn't he that elusive billionaire industrialist from Kazakhstan?"

"Indeed," Walker said. "The general knowledge you always seem to have at your finger tips is impressive, as usual."

"A little late for sweet talk, Buster," Penelope said sharply; then her eyes flew open.

Her reaction drew a smile from Walker. "Which apparently is only bested by your powers of deduction."

"You think he might be the one who attacked your compound." Penelope's comment came in the form of a statement and not a question. "That's why you want to meet him."

"He's on my short list. So, do we have a deal?"

"That depends."

"Depends on what?" Walker asked.

"How much of the evening will be on the record?"

"How much will it take to get me out of your doghouse?"

"I haven't even heard your second reason yet, but I can tell you, based on the first one, any restrictions at all and you can take Ian back there as your date."

Walker glanced over his shoulder at Ian who was still immersed in his handheld video game and, unlike the others, hadn't even noticed the grown-ups bickering at the front of the plane. "In that case, as far as I'm concerned, the entire evening is on the record."

Penelope felt a tingle go down her spine. She had not expected total surrender. She would have a front row seat, on the record, for two of the world's richest men and possible rivals having a stare down at a black tie ball surrounded by Washington's elite. It sounded like a scene from a thousand Hollywood movies. Visions of Cary Grant and Grace Kelly flashed through her mind's eye. She had no idea what little bombshell Michael Walker had left in his arsenal that he was going to drop on her next. It didn't matter. That was personal. This is business. There was absolutely nothing Michael Walker could say to her that could keep her from arriving at Josephine's party on his arm. Penelope extended her hand. "Deal."

Walker accepted the handshake but didn't release it. "I'm going to hold you to that."

"A deal is a deal."

"You haven't heard the other item on my list yet."

Penelope folded her arms across her chest and glared at Walker. "I can hardly wait."

"You're going to need to take this in the spirit in which it is intended..."

"Ominous start," Penelope muttered.

"This is vastly over simplified but here goes. At any given moment there are basically three types of people in the world. The first group, easily the largest, is possibly eighty to ninety percent of the population. These are people who live their lives at various levels of contentment and seldom if ever get a serious glimpse of their true inner potential. These are people who outwardly might even appear religious. They go to services, sing the songs, listen to lessons and try to live a good life. Most people intuitively know there is something more to life, but they let the act of actually living and the people and things around them to cause them to lose track of deeper possibilities."

"The next group," Walker paused to see if Penelope wanted to jump in with a question. When it was clear she was keeping up, he continued. "The next group is somewhere between ten and twenty percent of the population. These are devout people who are actively seeking a deeper understanding. This might be a priest, a rabbi, or even the woman on the mat next to you at your yoga class. These people will turn to organized religions, prayer, and meditation and so on in their hope of progressing to the third level. Mostly they just learn to release and let go, which greatly increases their level of day-to-day happiness. But, some of them will get flashes of a deeper reality, or get to spend even longer periods experiencing it. Unfortunately for them it doesn't last. You've been there too. Even Mother Theresa talked about this eloquently in her..."

"Me?!" Penelope exclaimed stopping Walker dead in his tracks. "What in the world are you talking about?"

"You had a flash of it in Jackson Hole last year."

Penelope felt a faint tingle dance up her spine as her mind leaped back to the glorious moment a year earlier. For an instant that could have been a second or a week, it was like a fog had lifted from her mind and she'd seen the universe and her place in it with perfect clarity. Beauty and simplicity. Her very own personal Fourth Awakening. Unfortunately, the moment had been fleeting and as soon as the demands and responsibilities of her daily life began to reassert themselves, the fog rolled back in. Each day since that place became fainter in her memory and more dreamlike, but the craving to return never faded.

She cleared her throat. "I remember."

"Most people spend their entire lives either ignoring level three and enjoying life or reaching for it and never quite grasping it."

"Let me guess," Penelope said with the snarkiest tone she could muster, "that third level would be where you live, right?"

"Yes."

"Is this a linear progression?"

"Not even close," Walker said with a soothing tone in his voice. "There are those who spend a lifetime in prayer and meditation and never obtain it and others who have it unexpectedly dropped in their laps without pursuing it at all. And, each level contains many different ways of experiencing reality, even the third one. There's no predicting where someone will land as they are jumping levels, especially for the third one.

"What did you mean when you said the people and things around us cause us to lose track of deeper possibilities?"

"Often those closest to us are our greatest impediment. Until we learn how to release the artificial restrictions we have allowed others to impose on us, we are stuck in an endless loop."

"You know how much I love it when you go all New Age on me."

"Actually that was more old school psychology than New Age. Overbearing parents, sibling rivalry, our struggle with our sexual identity;

we all carry different baggage. Learning how to release it makes a huge difference for our individual happiness. Just releasing on these types of things doesn't allow us to make the jump to the third level, though." Walker's eyes twinkled. "Of course, the force that binds us all can just get tired of our nonsense and slap us up side our heads."

"What?"

"There is always shock therapy. That's what happened to you."

"To me?"

"Back in Jackson, you felt completely trapped and were unable to either fight or flee. With your normal instinctive defense mechanisms blocked, mental circuit breakers started shutting down and in the quiet that produced you found a glimpse of one part of level three. We see it all the time when people have things like that happen to them. Then there is the 'near death' experience that has gotten more common as medical science has improved."

"What does that mean?"

"Often when people are clinically dead, and medics or doctors use a defibrillator to bring them back, they are very different when they reopen their eyes. It's almost as if they realize that where they are going, they won't need all the excess baggage they've been carrying around and they discard it. Instant release."

"Demented," Penelope muttered to herself.

"Pardon?"

"Nothing," she answered a bit louder. "So far you haven't said anything to me that I would find even remotely aggravating."

"Okay. But remember your promise."

"I am a woman of my word."

"Good." Walker drew in a deep breath and then let it out. "As I said earlier, people tend to bounce between living their lives and a deeper quest. You're a perfect example."

"Me?"

"Last year I pushed you too hard too fast. I thought you were ready to explore the third level, but I was clearly wrong."

"What are you talking about?"

"How often are you taking time to try and go deeper?"

Penelope's eyes narrowed. "What are you, the yoga police? I've been busy." Penelope could see where this conversation was headed, and she felt her defenses rising along with her temper. "I'm on the road a lot," she said with a terse edge to her voice.

"I hadn't expected you to maintain level three after having it forced on you the way I did, but..." his voice trailed off.

"But what?!" demanded Penelope.

"With everything you had seen and been through..."

"Spit it out," Penelope said between gritted teeth.

"I hadn't thought it possible that you would get so involved with your new life situation that you would completely abandon your spiritual quest." Walker grasped her hands again and looked deeply into her eyes. "In addition to not wanting to put you at risk, we are in such different places now that an intimate relationship wouldn't be fair to either of us."

Penelope pulled her hands away from Walker. She closed her eyes and tried to count to ten but only made it to three. "So what you're saying is I'm a nice enough girl but I am just not enlightened enough to date you!"

"Yes."

CHAPTER SIX

PENELOPE WOULD HAVE been less insulted if Michael Walker had slapped her face. Without another word, she unbuckled her seat belt, grabbed her bottle of water, got up and moved to the back row of the jet. Timothy Ellison, having seen the same look in Penelope's daughter's eyes before, beat a tactical retreat to the front and claimed the seat Penelope just vacated. Lucas Haley tapped Ian on the shoulder, breaking his bond with the portable game in his hands, and nodded that he should follow him. The two bodyguards claimed the seats behind Walker and Ellison, leaving an empty space separating the boys from the girls. Sally Winters plopped down in the seat across from Penelope.

"Nice," Winters said with a sympathetic smile. "I was wondering if you were ever going to stand up to him."

Penelope leaned in closer and spoke softly. "Let me ask you something?"

"Sure."

"Do you think I'm moving in the wrong direction, spiritually, I mean?"

"Personal growth is not a linear process."

"That's what Mr. Walker said."

Sally Winters made a face. "Ouch. You Southern girls are harsh."

"What?"

"You've gone all the way from Michael to Mr. Walker in a single five-minute conversation. He must have really hit a nerve."

"That would be a nominee for understatement of the year."

"This is just another part of that rough patch you've been going through and it isn't going to get any better until, one way or the other, you get tired of it."

"What does that mean?"

"From time to time we're all tested," Winters said. "As soon as we learn to release the problems confronting us and forget about them, the test is over."

"And if they are too much for us?"

Sally Winters sighed. "Then the universe will realize you are not ready, back off, and flunk you."

"Where's the downside to flunking if the problems go away."

"They don't go away. They regroup and start planning their next attack."

"I don't follow."

"Are you a Harry Potter fan?" Sally asked.

"Of course," Penelope answered as a puzzled expression covered her face. "Why?"

"You need to confront your personal boggarts."

"Boggarts? You mean those shape shifters who hide in wardrobes and dark places?"

"Exactly," Sally answered. "What happens when you cross the path of a boggart?"

"It turns into the thing you dread the most and paralyzes you with fear."

"What's the only way to get rid of a boggart?"

A smile broke across Penelope's face. "If you laugh at it, it explodes."

"The same rules apply here. As soon as you can laugh off your problems, humor takes away their power and you can release them. Once that happens, the stuff that you think will make you happy will step forward. The funny part is how often it doesn't. What you thought would make you happy before you released doesn't make you feel the way you thought it would. You're the perfect example."

"Excuse me?"

"For as long as you can remember," Sally Winters said, "what was the only thing you wished for?"

"I wanted to be the most famous journalist in the world and rub elbows with celebrities." Penelope waved her hand. "And fly around in private jets."

"How's that working out for you?"

"What is this? National Kick Penelope Day?"

"Look," Sally said as she leaned in closer. "You've reached the place where you've realized the stuff you thought would make the old you happy isn't necessarily what will make the new you happy. You've got the itch again."

"The itch?"

"If being the most famous and highest paid journalist in the world would make you happy, why haven't you signed your contract renewal with *The Washington Post*?" Penelope didn't have an answer. "Sweetie," Sally said softly, "I'm telling you this as a friend. Your life is about to turn into a nightmare. You are going to get hit from every direction imaginable. You're going to discover the past year was a wrong turn down the wrong street and there will be a price to be paid. If you can absorb these body blows and release them, you are going to be much happier." Sally shook her head in sympathy. "He really likes you, but he has to wait for you to find yourself before you can find him."

"It all sounds like a crock of crap to me." Fuming, Penelope turned her gaze out the window and reached again for the water bottle Timothy Ellison had given her. No sooner had she twisted off the cap than the jet hit turbulence and about a third of the contents spilled into her lap. She tried to jump to her feet but her seatbelt jerked her rudely back into the seat. By the time she finally disengaged the seatbelt and stepped into the aisle, Sally Winters was at her side with a towel. Penelope glared down at the dark spot in her lap and winced. "It looks like I peed my pants."

"Don't worry about it," Winters said as she continued to pat as much water out of Penelope's skirt as possible. "We're landing at the private end of Reagan and no one will see you."

When they had done the best they could, Penelope fell heavily back into the seat. "The disaster which is my life continues."

Sally's eyes danced a few rows ahead. "Here's a tip, trust Ian."

"Ian?"

"He wants to help you."

"Why?"

"He'll tell you when it's time, or better yet you'll figure it out for yourself first."

Penelope folded her arms across her chest again. She drew in a few cleansing breaths and slowly felt the tension leave her body. She leaned back in the comfortable seat and closed her eyes. Her elbows found the arm rests and she completely relaxed. Drawing in as much air as she could hold; she felt a surge of energy rush up her nose to the area behind her eyes then felt it plunge down through her body and settle a little south of her belly button. She held it for a moment, then released her anger at Michael Walker and let it flow out with the air as she exhaled through her nose. She hadn't been that relaxed in months. Opening her eyes, she saw the smiling face of Sally Winters who nodded her approval.

"Why don't you ask Ian to come back so I can get to know him?"

"Atta girl," Sally said as she left her seat and made her way up the aisle, leaning over to say a few words to Ian. The young man nodded that he understood. He walked to the back of the jet and claimed the seat Winters had vacated.

"Ma'am?"

"You can call me Penelope, or if that is too informal for your upbringing, I can live with Ms. Spence."

"Yes, ma'am."

Penelope's shoulders sagged. "You're not going to call me Penelope, are you?" He just smiled. It was a nice, friendly smile which Penelope found slightly off key. With the exception of Lucas, normally the bodyguards Michael Walker sent her way were humorless Robotrons who were all business. This one was different. From the twinkle in his eye, if she didn't know better, she might have thought his 'ma'am' routine was some kind of inside personal joke she didn't get. "What should I call you?"

"Whatever you like will work for me."

Penelope pulled back and continued the evaluation of her new shadow with a bemused smile on her face. "Everyone else seems to call you Ian." He nodded. "Do you have a last name?"

"Fleming."

A smile broke across her face. "Seriously?"

"Yes, ma'am. My father worked for the Central Intelligence Agency, and though many thought him to be an annoying jerk, he did have a whimsical sense of humor."

"You thought your father was a jerk?"

"I really didn't know him well enough to form an opinion. He worked all the time when I was growing up so he was seldom home. Plus, he died when I was fifteen."

"I'm sorry."

"Why?" Ian asked.

"Why what?"

"Why are you sorry?"

"I'm sorry you lost your father at such a young age."

"Ahh," Ian said. "Thank you. That is very considerate." Fleming scrunched up his face. "I did mention everyone thought he was a jerk, right?"

"You did," Penelope answered as she studied the young man next to her. He was certainly an odd one, even by Michael Walker and Hermes Project standards. Like everyone she'd ever met who was associated with Hermes, he was tan and fit. His eyes were chocolate brown with some depth to them. His hair, while fairly short, looked like it had seen some time pass since being in the same zip code with either a comb or brush. A lot of time.

"I understand you work for Homeland Security."

"Yes ma'am."

"Why exactly have you been assigned to me?"

Ian's face went blank. "If I tell you, then I would have to kill you." Penelope studied Ian's face to see if he was kidding; she got her answer when he chuckled to himself.

"So you're not going to tell me anything else?"

"What fun would that be?"

"Fun?" Penelope demanded.

"It will mean a lot when you figure out why I'm here."

The "Fasten Seat Belt" light clicked on and she heard the landing gear starting to lower. Penelope felt the knot in her stomach starting to reform. "Any clues to get me started?"

"Sure!" Ian said cheerfully. "I specifically requested to be assigned to you."

Penelope's hands tightened on the armrests as the jet's wheels bounced on the runway.

"Why?"

As Ian stowed his handheld game console in his backpack, he smiled and said, "If it wasn't for you, I wouldn't even be here today."

CHAPTER SEVEN

A S SOON AS it was apparent the corporate jet had safely reestablished contact with terra firma without bursting into flames or disintegrating into a million small pieces, Penelope released her iron grip on the armrests and turned to face Ian. "Where would you be if you weren't here, and what did I have to do with it?"

"Ahh!" he said brightly. "Now that's the riddle, isn't it?"

"I'm in no mood to play games."

"Okay," Ian said as he reached into his backpack for his Nintendo DS. "We can try again later."

As the plane taxied toward a private hangar, Penelope tried to gather her thoughts and make some sense of Ian Fleming. His dopey teenage persona appeared genuine, but the practical side of her brain screamed that he had to be a fake. How could he be a long-time Hermes Project person and also be working for Homeland Security? Clearly she did not have enough information. She shook her head and sighed. "Is Michael Walker putting you up to this?"

"No," Ian said with a puzzled expression on his face, his eyes never leaving the screen of his game. "Why would you think that?"

"He may be trying to make himself look good by comparison."

Ian burst into giggles more fitting for a junior high school girl than a Homeland Security assigned bodyguard. "You're getting colder."

"Have you experienced some sort of head trauma recently?" she asked sarcastically.

"Excellent! Now you're getting warmer."

"What?" Penelope shouted. Before she could form another question, the door to the plane began to open, and Ian was up and out of his chair like a bullet.

"Shotgun!" he shouted as he charged up the aisle.

Penelope watched in amazement as Ian was first out the door. What kind of bodyguard abandons the person he's assigned to protect? Shaking her head, she slowly gathered up the few items she had managed to grab before being whisked out of New York. Not wanting to bump into Walker, she lingered in the rear of the plane and was the last to exit. Waiting a few feet from the jet was a Black Cadillac SUV with dark-tinted windows. Ian was already in the front passenger seat, with Lucas Haley behind the wheel slapping Ian's hand away from the radio. Michael Walker had claimed one of the captain chairs in the middle row and motioned for Penelope to take the other one.

"No thank you," she said with her warmest Southern smile. "I believe I would be more comfortable sitting in the back with Sally. Timothy, do you mind?" Ellison scrambled out of the third row and made room for Penelope to get past him. The subtlety of the snub escaped no one. The short ride to the Washington office of the Hermes Project was draped in awkward silence.

At the curb in front of a squatty three-story glass and steel building, the Cadillac rolled to a stop. The world headquarters of the Hermes Project was located in a brackish section of the District where the old and dilapidated were mixed with the vacant and abandoned. The only signage on the building was the street number and 'Hermes' painted on each of the double glass doors leading to the lobby. The empty lots on either side of the building were littered with windswept garbage. There wasn't any foot traffic on the street, and few cars. It looked like every other underutilized building within a five block radius.

"I had forgotten how posh this place is," Penelope said to Winters.

"It looks even more inviting after dark." She nodded toward Lucas Haley. "He gets pretty antsy when Michael wants to come here late at night."

Penelope's forehead crinkled as she looked at the facade of the building. She hadn't been to the offices of the Hermes Project in months, but something was different. "Did you guys remodel?"

Sally nodded. "We had them put in new front doors."

"Why?"

Sally laughed. "Michael brought in a *fengshui* master who recommended the changes. His English wasn't the best, but it was something about a green dragon or a dark turtle. I never quite figured out what he was talking about. He also made us put mirrors all over the building to reflect the 'Chi' or some such thing."

"Mr. Walker believes in that kind of thing?" Penelope asked.

"As for the *feng shui* stuff," Sally said with a wink, "I think, *Mister Walker* is more into the school of 'why take the chance' than a true believer."

Once inside they headed to the center of the building where a large room with a glass viewing area was located. On an oversized table in the middle of the sealed room was a huge custom built aluminum crate. In front of the glass, engaged in an animated conversation, were Robert A. Smith and a woman Penelope had never seen before. Smith, the former Assistant Director of Homeland Security's Emerging Technology Division, had been hired away by Walker to oversee the Washington operations of the Hermes Project. In his late thirties, Smith was compact with the start of a muffin top hanging over the belt of his gray suit. His wardrobe fit in nicely with the several hundred thousand other mid-level bureaucrats and paper shufflers that populated the District. The woman was younger and quite pretty. She had a Hugo Boss blazer on with matching slacks. A Versace bag, which was obviously not a knockoff, hung over her slender shoulder.

"That can't be good," Winters whispered to Spence.

"Why? Who's she?"

"She's a junior press liaison for NASA."

"What's bad about that?" Spence asked.

"NASA was supposed to have a team of scientists here to look at the satellite." Winters nodded in the direction of the crate behind the glass, with "HERMES I" and "Walker Industries" painted on the sides. "I've crossed paths with her before and she's a shameless flirt. I'm betting they sent her over to soften the blow."

"Penelope," Walker said warmly as Spence and Winters caught up with the rest of the group, "I have someone I would like you to meet." The two women squared off and Penelope, still dressed in the casual outfit she had been wearing when she had been swept out of New York, felt underdressed. The remnant of the wet spot in her lap didn't help. "This is Catherine Willoughby of NASA."

Willoughby extended her hand and grasped Penelope's firmly. "No introduction needed, Michael. The Penelope Drayton Spence." She flashed a smile so bright it was obvious she had spent hours at the dentist's office to achieve a level of whiteness far beyond what was possible from the messy at-home strips. "I'm a big fan. I really enjoyed your book."

"Why, thank yooou," Penelope said as she let a bit of Dixie slip into her words. "You're too kind." While both women's lips were smiling, their eyes were telling a different story. They were sizing each other up as potential rivals.

Willoughby glanced quickly at Walker as she threw the first roundhouse. "Oh, yes. I remember first hearing about you during Women's History Week when I was a little girl in elementary school." Her smile grew bigger and her eyes narrowed as she went in for a kidney punch. "I thought it was exciting that you won your first Pulitzer Prize the same year I was born." A smug ear to ear smile covered Catherine Willoughby's face.

"How sweet of you," Penelope said as she set her feet to throw a counterpunch. "I've always hoped to be an inspiration to little girls like you so they will go out and be successful. I understand you're a junior assistant press liaison?" Willoughby nodded but never broke eye contact with Penelope. "Well, bless your heart. How cute is that? You just keep trying and I'm sure you'll make something of yourself someday." The younger woman winced.

Round One - Penelope Drayton Spence.

Penelope's smile vanished and she leaned in closer to Willoughby, her eyes focused on one of the younger woman's front teeth. Penelope grimaced, looked up at the woman, pointed to one of her own teeth and shook her head. Immediately Willoughby's smile vanished and she started running her tongue over her teeth in search of the offending nugget left over from her lunch. Penelope squeezed the woman's arm and leaned in close. "I'm sure no one else noticed." For the rest of their visit, Catherine Willoughby didn't flash another smile and talked mostly with her hand over mouth. Ms. Spence by a TKO.

Sally Winters leaned in and whispered, "You're my new role model," into Penelope's ear.

Spence nodded, "That one wouldn't work after second grade in Charleston. You Northern girls wouldn't last a week in the South."

"I think," Michael Walker said, "we are about to be told that NASA will not be able to help us launch our satellite."

"That's correct, Michael," Willoughby said softly. "I'm afraid we're going to have to decline."

"Is there a specific reason?"

"Your refusal to allow us to see the blueprints pretty much made it impossible to honor your request."

"Entirely understandable," Walker answered with his usual calm. "We did offer to bring it here and let your people look at it in person."

"Correct."

"And in the past that was enough for NASA."

"That is true," Willoughby said as she cleared her throat, "but the situation has changed recently."

Michael Walker's eyes danced as he toyed with the NASA Press Liaison. "What exactly has changed?"

Catherine Willoughby shifted her weight uncomfortably from one foot to the other. "I'm afraid the decision was made above my pay grade, and I wasn't privy to any of the details." While it was likely the decision came from the top of NASA, everyone in the room knew she was lying about not knowing the real reason. Walker's performance on cable TV had sealed the deal.

"Thank you for coming and telling us in person." Walker extended his hand to Willoughby, which she accepted, placing her other hand over his as well.

"I'm sorry I couldn't be more helpful."

"We will arrange to have the satellite picked up Monday morning and transported to the Boeing Sea Launch facility in Los Angeles so it can be included with our next launch." Walker patted her hand. "This will work out for the best for all of us."

"If there is anything I can do to help," Willoughby said, "please call me."

A puzzled look came over Walker. "Why would I do that?" he asked as he glanced over at Penelope. "If there was any negotiating room left, NASA would have a team of your scientists in here going over the satellite. Clearly the decision has been made and it is final, so you either drew the short straw or they thought a nice smile and a great pair of legs would soften the news." Michael Walker's face darkened. "Either way, tell your boss sending you instead of coming to tell me himself won't be forgotten anytime soon." Walker turned away from the NASA press liaison as he dismissed her with a wave of his hand. "Thank you for stopping in."

Willoughby flushed slightly and, accompanied by Robert Smith, headed toward the exit while she still had a bit of dignity left.

Spence sidled up to Walker. "Was that for my benefit?"

"What?" he asked innocently.

Penelope gave him her best *'how dumb do you think I am'* stare.

Walker blinked. "Did it work?"

Penelope had to force herself not to smile as she held her thumb and index fingers about a quarter of an inch apart while watching Catherine Willoughby and Robert Smith vanish around a corner. By no means had she completely forgiven Walker, but to her surprise, she no longer felt anger towards him. He had stated his feelings in a clear and concise manner, which was much more honest than stringing her along. It had stung but if their relationship hadn't blossomed in a year, who was she kidding? In a few days it would all be forgotten and they would both get on with their lives.

"Are we still on for Saturday?" Walker asked.

Penelope shrugged. "A deal is a deal."

"What about Friday?"

"The business dinner?" Penelope made a face as if she had caught a whiff of a foul odor. "I'll pass."

"Trust me," Walker said. "You don't want to miss this."

"What's so special about tomorrow night?"

"Let's just say," Walker said with a smile, "there are 50 financial reporters who would donate a kidney for a seat at this table."

"Seriously?" Spence asked as she looked around and saw both Ellison and Winters nodding their enthusiastic agreement. Ellison was Walker's man and apparently had just been dumped by Penelope's daughter, so his opinion was suspect, but Sally Winters had never steered her wrong. "Sally?"

"You'll kick yourself long and hard if you don't go."

"So," Walker's smile broadened, "are you in?"

"Will it be on the record?"

"Yes," Walker answered. "But, for legal reasons there may be an embargo on the story until the stock market closes on Monday."

"Why?"

"Clearly," Walker answered, "you don't have a lot of experience working the financial beat."

"That would be the understatement of the year," Penelope said with a laugh. "I think it is based out of *Post's* New York office and not

Washington." After waiting long enough to at least pretend she had some reservations in accepting the offer, Penelope nodded her head.

"Excellent," Walker said with his normal good cheer.

"Now what?" Spence asked.

"We're going to head over to Homeland Security," Walker answered, "and see if they have a line on who attacked the Wyoming compound."

As they turned to leave, Penelope saw something she had never seen before from anyone even remotely connected to the Hermes Project: red in the face anger.

CHAPTER EIGHT

ROBERT A. SMITH looked so angry as he approached Michael Walker that Lucas Haley stepped between them. Smith's ears were a fierce red and his face was a blotchy pink. He struggled to gain at least a bit of control over himself before he spoke. "Well," he said as he watched the NASA liaison leaving, "there goes six months of my life out the door."

As always, Michael Walker was calm and impassive. "We have contingencies for this, Robert. We'll have the satellite picked up first thing Saturday morning and moved to Long Beach. We'll see if Boeing can move our next launch slot up. Everything will be fine."

Penelope, standing slightly behind Robert Smith, started to speak but Walker waved her off with a barely noticeable shake of his head. So it wasn't a slip of the tongue. Spence put the nugget she had just heard in her mental vault, with a yellow sticky attached to ask about it when they were alone.

"I don't understand why you had me flying back and forth to Houston if you were just going to go out of your way to sabotage the deal?"

"Sabotage?" Walker asked with a wry smile.

"I think you knew exactly what you were doing when you went on cable and made a fool of yourself."

"That's a pretty bold claim, Robert."

"All I know is that I have a press conference scheduled for four o'clock where I expected to announce our partnership with NASA. I have no idea what I'll tell them now," Smith said as he shook his head.

Walker glanced at Sally Winters, and she nodded that she understood.

"I'll stick around, Robert," Winters said as she touched Smith's shoulder, "and help with damage control."

"You've had to do a lot of that lately," Smith muttered bitterly to Sally Winters as he continued to glare at Michael Walker.

Walker patted Smith on the shoulder. "Everything will work out fine, Robert." Smith looked unconvinced.

With a nod from Walker the group, less Sally Winters, headed toward the door. "What was that about?" Spence asked. Walker shook his head but didn't answer. She knew that meant it would be fodder for a future discussion. At the street Timothy Ellison, who had been judiciously avoiding Penelope and any potentially awkward questions about his relationship with her daughter, took a left as the others took a right.

"He has to pick someone up at the airport," Walker offered as he opened the rear door of the Escalade. Haley climbed behind the wheel while Fleming clamored in on the passenger side and immediately began fiddling with the big car's radio. Haley slapped the smaller man's hands away. "I told you before, you called shotgun not radio."

Penelope was stuck. Now, with only four passengers, if she claimed the rear seat and sat alone while making Walker sit alone in the middle one, she would appear rude. She wasn't going to give him the satisfaction. She even accepted the offered hand with a cool smile. While she had started to release her anger toward him, Penelope could still feel the sting of Walker's words. He had been right. She had gotten so wound up in her new life that she'd let many of the things she intuitively knew were important atrophy from neglect. She felt it in her body and, more importantly, in her soul. There was a great emptiness within her, and it was only deepening. Michael Walker, as usual, read her mental state perfectly and made no attempt at cutesy small talk. The man definitely had his strong points.

After a few minutes of plodding along in the District's usual snarl of traffic, Penelope's curiosity started to get the best of her and she broke the ice.

"About what Smith said?"

"Which part?"

"Where he thought you intentionally sabotaged your chance of having NASA launch your satellite."

An amused smile covered Walker's face. "What about it?"

"It didn't seem to upset you at all."

"Why should it?" Walker answered with a shrug. "It was true."

Penelope blinked her eyes several times in disbelief. "You're kidding!"

"There was no chance we were ever going to put this satellite in NASA's hands."

"Why?"

Walker laughed. "Why do you think?"

Walker often resorted to the Socratic Method instead of giving direct answers to direct questions. Penelope's eyes narrowed as she considered the possibilities. "You were afraid someone would leak the design."

"That was a concern, but not the reason. The design is pretty straightforward; it's the frequency settings that have the real value." Walker shrugged. "Here's a hint. We're at least a year ahead of everyone else in developing this technology."

Penelope curled her nose. "You are really lousy when it comes to..." Penelope nodded her head. "I retract my last statement. I get it now."

"As expected," Walker said with a laugh.

"They wouldn't need to destroy the launch vehicle; they would only have to delay the launch."

"Oops," Walker said. "A mechanic drops a wrench and the fuel tanks need to be checked for damage."

Penelope was getting into the swing. "Oops, there's a leak in the hydrogen coupling, which will take a few months to repair."

"A few hundred thousand dollars in the right hands at the right moment and my year lead disappears while my satellite is sitting in a NASA hangar."

"With you being so buddy-buddy with Noah Shepherd, why didn't you just have the Air Force or one of the spy agencies add it to one of their secret launches for you?"

"While I have many friends on Capitol Hill; I also have my fair share of enemies," Walker answered. "The same applies to Noah Shepherd. Homeland Security has a great deal of power, but it doesn't extend to the space program. Plus, there is considerable rivalry between agencies."

"So," Penelope said as she scratched her chin, "there are people at the CIA and NSA who would love to stick it to you and Shepherd if they get half the chance."

Walker shrugged. "Unfathomable isn't it?"

"Unimaginable." Penelope shook her head. "I'm guessing Robert Smith wasn't aware of your plan?"

Walker shrugged. "For a variety of reasons, Robert has been out of the loop on several things recently." Penelope was glad to see she wasn't the only one Walker kept guessing. "Before my little performance on *Hard Ball*, between Robert's tenacity and some large sums of cash changing hands in the House and Senate, we were about to get the green light from NASA."

"Smith was trying to bribe members of Congress?"

"Not with my money, but we're not the only ones with a stake in this game."

"Hold on. You think someone was trying to get the approval just so they could slow you down?"

Walker nodded. "I don't think, I know. Several members of sub-committees in both houses that control NASA's purse strings have been approached." Penelope was thunderstruck, which brought a smile to Walker's face. "Because of the size of my checkbook and my willingness to use it regularly, I've acquired a few friends here in Washington. I hear things."

"You're telling me someone besides you would be Machiavellian enough to think this far ahead and put up money to encourage NASA to include your satellite in a launch?"

Walker nodded again. "Politicians have the best return on investment in the world. For a few thousand dollars in campaign contributions or a part-time job for his mistress, you can get someone on Capitol Hill to do just about anything you want."

"That's pretty cynical."

"Have you ever tried to rent office space on K Street?" Walker said with a laugh.

"Granted, this town is full of lobbyists and influence peddlers, but you've been playing this game for a long time and..." Penelope stopped midsentence and turned to gawk at Walker.

"And."

"With all the money you've spent over the years and all the business Walker Industries does with the government, no outsider is going to come into your town and out maneuver you."

"Unless."

Penelope nodded. "Unless they thought you wanted to be on the NASA launch, and they were just trying to grease the wheels for you by getting you some added support from some fence sitters on the sub-committees."

"And." Walker motioned for her to continue.

Penelope's mind raced ahead at light speed. She started laughing so hard her eyes filled with tears. She shook her finger in Walker's direction. "And they tried to influence the wrong people!"

"Isn't this fun?" Walker said as he put his arm around Penelope and gave her a squeeze. Penelope, not feeling divine just yet, frowned at the arm draped over her shoulder and it was quickly removed. "They ignored our oldest friends completely since they assumed they would automatically throw their support behind us."

Penelope closed her eyes and shook her head. "Friends you could call privately to let them know that while publicly Walker Industries is seeking a spot on NASA launch, you would prefer it gets rejected."

"And?"

"There's more?" Penelope wiped a tear from her eye and leaned back in her seat to think. "I've got nothing. How about a hint?"

"It's an election year."

Her shoulders sagged and she shook her head. "You're awful," Penelope said as her hand flew to her mouth. "Your primetime meltdown was designed to give your supporters the political cover to vote the way you really wanted while letting them appear to be standing up to Walker Industries. They kept your financial support and were able to show the voters back home they're not in anybody's pocket. Especially some looney tune who is barking at the moon about the Fourth Awakening. Brilliant!"

"Thanks."

"Why did you tell that child from NASA the satellite is being picked up on Monday and then tell Smith Saturday?"

"I thought you caught that," Walker said with a laugh. "I was just sowing some seeds."

"What does that mean?" Penelope demanded.

"Let's just say if any of the seeds take root it will be clear soon enough and leave it at that," Walker answered.

They both looked up when they felt the Escalade begin to slow down as it reached the main gate at Ft. Meade.

IT TOOK LONGER to clear security at Ft. Meade than it had to drive there from Washington. Tucked between D.C. and Baltimore, the facility houses some of the federal government's most closely guarded secrets, and they intended to keep them that way. The offices of the Homeland Security Division of Emerging Technology, ET to both friends and foes, were in an unmarked and unremarkable building near the middle of the compound. You can't always judge a book by its cover. ET's annual budget rivaled that of the Environmental Protection Agency. With only a congressional select committee aware of exactly where the funds were going, ET's budget was approved by both houses of Congress by unanimous consent and without debate. The head of the Division, Noah Shepherd, was easily the most powerful man in Washington that no one had ever heard of. The President would take Shepherd's call ahead of half his cabinet secretaries'.

Emerging Technologies lavishly funded a broad range of research, but the money came with strings attached. If the research showed promise, ET had the option to take projects away from the individual scientists who were working on them and turn them over to major players in the military industrial complex. Walker Industries was one of the biggest players in that game and had inherited the Hermes Project from a Nobel winning scientist, Dr. Carl Altman, after Homeland Security cancelled the funding.

In the wild week when the story of Hermes had become public, Walker had managed to step on a few toes. The biggest pair of scuffed shoes was standing next to the final security checkpoint when they rounded the corner.

"Special Agent Wolfe," Walker said warmly while extending his hand. "I believe you know Ms. Penelope Spence."

Wolfe, after twice being bested by Walker, would rather have grasped the industrialist's throat than his hand, but settled for what was offered. As he started to bear down on Michael Walker's hand with his own, Wolfe felt a nudge and heard a soft voice say, "My turn." Wolfe turned and saw a grinning Lucas Haley with his hand out and a twinkle in his eye. Wolfe drew in a breath and loosened his grip on Walker's hand.

"Your people will have to wait out here," Wolfe said as his eyes locked on Penelope, "including her." Marcus Wolfe only had two smudges on his impressive resume as one of the quiet muscle men of Homeland Security. Both involved Penelope Drayton Spence, Michael Walker and the Hermes Project. Walker was nonplussed as he handed Wolfe a folded piece of paper. "What's this?" Wolfe asked. Walker didn't bother to answer and waited until the paper was unfolded. Penelope couldn't see what was written on the neatly typed document, but she recognized the blue artwork at the top of the stationery. She forced herself not to react but it wasn't easy.

Wolfe read the short note twice and then said, "I'll need to confirm this."

"Of course," Walker answered with a smile as he watched Wolfe disappear through the door behind him.

Penelope leaned in and whispered in Walker's ear. "Is that from who I think it is?"

"I got you a note from the principal," Walker answered softly.

"Why?"

"There are a couple more stories you might be interested in writing."

"Really? You know, Mark seems to have lost his love for Hermes stories."

"I guarantee Mark will want to print the story about our dinner meeting."

"Why is that?" Penelope asked.

"We'll be having dinner with Sal Trotta."

"Is that someone I should know?"

"I would be surprised if you did. He's in charge of the California Teacher's Union Pension Fund."

"And?"

"He controls more stock in Walker Industries than I do."

"Really?" Financial was not her usual beat, but she could see this had potential. "Does it involve those lawyers you were meeting with in New York this morning?"

"You'll just have to show up tomorrow and see for yourself."

Before Penelope could ask about the second story and if it involved Viktor Kursolov, the door on the other side of the security desk swung open. Instead of Marcus Wolfe they were greeted by Director Noah Shepherd. "Mr. Walker, Ms. Spence." He motioned toward the open door.

The room they entered was dimly lit. It had stadium seating with three tiers of overstuffed chairs in rows of four, each equipped with flat wooden arm rests large enough to hold a notepad. At the front of the room was a screen about half the size of an OmniMax. The screen was blank but there were four technicians seated unobtrusively in front of computers awaiting instructions.

Shepherd was the cover boy for the typical Washington mid-level bureaucrat. Fit and well dressed, he likely had a Yale or Harvard diploma hanging on his office wall. Penelope knew Shepherd on sight, having met him a few times at miscellaneous cocktail parties and once at the Kennedy Center. The one thing that always impressed her about him was his composure. If it were possible, he seemed to be even more in control than Michael Walker.

Shepherd handed the letter from the White House back to Michael

Walker. Shepherd's smile was warm but his eyes were cold. "You are always full of surprises. What can Homeland Security do for you today?"

"You can show me the satellite feed from the attack on my Wyoming facility this morning."

"What makes you think we would have something like that?"

"Because I know you've had a KH-13 spy satellite parked over my facility for the past year." Walker's eyes twinkled. "Do you need the transponder number? Encryption keys?"

Shepherd shook his head indicating that wouldn't be necessary. He nodded to one of the technicians and the screen filled with a crisp satellite image of the area around Jackson Hole, Wyoming. "We've determined," Shepherd said as he turned his attention to the screen, "the electromagnetic wave originated from the pull-off halfway up the pass over the Tetons between Wyoming and Idaho."

"That's nearly thirty miles from the facility."

"We calculated 31.8 miles," Shepherd answered as he motioned for a tech to zoom the satellite image in to the tourists' overlook midway up the pass. A white panel truck could be seen with its rear doors open and something that looked like a miniature sealed microwave dish extended.

"Excellent," Walker muttered softly, but loud enough for Shepherd to hear.

"That appears to be similar to the design we were using when the Hermes Project was still under Homeland Security's guidance," Shepherd offered.

"That's correct," Walker answered as he turned to face Penelope, "we abandoned that design over a year ago after we went to an array."

"They obviously knew we had a keyhole so they covered their faces and wore hats."

"Tracking?" Walker asked.

"No," Shepherd answered. "The EM field was so weak that, other than the avionics going screwy at Jackson Hole's airport for a few moments, with the limited population in the area, it didn't trigger any alerts until the alarms started going off at your complex. We were surprised by how far away they were from your compound. With nothing to triangulate, it took us nearly an hour to find their location." Shepherd sighed. "They were in and out in less than three minutes and long gone by the time we had figured out their position. By then it was too late to reposition the satellite, so we lost them on the other side of the Tetons. Very professional."

"Too bad."

"There is one thing which I think you'll find amusing." Shepherd motioned toward the screen as the men with the van were packing up to leave. When the last man pulled the rear doors of the van shut, the image zoomed in to the painted sign on the back. In bold black letters it said: Walker Industries.

THE WHITE VAN had been stolen from the Walker Industries distribution center in Salt Lake City. Even as they pulled into the underground parking lot of the Watergate complex, Michael Walker was still chuckling. "That was hilarious," he said for at least the fourth time. "This is really getting fun."

"You have the oddest sense of humor," Penelope said as she reached for the door handle.

"Thanks."

"It wasn't a compliment," she said shaking her head. "What time are you picking me up tomorrow?"

"I'll come down around seven."

Penelope stopped short and asked, "Down? What do you mean down?"

"My apartment is on the top floor, two up from yours."

"Whoa, whoa," Penelope said. "When did you move into the Watergate?" Walker looked at Haley. "Five years?"

"I'm thinking closer to six," Haley answered.

"Hold on, you're telling me you have lived in the same building as me for over a year and I didn't know it?"

"You're not here that much, I'm not here that much, plus this is a big place."

Penelope shook her head in disbelief. The three men, Walker, Lucas and Ian, accompanied her up the elevator to her apartment. Penelope turned the key and the doorknob at the same time. As she started to step inside she heard a noise; it was hushed voices. The sound was coming from the guest bedroom. The hair on her neck bristled as she stopped dead in her tracks.

"What is it?" Michael Walker asked.

Penelope leaned in closer and whispered, "There's someone in here."

CHAPTER NINE

A s Lucas Haley reached for his Glock, Ian Fleming was already gliding silently toward the door of the extra bedroom. Haley was one step behind and, despite his size, moved swiftly and confidently like a large cat on the prowl. The door was slightly ajar and each man took a position on either side. Ian took a quick look into the room and held up two fingers and then pointed toward his eyes. Lucas nodded that he understood. Ian had seen two people.

Walker had his hand on Penelope's arm and was ready to drag her out of harm's way if this turned ugly. Lucas Haley pointed at Fleming and then toward himself to indicate the order in which they would hit the room. Next he held up three fingers and began the silent countdown. When he had folded his last finger into his fist, the two men burst into the room.

"Jesus! H! Christ!" shouted a familiar female voice.

Penelope pulled away from Walker. "Carrie?"

"Are you guys crazy?" shouted a voice Walker immediately recognized. "Timothy?"

Walker and Spence exchanged glances. Both shook their heads and then trotted toward the extra bedroom. By the time they arrived, Carrie was standing in the middle of the room poking a finger in Haley's chest. Flames were coming from her eyes and smoke poured from her ears. "Put a leash on your pet," she shouted as she glared over her shoulder at Timothy, "before I take him to the vet and get him neutered."

A smile broke across Penelope's face. She doubted many would have the spine to dress down a former Navy SEAL like that, especially one who still had a gun in his hand. Penelope sighed. "*That's my girl*," she thought to herself.

Turning her attention to the late arrivals, Carrie's face changed instantly from the demon woman from Hell back to her normal self.

"Mom!" The two women exchanged hugs. Carrie was an honest three inches taller than her mother, with fair skin, an athletic build and blue eyes that, depending on her mood, men could get lost in or flee from in terror. "I almost wet my pants," Carrie whispered in her ear.

"Been there, done that." Penelope pulled back and examined her daughter from head to toe. "What are you doing here?"

Carrie glanced over at Timothy who had suddenly taken an unusual interest in his shoes.

"I..." Carrie grabbed Timothy's arm and pulled him to her side. "We actually..." Carrie's eyes welled up and she was near tears. The smile left Penelope's face; of all her children, Carrie was the toughest and hardest to make cry.

"What?" Penelope asked. "Are you sick? Has something happened?"

A single tear ran down Carrie's cheek as she reached into her suitcase, pulled out a magazine, and handed it to her mother. Puzzled, Penelope turned the magazine over. The instant she saw the title, she dropped it and screamed at the top of her lungs, "Ahhhhhhhhhh!!!!"

All of the men in the room flinched except Timothy who let out a big sigh. Penelope and Carrie were hugging, laughing, crying and bouncing. "Oh My God! Oh My God!" Penelope kept shouting. Penelope grabbed Timothy in a rib crushing hug and kissed him on the cheek. "This is why you have been acting so strange today." She patted both of his cheeks before returning her focus to her daughter.

Walker looked at Ellison and asked, "What just happened?" Timothy Ellison bent down, picked up the magazine which had landed face down on the floor, and handed it to Walker. It was the most recent copy of *Modern Bride*. "Ah," Walker said as he extended his hand. "Congratulations." Timothy Ellison accepted Walker's hand but didn't shake it with much enthusiasm. Walker pulled him aside and asked, "What's going on?"

Ellison held up a single finger indicating the second shoe was about to drop.

Penelope broke away from Carrie and gave Timothy another hug and a quick peck on the cheek before turning again back to her daughter. "Have you told your father?"

"Not yet."

"What about your brother and sister?"

"Kelly and William know."

"Have you set a date?"

Carrie shot Timothy a glance that escaped Penelope but not Walker. "Not yet."

Walker slid over to Haley and Fleming and softly said, "Why don't you guys give us a minute?" Haley nodded he understood and motioned to Fleming, and they quietly made their exit.

Penelope's eyes flew open. "Let me see the ring."

There was another quick exchange of glances between the betrothed.

"We don't have a ring yet," Carrie answered in a flat monotone.

A puzzled smile covered Penelope's face as she pulled back and looked first at Carrie and then at Timothy. "What do you mean you don't have a ring? How can you ask someone to marry you without a ring?"

Walker leaned over and whispered in Timothy's ear. "You may want to take a few steps back. She's stronger than she looks, and she's having a really bad day." Timothy nodded and inched toward the door.

"Kelly and William both insisted we had to tell you this in person."

"Tell me what?" Penelope demanded.

Carrie's eyes filled with tears and her lower lip began to quiver. "Don't yell at me!" She broke into uncontrollable sobs. Penelope was stunned. She had never seen her daughter this emotional before. Suddenly Carrie's face went ashen. Her eyes grew large. Her hand flew to her mouth and she bolted toward the bathroom. Through the door they could all hear her retching.

Penelope wheeled and her eyes locked on Timothy Ellison. "What the hell is going on?"

In a barely audible voice, Timothy answered. "Morning sickness."

PENELOPE HAD CALLED in reinforcements. Josephine Middleton Mitchell, Penelope's lifelong friend, whose philandering first husband had walked out on her for a curvy twenty-something, was sitting across the table. Thankfully, because of her recent marriage, she only lived a few miles away. A bit over a year ago Joey had met Franklin Mitchell, CEO of *The Washington Post* Group, at a party held for Penelope and the Hermes Project in Jackson Hole. With both between spouses it only took about six months for her Southern charm and incredible aerobicized body to win over Mitchell's heart, and the various other parts of his anatomy.

He considered her his ultimate trophy wife. Not only did she look spectacular in an evening gown, but she was also a holy terror in the sack and, being roughly the same age, they shared a common history. From impressionist art to Watergate to obscure Eastern religions, Josephine could hold up her end of a conversation on nearly any subject. Mostly, she made him laugh, a lot. Since she decamped from a lifetime in Charleston to Washington, she'd let her hair return to its natural color of chestnut from the fire engine red she had favored during her post-divorce recovery period. She had also reverted to preferring Josephine rather than her mid-life-crisis alias. 'Joey' was now limited to longtime friends who had grown up with her in Charleston, like Penelope. While almost exactly the same age as Penelope, thanks to the magic hands of her plastic surgeon and a lady of leisure's ten hours a week at the gym, she looked several years younger.

Josephine was having trouble keeping the smile off her face. Walker and Haley had beaten a tactical retreat the moment Josephine arrived, while Timothy and Carrie had retired to the guest room to regroup. Ian was parked in front of Penelope's sixty-inch flat screen watching television. Unlike Penelope, Fleming had quickly mastered the remote and was flipping around watching snippets of one show before moving on to another. "What's with him?" Josephine asked. "Has he got Attention Deficit Disorder or something?"

"Not a clue," Penelope answered with a sigh. "He was Michael's idea."

Ian Fleming broke into a fit of giggles from the other side of the room and leaned in closer as Bugs outsmarted Daffy. Penelope shook her head and Josephine rolled her eyes before they turned their attention back to their glasses of Merlot.

"You brought all of this on yourself, you know," Josephine said with a laugh.

"What are you talking about?" Penelope asked as she put her elbows on the kitchen table and rested her chin on her hands.

"With all of your Power of Thought and Law of Attraction hocus pocus."

"I'm still not tracking."

"You're the one who keeps telling me how much you were wishing for your daughters to get married and start having grandkids."

"I was thinking more along the lines of them getting married and THEN having the grandchildren."

"Maybe you weren't specific enough when you were communicating telepathically with the Wizard of Oz or whoever it is you talk to when you're in one of your little trances."

"You're not being much help," Penelope announced. "Besides, I haven't had much time for that kind of stuff lately."

Josephine's eyes twinkled. "At least there's one good thing."

"Pray tell."

"I'm happy to see that not all of the Drayton women have taken a vow of celibacy."

Penelope stuck her tongue out at Josephine, picked up her glass of Merlot and took a sip. "Remind me again why I called you?"

Josephine clinked her glass with Penelope's. "No one can abuse you like an old friend."

Penelope sighed. "I just can't believe the way Carrie is acting. I've never seen anything like it."

Josephine's eyes grew large with amazement. "Excuse me?"

"What?"

"Apparently you've dropped your own pregnancies down the memory hole."

"What does that mean?"

"Okay," Josephine said as she leaned back in her chair. "We lovingly called Carrie's pregnancy your '*Muy Loca*' period."

"What are you talking about?"

"Remember that housekeeper you had from Costa Rica?"

"Evita?"

"About half way through your first pregnancy she threw up her hands and left muttering, '*muy loca, muy loca*'. Apparently she decided she would rather take her chances with the immigration authorities than have to put up with you."

Penelope took another sip of wine. "I always wondered what happened to her."

"Kelly was the 'Kimberly Clark' pregnancy."

"Kimberly Clark?"

"They manufacture Kleenex," Josephine said. "Once you were past the post-partum blues, their stock dropped 15%."

Penelope shook her head as she took another sip of wine. "If you say so."

"Ah," Josephine said with a smile. "But the *pièce de résistance* was William and the 'Vampire' pregnancy."

"The what?"

"Having elected to have three children in four years, you were not exactly going to win the swimsuit competition, pumpkin. You were so upset with the shape of your body." Josephine took a quick sip of wine. "You hung drapes over every mirror in the house so you didn't have to look at yourself."

"I'm sorry," Penelope said with a sigh, "I don't remember any of this."

"Honey, you were so juiced up on hormones, you didn't know what year it was."

"You're not being very helpful here," Penelope said as she ran her finger around the rim of her wine glass. "Don't you have a party to plan?"

"Frankie and *The Post* have a full time staff person to deal with stuff like that. I was just in the way." Josephine began fanning herself and her voice reverted to her best Vivien Leigh. "Besides a fine Southern lady of good breeding is much too silly to handle something that complicated. Just ask anyone in here in Washington and they'll tell you. As you know, I have always depended on the kindness of strangers."

"Do these people realize you were valedictorian of Wellesley?"

Josephine pressed her index finger to her lips. "I haven't had this much fun in years," her voice returning to normal. "Frankie is in on the joke and thinks I'm hilarious. Apparently every Yankee, particularly those with Ivy League diplomas on their office walls, believes anyone with the slightest bit of twang in their speaking voice is an inbred imbecile playing *Deliverance* on the banjo." Josephine raised her glass. "To the breathtaking arrogance of Northerners." Penelope clinked her glass.

"Amen. One of my New York editors always talks more slowly to me than she does to anyone else in the room simply because I'm from Charleston."

Josephine shook her head. "And they think we're the ones with the monopoly on prejudice." Josephine looked past Penelope and nodded toward Carrie who had emerged from her cave, Timothy Ellison in tow. She leaned in and whispered, "Incoming."

Carrie stopped directly in front of Penelope and announced, "Mom, Timothy and I have decided we want to get married at Drayton Hall."

"Carrie," Penelope answered, "the family doesn't own Drayton Hall anymore. We deeded it to the National Trust for Historic Sites years ago."

"I'm not stupid, mother, I know that." Carrie snapped. "You were married there after we gave it to the Registry so I know it can be done." Carrie squared her shoulders and announced, "I will NOT be the first

Drayton woman in fifteen generations to be married someplace other than Drayton Hall." She folded her arms across her chest, indicating no further discussion would be necessary or tolerated. "I talked to Grandma..."

"You called my mother?" Penelope asked as her eyes grew large.

"Oh, boy," Josephine said softly as she poured the last of the Merlot into Penelope's glass. Penelope emptied the glass in a single gulp.

"Yes. Grandma has talked to Uncle Rob..."

Penelope held up her hand and closed her eyes. "You brought my brother into this?"

Josephine slid off her chair, headed toward the wine cabinet, grabbed another bottle of Merlot, and began fishing in a drawer for the corkscrew. "We are definitely going to need more wine."

"Grandma and Uncle Rob both agree that with you being such a celebrity and all, you could call the National Trust and get it all arranged."

Penelope forced a smile. "Remind me to call and thank them for their vote of confidence." Out of Carrie's line of sight, Josephine was rolling her eyes and mouthing "Muy Loca." Penelope, with as much calmness as she could muster said, "When is this wedding supposed to take place?"

"We've decided four weeks from this coming Saturday."

Behind them, Josephine lost her grip on the corkscrew. It fell with a clatter back into the drawer and disappeared. "Sorry," she muttered as she forced a smile.

Penelope tried to control her voice and the expression on her face. There was no telling what would launch Carrie into another emotional jag. "Four weeks is not very much time to plan a wedding sweetie."

"You think I don't know that, Mother?" Carrie answered, exasperated with the incredible density her mother was showing. "I don't want to look pregnant in my wedding pictures."

"But, honey, you are pregnant."

Carrie's lower lip began to quiver and tears started streaming down her cheeks. She turned on her heels, bolted toward the guest bedroom and slammed the door. The muffled sounds of her sobs could be heard through the door. Timothy Ellison was like a deer in the headlights, frozen to his spot.

Josephine patted him on the shoulder. "Don't worry. If she is anything like her mother, the first trimester will be the worst. She'll run along fine ninety-five percent of the time, and then something will set her off. You've already seen her as bad as she is likely to get. Once this wedding thing is behind her, I'm sure she'll be just fine."

"Thanks," Ellison said as he drew in a cleansing breath to brace himself.

A broad smile covered Josephine's face as she studied Ellison. "You really love her, don't you?"

"I've never met a woman like her before."

"You haven't spent much time in the South, have you?" Josephine asked rhetorically as she patted his cheek.

"No, ma'am."

"You're in for a treat." Josephine nodded toward the bedroom. "You run along now. It's probably best if she is not alone too much right now."

Timothy Ellison nodded his head in agreement and trotted off toward the guest bedroom.

After he was out of earshot Josephine said, "I didn't have the heart to tell him that a Southern woman can make a man deliriously happy or his life a living hell, nor that there is seldom any middle ground."

Penelope could feel a headache starting to build behind her left eye. "Was it true what you said about the first trimester being my worst?"

"Lord, no," Josephine said with a laugh. "You didn't even build up a good head of steam until the middle of the second trimester. I didn't want the boy running out of here screaming before he says 'I do.'" Josephine scratched her chin. "You know, they always say sequels are never as good as the original but '*Muy Loca II, The Revenge of Carrie*' has real potential."

Josephine was just about to start foraging again for the corkscrew she had dropped when the phone rang.

"Will you get that?" Penelope asked as she started softly banging her forehead on the table. "How," she said to no one in particular, "could this day possibly get any worse?"

"Could you hold the line for one little bitty second? Thank yooou." Josephine put the phone on the kitchen counter. Penelope watched as her friend put the Merlot back in the rack, grabbed a bottle of Scotch from the cupboard over the refrigerator and poured four fingers' worth in a highball glass. She handed the phone and the glass to Penelope. "It's your ex-husband."

CHAPTER TEN

PENELOPE WOKE WITH a start. It was still dark outside, but she could make out that the first digit of the clock on her nightstand was a three. She was having trouble making her eyes focus enough to get anything beyond that. As she gingerly tried to sit up, the throbbing in her skull sent her hand to her forehead and her head back to the pillow. Closing her eyes again, she ran her tongue around the inside her mouth just to be sure the source of the awful taste wasn't a sock from the bottom of her gym bag. Obviously Merlot with a Scotch chaser, especially when consumed in bulk, was not the best combination for her.

Penelope knew she was going to have to get up. In addition to feeling an irresistible need to brush her teeth, there was another bathroom duty which needed urgent tending. She figured she could either try to stand up slow or fast. Slow had already crashed and burned, so she opted for fast. Closing her eyes and taking in a deep breath, in one motion she sat up and swung her legs over the side of the bed. She held that position with her eyes closed for a few moments to be sure there wasn't going to be an uprising from her intestinal tract. While her stomach was queasy, it didn't seem to have any urge to relocate its contents. So far, so good. Bracing herself with her hands on the bed, she stood up. While shaky, everything still appeared functional. She shuffled her way to the bathroom. Not wanting to see the state of her hair, Penelope didn't bother with the overhead lights and opted instead for the much lower wattage light in the shower stall. After a few minutes with a toothbrush and washcloth she was actually starting to feel better. Not good, just better.

"Water," Penelope muttered to herself and she pulled on her terrycloth robe, opened the door to her bedroom and padded barefooted toward the kitchen. She was only a few feet into the hallway when she noticed the glow from the television in the living room. Approaching, she discovered Ian and Timothy sitting on the couch watching an episode of *The Dog Whisperer*. Cesar Millan was trying to convince a weepy, collagen-enriched Southern California lady that maybe the problem was with her and not the brainless fluff ball in her lap. He wasn't making much headway.

A smile broke across Penelope's face. Watching Ian and Timothy reminded her of her only son, William, when he was perched on the edge of the nest ready to be the last of her children to fly away. Penelope had discovered his night owl tendencies when he was discussing "stupid pet tricks" with one of his sisters over a bowl of Cheerios at age eight. Apparently he had been sneaking downstairs and watching "*Letterman*" from the time he had mastered rappelling from his crib.

Penelope froze in the shadows when she saw the door to the guestroom open. In the doorway, with her arm extended seductively and dressed in a teddy that left nothing to the imagination, was Penelope's eldest. "Timmy? When are you coming back to bed?" Carrie purred. When she noticed Ian, she squeaked and mounted a hasty retreat.

"She has been insatiable since she got pregnant," Timothy said to Ian. A few feet behind him Penelope cleared her throat. Timothy closed his eyes and his chin fell to his chest.

"That's my daughter we're talking about."

"Yes ma'am."

"You remember my daughter?"

Timothy flinched when he felt his future mother-in-law's hands on his shoulder, but he was too afraid to turn around and make eye contact.

"The pregnant one?" Penelope leaned over and whispered in his ear. "I would love to hear your explanation of how in this day and age, with so many contraceptive options available, this blessed event occurred."

"Timmy!" cooed Carrie from the guest room. "Come back to bed."

Penelope squeezed Timothy Ellison's deltoids hard enough that he winced. "Why don't you run along? We'll chat again later." Given the choice between the frisky Drayton kitten in the guestroom or the angry Drayton lioness in the living room, Ellison was gone in a less than a heartbeat.

Ian Fleming, with a large bowl of fruit in front of him, was busy peeling a banana. "This is a lively place."

"A little too lively of late," Penelope said with a sigh as she fell heavily into the still warm spot on the couch Timothy had just vacated.

"I really like your friend Josephine. She's funny."

"She's twice your age and married," Penelope said as she declined a banana and reached for an Asian pear instead.

"You really need to stop that."

"Stop what?"

"I spoke in simplicity, but you were listening with complexity," Ian answered without taking his eyes off of the television screen.

"What are you talking about?"

"You hear what you want to hear instead of the actual words. You listen through the story that is already playing in your head."

"Explain," Penelope said.

"I said your friend was funny and you told me she was too old for me and married."

"So?"

"What does being funny have to do with her age and her marital status?" Ian asked as he popped a piece of cantaloupe in his mouth.

"You are very odd."

"I get that a lot."

"I don't doubt it for a second." Penelope bit into her pear. It was like nectar. "Where did you get this?"

"I know a little twenty-four hour green grocer in Georgetown."

"Do they deliver?" Penelope asked as she took another bite of pear and had to wipe some juice off of her chin.

"No, I walked over."

Penelope nodded as she slowly chewed the pear. After a few moments a puzzled look covered her face. "You just got up and left?"

"Yes. There was nothing in your refrigerator worth eating and I was hungry."

"How did you get back into the apartment?" Penelope asked.

"I left the door unlocked."

Penelope nearly choked on her piece of fruit. She finished chewing, swallowed and turned to face Ian. "You left my apartment door unlocked?"

"Yes," Ian answered innocently as a smile broke across his face and he pointed toward the television show that seemed to have him transfixed. "I love Cesar."

Penelope was torn between screaming and strangling Fleming, but with Carrie in the next room she leaned in and hissed instead. "What kind of idiot leaves an apartment unlocked in downtown Washington in the middle of the night?"

Ian shrugged. "Tim was here and they've got security downstairs."

Penelope had lost her appetite for fruit and tossed the half eaten pear in the scrap bowl Ian had placed on the coffee table next to the larger bowl of fruit. She shook her head and glowered at Fleming.

"May I make a suggestion?" Fleming offered.

"Will it keep me from strangling you?"

"Maybe." For the first time Ian turned his full attention from the TV and focused on Penelope. Seeing the expression on her face, he scooted a few inches away. "Then again, maybe not."

"Spit it out," Penelope said impatiently.

"I've only been around you for less than a day, so please don't take this the wrong way."

Penelope drew in a deep breath and slowly released it through her mouth. She had heard the bodyguard lecture before. *'I'm here for your protection.' 'Don't tell me how to do my job.'* Blah, blah, blah. Michael Walker and Sally Winters had explained to her a dozen times that having a bodyguard was a part of being a celebrity and that she needed to get past it. She was confident she knew exactly what Ian would be saying next. She was wrong.

"You really need to release your anger."

Penelope blinked her eyes a few times and shook her head in disbelief. "Excuse me?"

Fleming's face was devoid of emotion; his voice was so calm it had a soothing musical quality. "You just won an unheard of three Pulitzer Prizes, and your beautiful daughter has informed you that she will soon be giving you a grandson and marrying a man you know in your heart will always be there for her. This should be the happiest day of your life, but instead you're making yourself and those around you miserable."

Penelope was stunned. Her mouth started to move, but she was unable to form any words. In less than a second Penelope's mind went from *who does this pup think he is?* or the better question of *who is this pup?* to realizing that Fleming's words, with a simple honesty and serenity, had summed up the current state of her life. Instead of dressing Ian down for his impertinence she heard herself, much to her own surprise, ask, "What do you recommend?"

"Have you ever tried the straw method of release?" She shook her head. "This is a great simplification. Lie in bed and pretend there is a straw sticking out of your chest or solar plexus and just imagine all of your anger and frustration flowing out of the straw. Once you have let the problem go, the universe will take care of it for you."

"Do you know how silly that sounds?"

"Yes, ma'am."

"Do you have a recommendation of where I should start?"

"Yes, ma'am."

Penelope waited a few beats and when it was clear no additional information was coming, said, "Well? What do you suggest?"

"Release your feelings toward your daughter and the situation she finds herself in. It will make you feel better and will do wonders for her."

"What does that mean?"

"This is her entire life and she is terrified. From you, all she is asking for is a bit of your time, a few dollars for a wedding, and your love and understanding."

"I'm giving her all of that."

"True, but at an emotional cost to both of you. If you truly love your daughter, you need to release her. Use the straw. Let the universe know you love your daughter and will support her in all things, and then forget about it."

"It's that simple?"

"All of the important things usually are."

"You are a very odd person."

"You've mentioned that before."

With her head swimming, Penelope returned to her bedroom. The clock by her bed still hadn't progressed enough to make the first digit a "four" instead of a "three". It was too early to get up, and after her little chat with Ian, Penelope was too wired to go back to sleep. With a sigh, she reached blindly under the bed for her yoga mat, but it wasn't there.

"That's odd," she muttered as she dropped to her knees and lifted the dust ruffle. It had been so long since she had used it, the maid's vacuuming had pushed it up near the top of the headboard. Flattening herself on the floor, she slid part way under the box springs until she was able to grab enough of the mat to pull it out. A herd of dust bunnies followed in its wake. She rolled the pad out on the floor next to her bed, but it had been so long since it had been used that the edges curled up and it wouldn't lie flat. Flipping it over left it bowed slightly at the ends but serviceable.

For about ten minutes she did a series of yoga stretches and was disappointed but hardly surprised at how much flexibility she had lost in the past year. She could already feel her hamstrings and lower back drafting a letter of protest, which they would be delivering later in the day.

Penelope sighed as she lowered herself to the mat and tried to get into a lotus position, but her knees declined to help in the effort. It had been too long. She settled into a half-lotus instead. She drew in a cleansing breath, closed her eyes and tried to relax. After ten minutes, Penelope decided this wasn't working, rolled the mat back up, and tucked it under her bed. Back in bed and lying on her left side in a fetal position, she flashed back to what Ian had said. Closing her eyes, she imagined a straw extending from the middle of her chest and tried to imagine all of the negative energy and emotion she felt there flowing out of it. At first it was a drip, then a trickle, then a torrent. When it seemed like only trace amounts were left, she silently affirmed, "I love my daughter. This is going to be fine."

Before she was even aware of it on a conscious level, the thought evolved into a mantra. "I love my daughter. This is going to be fine. I love my daughter. This is going to be fine." Penelope felt her body relaxing and visualized her last remnants of tension flowing away through the imaginary straw in the middle of her chest. Before long she had released the thought and fallen into a deep sleep.

HAVING LIVED ALONE since her divorce, Penelope woke with a start at the sound of hushed voices in the kitchen. The clock next to her bed told her that she had slept for over five glorious hours. Penelope threw on her robe and stuck her head out the door. Ian did not appear to have moved from his parking spot in front of the television. His wingman, Timothy, had returned but neither were the source of the mysterious voices. Sitting at the small glass top table in the breakfast area were Carrie and Josephine.

"Morning, sleepy head," Josephine said with a laugh.

"How long have you been here?" Penelope asked as she reached for the coffee pot and poured all that was left into the "Bubba's Bar-B-Que" mug she had picked up on her last visit to Jackson. The dregs only filled her mug about two thirds of the way.

"Long enough." Josephine and Carrie broke into a fit of the giggles.

"What's wrong with you two?" Penelope asked.

Josephine tried to wipe the grin off her face, with mixed success. Carrie, with the worst poker face in the galaxy, was trying so hard not to laugh that her whole body shook. "Apparently your daughter has never heard any of the exploits of 'Bad Penelope'. I've been bringing her up to speed."

Carrie broke into another fit of giggles and had to wipe a tear from her eye. "I had no idea you were such a wild child when you were in high school and college."

Penelope's eyes narrowed as she shot an angry stare in Josephine's direction. As was usually the case, her best look bounced right off leaving no measurable impact on her old friend. Knowing a lost cause when she saw one, she took a sip of the coffee and made a face. When Josephine was the barista, the coffee was always way too strong for her taste. Penelope opened the refrigerator door, pulled out a carton of skim milk, sniffed it to be sure it was safe, and poured a generous portion into her mug. "In my defense, during that period some people were more inclined to get into trouble than others."

"True," Josephine said with a laugh, "but I had a heck of a partner in crime."

Penelope joined them at the table. "Don't believe everything you hear, sweetie. Some people are prone to exaggeration."

"Did Grandma know?"

"Of course not," Penelope answered instantly but without much conviction.

"Ha!" barked Josephine. "The old biddy isn't as dense as she acts, and we did provide her with a few clues."

Carrie propped her elbows on the table and rested her chin on her fists as she focused her full attention on Josephine. "What kind of clues?"

Penelope pointed a warning finger at Josephine. "Don't go there."

Josephine waved her off. "I guess the first clue was when she had to show up with bail money..."

"What?" Carrie shouted as she looked at her mother with open-mouthed wonder. "You got arrested! Oh! My! God! Grandma must have had kittens. What happened?"

"Josephine Antoinette Middleton," Penelope hissed as she stood up, leaned across the table and shot a look at her lifelong friend that could stop the average pacemaker, "how can you tell this story?"

"That's the difference between you and me, pumpkin." Josephine was beaming. "I'm proud of it."

Penelope picked up her coffee mug and headed back toward her bedroom. "I'm going to take a shower." As she started to close the door, she heard an eruption of co-ed laughter. Apparently the boys had found this nugget from her misspent youth more interesting than cable.

"No way!" shouted Carrie.

"Seriously?" Timothy asked.

"It gets better..." Penelope heard Josephine say as she closed the bedroom door. Penelope rubbed her forehead. Her headache was coming back.

After a solid half hour of grooming, Penelope rejoined the giggle fest taking place in her breakfast nook. Carrie couldn't make eye contact with her mother without breaking out in fits of laughter. Penelope shook her head and got herself a large glass of water. Josephine's coffee had more than satisfied her daily, possibly weekly, requirement for caffeine.

"So," Penelope said as she put her arm around Carrie's shoulder, "are you finished shattering my daughter's illusions of her sainted mother?"

"We moved past you a long time ago," Josephine said with a laugh and a wave of her hand. "You had your moments but they were unfortunately few and far between. Besides, there is so much low-hanging fruit on the Drayton family tree it was hard to know where to begin."

Penelope eyed Josephine with suspicion. "What kind of low hanging fruit?"

Before Penelope could get a description of which skeletons Josephine had decided to pull out of the Drayton family closet, there was a soft tap on the apartment door. As the three women turned to look in the direction of the foyer, they saw Ian Fleming looking through the eye piece.

Josephine leaned into Penelope and asked, "Wasn't he just sitting on your couch?"

"I thought so."

"How did he do that?"

"No idea," Penelope answered.

The door burst open. Sally Winters and four of her top assistants marched in. When the story of the Hermes Project and the Fourth Awakening broke, for nearly a month this posse had surrounded Penelope and helped maintain her sanity. Penelope waved to them as they surveyed her apartment looking for the best place to start setting up. They opted for the dining room table.

"What's going on?" Penelope asked with an expression somewhere between puzzled and amused.

"The cavalry has arrived."

"What in the world are you talking about?"

"We've got a wedding to plan," Sally Winters said as she located an outlet to plug in the printer she carried under her arm.

Penelope blinked and shook her head. The wedding. It had completely slipped her mind since falling asleep after her meditation the night before. She glanced at Ian Fleming, who was nodding his head in approval. Just like her new and extremely odd bodyguard had said, release the problem and the solution will find you.

Carrie came over and draped her arm around her mother. "Thanks," she said softly as she kissed Penelope on the cheek.

Penelope sighed. "There is still a problem we need to work out."

Carrie squared her shoulders and said, "I would love to get married at Drayton Hall, but it won't be the end of the world if I don't."

Penelope pulled Carrie tight. "It's something worse than that."

CHAPTER ELEVEN

JOSEPHINE, WHO HAD served the dual role of bartender and understanding old friend the night before, knew what was coming. As Timothy emerged freshly showered from the guest bedroom, Josephine cut him off with her eyes and a shake of her head. He stopped short, and one glance told him he wanted no part of the conversation between his blushing bride to be and his future mother-in-law. He pivoted on his heels and retreated back to the safety of the guest room. "Come along," Josephine said as she hooked her arm under Ian's and guided him in the direction of the dining room where Sally Winters and her staff were still busy setting up.

"What?" Carrie asked with a touch of panic in her voice.

Penelope pulled Carrie aside and sat her down on the couch. "I talked to your father last night." Penelope brushed a wisp of hair away from her daughter's face and took in a cleansing breath. "As you know, the real estate market has been a disaster for the past few years." Carrie nodded but didn't speak. "Your father was planning on filing for bankruptcy this week, but I convinced him to wait until at least after the wedding."

Carrie Drayton Spence blinked a few times as she absorbed the bad news. "Well," Carrie said with her normal take charge attitude. "We'll just have to scale back a bit."

"I have plenty of money, dear. We'll make this all work out."

When the subject of money came up, Sally Winters wandered over and asked, "I'm not interrupting anything, am I?" Carrie and Penelope both shook their heads. "Okay," Winters said quizzically as she studied the two women. "I have something for you from Mark."

"My boss," Penelope answered before Carrie could ask. "You met him last year." Carrie nodded that she remembered as Winters handed Penelope a business envelope with her name handwritten on the front. "What's this?"

"He said it was your bonus for winning your Pulitzers."

"Bonus? What bonus?" Penelope tore the envelope open, and inside was a smaller envelope, the kind *The Washington Post* uses for one-off payroll checks. She had gotten two of them before she had gotten around to submitting the paperwork to Human Resources for direct deposit. She could see her name through the glassine window but the amount was hidden.

Inside there also was a note from Mark:

Nellie:

Since no one had ever won two Pulitzers in the same year, much less three, legal didn't squawk when your lawyer friend Amy added these bonus provisions to your last contract. They actually laughed at her for being so naïve. Needless to say, they are not laughing now. FYI: the multi-Pulitzer provision has been deleted from your new contract.

WHICH I HAVEN'T RECEIVED BACK FROM YOU YET!!!

If you don't buy Amy a month in the south of France, you are a shameless cheapskate.

Mark

Penelope tore open the envelope and her eyes nearly popped out of her head. Carrie looked over her mother's shoulder and said, "Holy Crap! I've never seen that many zeros on a check before."

Penelope's heart was racing as she turned the check over to be sure it was real. "Me either." Out of the corner of her eye she saw that Ian had broken away from Josephine and was looking over her shoulder.

His eyes grew large when he saw the check in her hand. "What size straw did you use?" he asked, drawing a puzzled look from both Carrie and Josephine.

"Ignore him," Penelope said as she handed the check to Sally Winters. "This should cover the cost of the wedding."

Winters pulled back when she read the amount. "And end world hunger with change to spare."

"You'll be surprised how much something like this can cost," Penelope said firmly. "I had two ex-presidents and the entire South Carolina congressional delegation at my wedding. I expect nothing short of that for Carrie. Also, I've been getting pestered by a bunch of people in Hollywood who want the movie rights to my book. Make it clear that anyone who RSVPs with regrets is out of the running. That goes for actors too. If their butts are not in a white folding chair in South Carolina four weeks from now, they can forget being in the movie. Figure out what it's going to take to get Drayton Hall for that weekend, and if you need more money, let me know."

Sally gave a small salute and started to walk away, but Penelope pulled her back and turned her attention to her daughter. "For the next 30 days you do what this woman's team tells you. If they say eat, you eat. If they say sleep, you go take a nap. If they say..."

Before Penelope could finish her thought, Carrie threw her arms around her mother's neck and burst into body-shaking tears.

*T*HE *WASHINGTON POST* Building on 15th Street NW, by any measure, was ugly. It was squat and lifeless and looked as if it had been designed and built by bored Cold War Russians on the cheap. As Penelope waited by the main entrance for Ian to finish his conversation with the driver of her company car, she had to smile. Through the scratched glass of the bright yellow newspaper box that was chained to a light pole in front of the building she could see the morning edition of *The Post*. Her picture was in the left hand column with a headline about her winning three Pulitzers.

"Hey," Ian said as he caught up and pointed at the news box. "That's you!" Penelope sighed as they headed inside.

Since it was well after the arrival of the Monday through Friday day shift but an hour before the building began to empty for lunch, the lobby was nearly deserted. This meant Penelope's entrance only caused a small commotion instead of a full scale riot. Every face flashed with recognition the moment people saw her. Brave ones offered verbal congratulations, and a few extended their hands. As Spence and Fleming approached the security area, the crowd reverently parted to allow her to be next in line to walk through the metal detector. Penelope handed her over-sized purse to the guard, who didn't bother to look inside before handing it back to her. Fleming had nothing to declare and strolled through the pylons without generating a single chirp.

Penelope was two steps toward the elevator when it hit her. She wheeled and faced Fleming.

"You didn't set off the metal detector."

"No ma'am."

"That means you're not carrying a gun."

"I never carry a gun."

"Never?"

"Not since I got back, ma'am."

"Back from where?"

"No. No. No," Ian said with a laugh, "that's for me to know and you to find out."

"Whatever," Penelope answered with a hint of exacerbation in her voice. "You left me sitting alone on Walker's jet. You went out for a moonlight stroll and left my apartment unlocked, and you never carry a gun. Exactly what kind of a bodyguard are you?"

Ian made an odd, surprised face. "Who said I was a bodyguard?"

Before Penelope had time to process a response to this little nugget, Fleming took two quick steps and stuck his hand between the closing doors of one of the elevators, causing them to reopen. When Penelope stepped in, all conversations stopped and all eyes locked on her. Fleming pushed the only button which wasn't lit, the top floor.

Penelope had to step aside when the doors opened on the newsroom floor so two young reporters could join the chaos of a major newspaper's next edition being created. She sighed as the doors started to close and found herself leaning to peer through the rapidly shrinking opening so she could see the newsroom for as long as possible. She and Fleming were the only people still in the car when it reached the seventh floor. The rank and file in the newsroom called this 'Mount Olympus'. It contained the offices for the editorial board, columnists and, of course, people like Penelope. Unlike the newsroom three floors below, the floors were carpeted, the lighting was indirect and the only noise was classical music playing over well-concealed speakers.

Stepping off the elevator, the first thing one would notice was "*The Washington Post* Wall of Fame." It had about eight dozen portraits, some over 100 years old, in ultra modern frames mounted in chronological order as one approached the receptionist. Penelope smiled when she saw that a workman had finished hanging her picture and was busy screwing the last of the brass plates under it. As she walked by, the workman looked at her and then at the portrait and then back at her. "Good likeness," he muttered.

"Thanks," Penelope answered as she lingered for a moment and read the inscription.

Pulitzer Prize – Investigative Reporting
Pulitzer Prize – Breaking News Reporting
Pulitzer Prize – Explanatory Reporting

Apparently the Pulitzer for Investigative Reporting she had won years earlier while working for *The Post and Courier* in Charleston didn't count for anything in the hallowed halls of *The Washington Post*.

The duo approached the reception desk where an attractive woman in her mid-thirties was just finishing up a call. The nameplate at the center of her desk identified her as Mary Garrett. "Good morning, ma'am," she said while handing Penelope a stack of pink *'While You Were Out'* phone messages. "They are in order of importance as usual."

Penelope held up the one from the top of the stack. "Seriously?"

"Yes, ma'am. I didn't believe it myself," Garrett answered. "Mark Hatchet left a message that he wanted to see you the moment you arrived."

Penelope nodded. "Call and tell him I'm on my way."

Mary Garrett reached for the phone on her desk as Penelope and Ian headed back toward the elevators.

THIS WAS PENELOPE'S first visit to the newsroom since the announcement of her multiple Pulitzers, and she had no idea what kind of reception to expect. There always seemed to be an unspoken level of tension between those who worked on 'Mount Olympus' and the rank and file reporters who toiled in the newsroom bullpen.

The moment Spence and Fleming stepped off the elevator the noise level in the newsroom began to drop. With around 50 desks tightly crammed into an area better suited for, at most, 40; the available floor space was precious and had been claimed by knots of reporters discussing stories. As conversations ended mid-sentence and heads turned, Penelope felt self-conscious. Everyone in the bullpen was closer to Ian's age than to her own. As more and more left their chairs for a better look, she felt like a judge walking into a crowded courtroom. With over thirty pairs of eyes sizing her up, Penelope nervously brushed a stray hair out of her face.

Penelope gave a weak smile and wave to those faces she recognized, dropping her head as she tried to avoid any further eye contact while making her way to Mark Hatchet's office. Then Penelope heard a sound that stopped her in her tracks. It was first one rhythmic beat, then five, then twenty. Lifting her eyes, she saw that everyone in the newsroom of *The Washington Post* was on their feet. Applauding.

Penelope's hand shot to her mouth as she gasped in surprise. Tears started to well up in her eyes. In a flash she was surrounded by Fourth Awakening alumni who had helped her write the original story, all offering their congratulations. Penelope sheepishly made her way to the fish bowl Mark Hatchet called his office.

Hatchet glanced up as Penelope and Fleming entered the cramped space. A young man in his mid-thirties was sitting in the chair across the desk from Hatchet. He looked familiar but she was sure she had never met him before. He glared at her with intense blue gray eyes as she entered. "Close the door," Hatchet said with an unexpected stern edge to his voice. "We've got a problem."

CHAPTER TWELVE

Penelope's defenses immediately went up. She had known Mark for years and, having spent the last year working closely with him, she knew his body language well. Since he kept avoiding eye contact, this wasn't going to be good. "If this is about my contract..." she said hopefully but already certain it was not the reason the meeting had been called.

Hatchet waved her off. "No, that's not it." Hatchet motioned toward the second chair in front of his desk. "Please, sit down."

The young man already in the chair next to her glanced up at Penelope as if she had something unpleasant stuck to the bottom of her shoe. To Penelope's surprise and great relief, Ian's demeanor had completely changed. The man child who had accompanied her into Mark's office had vanished and been replaced with something very different. Fleming's smile had vanished and his eyes were locked on the unknown but obviously hostile stranger. Fleming perched himself on the arm of Penelope's chair. Whoever the young man was, to get to Penelope he would now have to go through Fleming first. Previously that would have appeared to be light work, now she wasn't so sure. While completely calm and relaxed, Fleming looked like a coiled cobra ready to strike at the first sign of movement in Penelope's direction.

"You, of course, know Kent," Hatchet said. Penelope shook her head. "You don't know Kent Lazlo?" Mark Hatchet's mouth fell open. "How is that possible?"

"That's your ace reporter for you." Lazlo folded his arms across his chest and pivoted in his seat so his back was nearly pointed at Penelope. "She doesn't miss a trick."

"I'm sure," Penelope, ignoring Kent Lazlo, answered in her defense, "that there are dozens of reporters here I've never met." Her eyes narrowed. "What makes him so special?"

"Jeez, Nellie," Mark Hatchet said as he leaned back in his chair, "you've never met Kent or even know anything about him?"

"No," Penelope answered as she felt the color rising in her cheeks. "I repeat. What makes him so special?"

Kent Lazlo pointed at Penelope but kept his eyes locked on Mark Hatchet. "Explain to me how they can give multiple Pulitzers to someone with her head so far up her..."

"Calm down, Kent," Hatchet said firmly as he cut him off before he could finish his thought. "I'll handle this." In the year since Mark Hatchet had stepped inside the "Cube" at the Hermes Project he was a different man. His weight was down over thirty-five pounds and his waist had gone from 44" to 38". He was off both his blood pressure medicine and Lipitor. Fresh had replaced fast as the most common word used to describe his food preference and he was seriously considering training for a marathon with no one snickering behind his back. Having known him since their college days, Penelope had never seen an expression quite like the one he had on his face. It was an odd combination of disappointment and disbelief. Who was Kent Lazlo and why was it so astounding that she didn't know him?

Still refusing to even look in Penelope's direction, Lazlo demanded, "Go ahead and ask her."

"Ask me what?" demanded Penelope.

Mark Hatchet took a moment to gather his thoughts before speaking. "Are you meeting with Walker and Trotta tonight?"

Penelope was confused. "Yes, we're having dinner..."

"See! She admits it!" Lazlo shouted as he started to his feet, but Ian Fleming made a sharp hissing sound as he pressed his thumb onto Lazlo's sternum and pushed him back into his seat. "What the hell is wrong with you?" Lazlo demanded as he rubbed his chest.

Ian Fleming hissed again as he pointed a warning finger in Lazlo's direction before saying, "Sit." Lazlo blinked several times but didn't try to get up again.

Mark Hatchet drew in a deep breath and his cheeks puffed out when he exhaled. "Did you ask to be a part of this meeting?" Hatchet asked softly.

Penelope's eyes danced back and forth between Mark Hatchet and Kent Lazlo. She couldn't believe it, all of this because she had been asked out on a date? "No," she said slowly, still unsure where this was headed.

"Michael Walker asked me to join him for dinner tonight and I accepted. He said there may be a story in it for me, but he didn't provide any details."

"Oh my God!" Lazlo groaned. "Here we go again." Lazlo started to his feet but a threatening hiss from Fleming and a thumb poised inches from his rib cage caused him to reconsider. Penelope had a new-found respect for Ian's bodyguard skills. If it wasn't for his presence, Penelope had the distinct impression that right about now she would be on the floor with Kent Lazlo's fingers wrapped around her throat.

"What's going on, Mark?" Penelope asked.

"Kent is on the financial desk," Hatchet answered, "and he has been working on a story about the problems at Walker Industries for the past couple of weeks."

"Six weeks to be exact," Lazlo corrected. He obviously wanted to be up pacing, but the presence of Fleming limited his options to squirming in his seat. "And the board of directors votes on Monday."

"What does any of this have to do with me?" Penelope asked.

"Don't play innocent with me, cupcake," Lazlo barked at Penelope. "You can't possibly be that naive."

"I got invited to dinner!" Penelope felt her blood pressure starting to rise. "I said yes. Where is the problem here?"

"This may be the single most important business meeting for any of the Fortune 50 companies in over a decade." Kent Lazlo rolled his eyes and shook his head. "And you expect me to believe princess here gets invited and doesn't even have a clue what's going on? Unbelievable!"

"So, Nellie," Hatchet said softly, trying to lower the tension in the room. "You didn't ask to be invited and you had no idea there may be a potential conflict with another reporter?"

"I did not ask to be invited."

"Do you have any idea what may happen at this meeting?" Hatchet asked.

Penelope's cheeks flushed. With the disaster that had greeted her in her apartment the previous evening, Walker's business dinner had been the furthest thing from her mind. "Michael Walker is meeting with Sam Trotta..."

"Sal Trotta," Lazlo corrected rudely.

"Excuse me," Penelope said. "Michael Walker is meeting with Sal Trotta and he invited me along."

"As his date or as a reporter?" Hatchet asked.

"What does that mean," Penelope asked.

"Will it be on or off the record?"

"He said something about a potential embargo period having to do with the SEC and insider trading," Penelope said, "but he said it would be on the record."

"What!" Lazlo shouted but, catching a glimpse of Ian out of the corner of his eye, stayed seated.

Mark Hatchet turned his focus on Kent Lazlo. "Did you get invited to this on the record sit down?" Hatchet asked.

Lazlo fell silent and shifted uncomfortably from side to side in his seat for a few seconds. "No," he answered bitterly in a barely audible voice.

Mark Hatchet leaned back in his chair and pressed his lips tightly together. Finally he said, "Kent..."

"No! No! No!" he shouted as he started to his feet. This time Fleming not only hissed and jammed his thumb on Lazlo's sternum, but also, with his other hand, grabbed the back of Lazlo's collar and roughly pulled him back into the chair.

"Sit," Fleming said, his voice like the crack of a whip. "Stay."

Lazlo wheeled and glared at Fleming but made no attempt to get up again. "Touch me again and I'll break your arm off and shove it ..."

"That's enough!" Hatchet barked with enough authority to cause the room to fall silent and heads to turn in the bullpen just outside his office door.

Lazlo's head pivoted back and forth between Spence and Hatchet. His voice softened to a whisper. His eyes finally decided on Penelope. "I'm not going to let you waltz in here and steal another story from me."

Penelope held her hands up in mock surrender. "What story did I ever steal from you?"

Kent Lazlo rolled his eyes in disbelief. "Oh, I don't know," he said with venom dripping from every word. "How about the one that got you all of your Pulitzers? You remember; the one about Michael Walker and the Hermes Project and the Fourth Awakening?"

CHAPTER THIRTEEN

"WHAT?!" PENELOPE SHOUTED as she turned her focus to Hatchet. "What is this lunatic talking about?"

Before Hatchet could answer, Lazlo jumped in. "Maybe he's talking about the fact that I had been on the Hermes Project story for months, and just when I was starting to make enough progress to get everybody nervous, *The Washington Post* spiked the story."

"That decision," Hatchet said, "was made by the publisher and not by me."

"Right," Lazlo answered while shaking his head bitterly. "Then the next thing we know, your old college sweetheart, who hasn't had a byline since V-J Day, appears out of nowhere having the story spoon-fed to her by Michael Walker. I do all the real reporting and she gets the book deal and the Pulitzers, while I get hosed."

Mark Hatchet shook a finger in Lazlo's direction. "You're getting very close to that line, Kent."

Penelope was stunned. When Mark had contacted her about the story he had told her *The Post* had agreed to officially quit looking into the activities of Michael Walker and the Hermes Project. She knew Mark had risked his career bringing her in on the story. It had never occurred to her that the background information he gave her might have been from another reporter's notes.

Penelope's eyes narrowed and locked on the Managing Editor of *The Washington Post*. "Mark, was he working on the Hermes Project story before you gave it to me?"

"Hallelujah!" Lazlo said with a sneer as he threw his hands up. "Miss Scarlett finally starts asking a few questions instead of worrying about what to wear for her next TV appearance."

"What does that mean?" Penelope demanded.

"Look," Lazlo answered as he pointed a finger at Spence, "you can either be a celebrity or a journalist but not both. Journalists ask questions and piss people off. We're curious. We want to know things. Celebrity journalists like you walk around with so many bright lights in your face you can't see anything that is going on around you. The only thing a celebrity is curious about is if they made *Page Six* or got mentioned in *People* magazine." Lazlo motioned toward the people in the newsroom bullpen. "You got your little standing ovation, but those people all hate your guts and none of them have an ounce of respect for your reporting skills." Lazlo's eyes narrowed and his voice was somewhere between a whisper and a hiss. "This time next week a bunch of those real reporters will be out of work. Do you know why?" Penelope shook her head. "So *The Washington Post* can afford to pay you enough to keep their precious prize winning reporter on staff."

"What are you talking about?" Penelope asked.

"My God, woman, do you even bother to read the newspaper you work for?" Lazlo shouted. "Budget cuts. Layoffs. Any of this ring a bell?" He shook his head in disgust again. "The people out there have spent years turning over rocks and chasing down bad leads that end up nowhere. They see some friggin' Southern Belle housewife who swoops in from Charleston and cherry picks the biggest story of the year." Lazlo's eyes turned toward Mark Hatchet. "Just because you're buddy-buddy with the boss."

The hint of smile flickered across Penelope's face. The Mark Hatchet she knew wasn't going to take that from some wet behind the ears reporter. Her eyes locked on Kent Lazlo as she waited for the bomb to drop. Silence. "Mark?" Penelope said as she turned toward Hatchet. His deadpan expression indicated he would not be racing to her defense. Penelope slumped back in her chair and shook her head. Her eyes lingered on Hatchet before turning her full attention to the man in the seat next to her. It looked like it would be up to her to add some clarity to this discussion.

She straightened her shoulders and said, "I occasionally glance at *The Post* and I've noticed that since I've joined the staff we are the only major daily in the country that has shown a circulation increase, and our top ten circulation days were when my stories were on the front page." Penelope leaned in close to Kent Lazlo. "So you might want to consider how many people would have been laid off if I hadn't come along." She held Lazlo in an icy stare, giving him an opportunity to reply. He folded his arms across his chest and crinkled his nose as if he had just noticed a foul odor.

"Next," Penelope said slowly and softly. "This is the first I've heard about you being on the Hermes Project story before me. I got a call about a story and I took the assignment."

"A real journalist would have asked a few more questions," Lazlo said with a sneer.

Flames leapt from Penelope's eyes. She had heard quite enough. She rose slowly to her feet and started yelling loud enough that, even with the door closed, everyone in the bullpen could hear every word. "Let me tell you about real journalism, you little pup. I won my first Pulitzer when I was the only woman in the newsroom. I took on politicians who wouldn't have lost a minute's sleep after turning fire hoses and German shepherds on their own citizens. I've had a cross-burning in my front yard and bricks through my window. I did all of that when your mama was still sprinkling baby powder on your butt after changing your diapers."

Penelope's arm swept toward the newsroom bullpen and pointed to the mass of reporters on the other side of the glass who were now hanging on her every word. "They may not like me, they may even hate me. But I'll tell you this, if it wasn't for people like me breaking through the glass ceiling, half of them wouldn't even be out there." Penelope's eyes narrowed and she growled, "It looks to me like you're upset because one of those celebrity journalists you hold in such low regard managed to get a story in five days that you hadn't been able to break in five months." Penelope pointed her finger at Lazlo and leaned into his personal space close enough that their noses almost touched. "Man up if you want to play in the big leagues, little boy. You had your shot, rookie, and you fumbled the ball. Just because you got your hat handed to you by a little ole Southern belle, don't come crying to me."

Kent Lazlo did something totally unexpected. He blinked his eyes a few times, and then the frown left his face and was replaced by first a smile and then a grin. Lazlo's body relaxed and he started laughing. It was one of those throw back your head laughs that causes others to want to join in.

Penelope looked across the desk at Hatchet while pointing to Lazlo. "He's nuts."

Hatchet shrugged. "It's part of the job description." He motioned toward the newsroom on the other side of the plate-glass window. "Everyone working at this level is wound a little tight and goes crazy from time to time. Half my job is keeping the inmates from killing each other over the good story assignments."

Penelope returned to her seat. "This happens all the time?"

"On a scale of ten," Hatchet said with a sigh, "I'd give this one a six and maybe the third best of the week." Hatchet glanced up at Fleming. "It might have gotten to an eight if your friend hadn't been along."

"What does a ten look like?"

"We call in the glazier to replace the glass in my window." Turning his attention to Ian, Hatchet asked, "What was the deal with the finger poke and that noise you made?"

"I saw it last night on the *Dog Whisperer*," Ian answered.

"Cesar Millan. I like it. I may use that next time."

"Thanks, by the way," Penelope said, sarcasm dripping from every word, "for all of your support."

Hatchet shrugged. "The financial desk guys are all wimps. I've seen you in action before when you were mad and figured if anyone was going to need any help it would be Kent. Besides," Hatchet motioned toward the newsroom, which had started to return to normal now that the floorshow was over, "I know you and they don't. Your little performance just got you more street cred with that crowd than all of your Pulitzers combined."

"You set me up."

Hatchet shrugged as he leaned back in his chair. "Naw. Let's just say I gave you the opportunity to enhance your standing with your peers."

"Amen," Lazlo said as he wiped a tear from his eye and extended his right hand. "Let's try this again. I'm Kent Lazlo, nice to meet you."

"Penelope Spence," she answered as she gripped his hand.

"Now that we've got that out of our systems," Hatchet said, "Let's get back to this Walker story." Lazlo and Spence exchanged glances and both nodded their agreement. "Here's the way this is going to work," Hatchet said with authority. "You are now both on this story." Hatchet held up a finger of warning to Lazlo causing him to swallow his protest before it was even registered. "Kent, if you can get yourself a chair at this meeting you are the primary reporter and will get the top byline. If not, Penelope takes the lead and you get the second byline."

"That sucks," Lazlo muttered.

"Yeah, yeah," Hatchet said firmly. "Take a second to get over it. Your only other choice is to watch me give it all to her. Take it or leave it."

With a sigh, Kent Lazlo said, "I'll take it." He stood up and nodded in Penelope's direction. "Let's go, Miss Scarlett."

"Where?" Spence asked.

"To talk to Michael about getting me invited to dinner."

F LEMING SAT IN the front seat with the driver of the town car *The Washington Post* provided for Penelope whenever she was in town. Unlike Lucas Haley, the hired help let Fleming pick the radio station. Lazlo and Spence sat in the back. They had stopped by the desk Lazlo shared with three other reporters when he was in Washington instead of New York and picked up his notes on what was happening at Walker Industries.

"I guess," Lazlo said as he admired the plush interior of the town car, "there are some advantages to being a celebrity journalist."

Penelope was rereading Lazlo's background notes and answered without looking up, "It's not as glamorous as it looks." She finished and handed the dog-eared stack of pages back to Lazlo, who crammed them into his battered briefcase. "I had no idea Michael was in so much trouble with his board of directors."

"Sales are down nearly twenty percent over last year and the projections for the next fiscal year don't look any better."

"What's causing the decline?"

"You, mostly."

"Me? What did I do?" Penelope demanded.

"Your stories about the Hermes Project and Walker's rants about a Fourth Awakening have spooked a lot of Walker Industries' clients and a lot of people on Wall Street."

"Why?"

"You have to admit, Walker does come off as a bit of a flake in your book."

Penelope sighed but didn't offer a defense of the quirks and ticks of Michael Walker's personality and beliefs. She had written the story straight, but to those who didn't buy into his concept that mankind was on the cusp of a new Awakening that would change the world forever, 'flake' might be the nicest word they would use. "I guess you have to know him." Kent Lazlo's eyes twinkled in a way Penelope found oddly familiar. "What was that look for?"

Lazlo smiled like a Cheshire cat but didn't answer. "I wouldn't spoil this for the world."

"Spoil what?"

"It's not important," Lazlo said with a laugh. "Besides, your stories were the least of his problems."

"What does that mean?"

"Walker Industries does a great deal of top secret research and after the way he pushed Homeland Security around to declassify the Hermes Project, no one trusts him anymore."

"Why do you say that?"

"Michael Walker built the company by staying out of the spotlight and under the radar. For years, Sally Winters' primary job was keeping Walker Industries out of the news and not in it. He was the mysterious billionaire, and this Hermes thing made him look bad. Every time a story with your byline runs, it reminds everyone how far around the bend he might be and the stock price drops another point or two."

"Really?" Penelope asked.

"Yes, really," Lazlo answered. "There's a board meeting in New York on Monday and Walker is about even money to lose his CEO title. That's obviously why the meeting with Trotta is such a big deal."

"Obvious to you maybe," Penelope said with a laugh, "but certainly not that obvious to me."

"When Walker told you who you were meeting for dinner, you didn't even bother to do a background search?"

Penelope felt her cheeks darken with embarrassment, and she wanted to start banging herself in the head. Yet another example of her losing her journalistic edge. Walker had told her this was an important meeting, and she hadn't even bothered to do the minimum you would expect from a cub reporter. "We had a bit of a family crisis last night."

Lazlo nodded that he understood but his eyes clearly indicated that he didn't. "It must have been some crisis."

"I arrived home to have my twenty-seven year old daughter announce she was pregnant and wanted to get married in four weeks."

"Ouch."

"That's just the appetizer," Penelope said with a laugh. "She wants to get married at Drayton Hall, which the family deeded to the National

Trust decades ago, and my ex-husband called to let me know he was filing for bankruptcy."

"Okay, okay..." Lazlo said with a laugh.

"So, who is Sal Trotta?"

"Trotta represents the California Teacher's Union Retirement Fund, which is the largest share holder in Walker Industries outside of family members. He is very respected and tough as a two-dollar steak. I can't say for certain, but he probably already has the proxies of enough other retirement funds in his pocket to be over halfway to showing Walker the door, if he is so inclined. Without Trotta's blessing, Walker is toast."

"Do you think he'll get dispensation?"

Lazlo shrugged. "Walker Industries has always been a good investment, and Michael Walker has been a top flight CEO who puts dollars on the bottom line. He still has some goodwill to draw upon, but it has started to reach its limits. A few more quarters like the last three and his goose is cooked with or without Trotta's support."

"Really?"

"Right now Trotta is the king maker," Lazlo said as he rubbed his chin. "There are fifty financial reporters who would give up their first born for a seat at that table."

"I heard it was a kidney," Penelope said gloomily.

"What?" Lazlo asked.

"It's not important. Please continue."

"A Fortune 50 company tossing their CEO overboard with a hostile proxy battle is big time stuff. In the financial world, this is as big a story as your Hermes Project reporting."

"I had no idea," Penelope said with a sigh. "I wish I had paid more attention when I took that economics class in college."

"That's why *The Post* assigns stories like this to guys like me."

"MBA?"

"Wharton," Lazlo answered.

"With that background why did you get into journalism?"

Lazlo sighed. "Let's just say I was being groomed from about age six to take over the family business but decided it wasn't right for me."

"Ah," Penelope said with a smile. "There is a rebel inside with a burning desire to be a reporter."

Lazlo didn't answer as the town car rolled to the curb in front of the Hermes Project building. Before the heavy car came to a complete stop, Fleming was already on the curb and opening the door for Spence. She refused the offer of a hand but adjusted her skirt before making her exit.

Once inside, they turned a corner and saw Michael Walker in an animated conversation with Robert Smith. At least Smith was animated, Walker was his normal calm self. When Walker saw Spence and Lazlo heading in his direction, he excused himself with a huge smile on his face. *That's better*, Penelope thought, smiling back as she felt her hand dart to her hair to check for any strays. Perhaps, after sleeping on it, Michael had realized what a jerk he'd been, and her threat to walk away and never look back had brought him to his senses. If he was going to offer her a sincere and heartfelt apology, should she accept it or make him squirm a bit? As they got closer, Penelope's smile began to fade as Walker's got bigger. The smile wasn't for her; it was for Kent Lazlo.

"Kent!" Walker said as he gave Lazlo a quick hug. "What has it been? A year since we last saw each other?"

"Yes," Lazlo answered with a nod in Penelope's direction, "and I'm still upset about the way you gave the Hermes story to her instead of me."

"I remember the conversation," Walker said with a laugh. "Such language, your mother would have been horrified. How is the Duchess?"

"Mad as hell at you, as usual," Lazlo said with a laugh.

"GOOD!" Walker exclaimed with more emotion and enthusiasm than Penelope thought he would ever be able to muster. "Then the universe is still in balance." After a moment, Walker finally noticed that Penelope was also there. He gave her a small nod of the head.

Penelope blinked a few times as she tried to make sense of all of this. "Who is the Duchess?"

"Her Grace, Gabrielle Brocklehurst-Gardiners," Walker said as he turned his attention back to Lazlo and gave him a shake to be sure he was really there. "It's good to see you again."

Lazlo returned the smile but also read the confusion on Penelope's face. "My mother's current husband is Albert Brocklehurst-Gardiners, The Ninth Duke of Leinstershire." The lights were still out in Penelope's eyes. She had no idea who they were talking about or why it mattered.

Walker caught up and pointed at Spence. "She doesn't know?" Lazlo shook his head and had to bite his lower lip to keep from laughing out loud. Walker took a moment to compose himself before turning his full attention to Penelope. Clearing his throat, he said, "The Duchess is my older sister."

Penelope's eyes flew open and her cheeks turned crimson. "You mean?"

"Yes," Walker answered. "Kent is my nephew."

CHAPTER FOURTEEN

W ITH THE TWO men standing together in front of her, it was obvious
why Kent looked familiar; he was a younger, slightly heavier version
of his uncle. Side by side the resemblance was striking, especially around
the eyes. Walker had a lean, sun baked look while Lazlo was office soft and
a touch pale. Other than that they could be teeing off together at a father/
son golf tournament. How could she have been so dense?

"What merits this visit?" Walker asked.

"Are you having dinner with Sal Trotta tonight?" Lazlo asked.

"Yes."

"Can I come?"

"That depends," Walker answered. "Will you be there as a reporter or
the sixth largest shareholder in Walker Industries?"

Penelope felt her cheeks darken even more. She started wondering
about the length of the list of obvious things she had failed to notice as
she had focused so intently on her new life. Was there any end in sight?

"You know perfectly well I put my entire stock portfolio in a blind trust
the day I started at *The Post* to avoid any potential conflicts of interest, so
I'd be there as a reporter."

"Okay," Walker said calmly. "Are you still at the same address in
Georgetown?"

"Yes...," Kent Lazlo said as he eyed his uncle with suspicion, "but that
was way too easy. What are you up to?"

"Me?" Walker answered innocently. "Why does everyone always think
there is always an ulterior motive?"

Lazlo glanced at Penelope for support and received it in the way of an
enthusiastic head nod.

"Because there always is," the pair said nearly in unison.

Lazlo and Walker locked eyes and held it for a moment before both burst
out laughing. Penelope gave herself another mental head slap. They even

had the same laugh. She closed her eyes and sighed. This was fast moving beyond simple embarrassment and was starting to approach humiliation.

"I'm not coming back, Uncle Mike."

"If memory serves," Walker answered with a mischievous twinkle in his eyes, "the last time the offer was extended, you suggested I do something that was anatomically difficult if not impossible."

"The same sentiment still applies."

"No problem," Walker said as he patted his nephew on the back. "Lucas will pick you up and we'll all take one car."

"Sal's usual place?" Lazlo asked.

"You know Sal," Walker said with a laugh. Walker lowered the bass in his voice in an apparent Trotta mimic. "If you want ta talk to me, you gotta buy me some dinner at the best damn restaurant on the entire East Coast or forgetaboutit!"

AFTER THEY DROPPED Lazlo off at *The Washington Post*, Penelope motioned for Ian to join her in the back seat. Fleming glanced longingly at the radio in the dashboard, before he climbed into the back seat. The driver didn't look like he was going to miss Ian's company. As the heavy car pulled away from the curb, she turned to face him.

"I want to ask you something."

"Sure."

"You've been my shadow for the past 36 hours. What impressions have you gotten?"

"Ma'am?"

"You were part of the Hermes Project, right?" Penelope asked.

"Yes, ma'am."

"So you must know Michael Walker pretty well."

"No." Ian shook his head. "Not really."

"What?" Penelope was stunned. "How is it possible that you worked for the Hermes Project and didn't know Walker?" When it was clear that Fleming was not going to provide an answer, she provided her own. "Right. Classified." She leaned back in the plush seat and sighed. "You must have formed an opinion."

"An opinion of what?"

"Me and my life."

"Why would you care what I think?" Ian answered with a befuddled look on his face.

"Two reasons," Penelope answered. "First, you gave me some very helpful advice last night. Second, Michael Walker obviously has one of his little plans in motion and I'm pretty sure he didn't just pick your name out of the Yellow Pages. He put us together for a reason."

Fleming shook his head. "There you go again."

"What does that mean?"

"You keep allowing the stories in your mind to make you jump to way too many conclusions. Actually, I was the one who approached Mr. Walker and not the other way around."

"Really? This wasn't Michael Walker's idea?"

"All me," Ian said brightly.

"Why do you have any interest in my well-being?"

"You'll figure it out."

"What if I don't figure it out?"

Ian shrugged. "Release and it will come to you."

Penelope rubbed her forehead as she felt a headache starting to build. The jury was still out on whether she had a hangover or if being around Hermes Project people again was the culprit. "I need to start carrying Ibuprofen."

"Let me ask you something," Ian said.

"Sure," Penelope said as she leaned back in her seat.

"Why did you assume I was your bodyguard?"

"Gee, let me think. First, you show up with Walker's personal bodyguard and the trigger happy Earp Brothers fresh from the O.K. Corral. Second, Walker has assigned me other bodyguards before. Third, you were introduced as being from Homeland Security. I can't imagine why I would jump to such an outrageous conclusion."

"It's interesting how our minds tend to combine experiences that seem related into stories that aren't even close to correct isn't it? And then we try to use those stories to guide our lives with predictable results."

"Meaning?"

"The most powerful and important form of release is one that is both the most obvious, and the most difficult to see and understand."

"You're reminding me more of Walker every minute."

"Maybe, but you've already experienced it." Fleming said with a laugh as he pulled a pair of kumquats out of his pocket and offered one to Penelope. She declined and he put the extra one back in his pocket, before beginning to roll the remaining fruit between his fingers and popping it in his mouth. "For the record, with my background and training at Homeland Security and a few other places, I am well qualified to be your bodyguard."

"I noticed that in Mark's office?"

"I have skills I would rather I didn't have."

"Such as?"

"The ability to pick handcuff locks with toenail clippings."

"Seriously?"

"Of course not!" Ian said with a snort. "My background is classified but you can take comfort in the fact that if you're really in danger I'll probably be there for you."

"Probably? That's not the level of reassurance we're looking for here."

"It's the best I've got. Besides, I'm not here to be your bodyguard. I'm here to help you find your way."

"My way where?"

"To the place you need to be."

Before Penelope could respond, the town car pulled to the curb and Fleming was out the door.

PENELOPE'S INTEREST WAS piqued but she didn't get the chance to quiz Fleming further. It was a conversation she didn't want overheard. They were not alone in the elevator, and her apartment was a madhouse. Josephine was there and had brought her massage therapist with her. Carrie was lying face down on a portable massage table making noises like a puppy having its belly scratched, as an Oriental woman roughly half her size was working on a knot in her back. Sally and four female members of her staff had commandeered the dining room, which had the quiet buzz of well-organized efficiency.

"Any progress on getting Drayton Hall?" Penelope asked as she walked past Sally on her way to the kitchen.

"Not yet," Sally Winters said as she glanced up from the keyboard of her laptop, "but I think we've figured out who can make the decision. A guy named Abernathy. He lives down in Charleston."

"David Abernathy?" Josephine asked. Winters checked her notes and nodded. "Interesting," Josephine said.

"Do you need my help?" Penelope asked Winters.

"I'll let you know."

Timothy Ellison sat quietly on the couch, drowning in a sea of estrogen. His eyes brightened when he saw Fleming come through the door. Finally, he would have someone to talk to that didn't want his input on china patterns or the color of bridesmaid's dresses. Fleming flopped down on the couch. Ellison handed him the remote.

Josephine held up a bottle of Merlot but Penelope waved off the offer. "So, how was your day?"

"Well," Penelope said as she joined Josephine in the breakfast nook, "I threw a hissy fit in Mark Hatchet's office when some pup of a reporter accused me of stealing the Hermes story from him."

"Why did he accuse you of stealing the story?"

"Because I pretty much did."

"Goodness."

Penelope sighed. "Mark had neglected to mention that when senior management spiked the story, someone else had been working it before he gave it to me."

"Senior management as in my Frankie?"

"Exactly. Then I made a complete fool of myself when I didn't realize the pup was Michael Walker's nephew until they were standing next to each other."

"Oh my!" Josephine answered. "We are having a day, aren't we?"

Penelope glanced over at Fleming. "Did I leave out anything?" Fleming's eyes never left the television but his finger pointed toward the ceiling. "Thank you, I had forgotten that one." Turning back to Josephine, "The entire time I've been living here, I never realized Michael Walker has an apartment two floors up."

Josephine Mitchell burst into laughter. "Forget the Merlot. We need to get some Scotch into you."

"No," Penelope said as she eyed the nearly empty green bottle on the counter. It was clear why she had a headache, that bottle had been full this time yesterday. "I'm having a business dinner later with Michael, his nephew, and some guy named Trotta..."

"Salvador Trotta?" Josephine asked. "The guy from the California

Teacher's Union Pension Fund?"

"How did you possibly know that before me?" Penelope demanded.

"Frankie gets all pouty if he asks me about something in his newspaper and I haven't read it." Josephine shook her head. "I can't believe you didn't know that Kent Lazlo was Walker's nephew..."

"What?" Penelope was incredulous. "I didn't tell you Lazlo's name!"

"Pumpkin," Josephine said as she patted Penelope's arm, "it's not like they've tried to keep it some great secret." Josephine grabbed a copy of *The Washington Post* off the coffee table, pulled out the financial section, and handed it to Spence. "Read the disclaimer at the bottom."

Are Michael Walker's Days Numbered?
By Kent Lazlo

Penelope was mentally kicking herself. How a story this big could have completely missed her radar screen was unimaginable. She had been so enamored with the events of her own life that she had lost focus. If it wasn't about her, it just didn't get through the mental filters. The self-flagellation only got worse when she read the disclaimer at the bottom of the story about the insurrection at Walker Industries.

Kent Lazlo earned his MBA from Wharton and a PhD in Economics from the University of Chicago. While he is the nephew of Michael Walker and a major shareholder in Walker Industries, his entire portfolio is in a blind trust.

"I am such an idiot," Penelope said as she skimmed the article.

Josephine shrugged. "I have to admit, lately if the world was about to come to an end and the story didn't have your byline, you might not know about it."

"Thanks. That makes me feel much better," Penelope said.

"Besides," Josephine said as she waved it off, "you're a political animal and the financial stuff bores you to tears."

"What does that mean?"

"Who was Grover Cleveland's Vice President?"

Without a moment's hesitation, Penelope said, "His first term it was Thomas Hendricks and his second term it was Adlai Stevenson."

"Who is the CEO of Ford?" Penelope's face was blank. "IBM? Exxon?"

"Okay," Penelope said. "You've made your point."

"When it comes to politics, you're like Rain Man. It's the only thing I've ever seen you be passionate about other than shoe shopping. I bet you haven't read the financial page in twenty years."

Penelope claimed her laptop from the clutter on the dining room table and trotted off toward her bedroom. "That's about to change."

FOR THE NEXT two hours, Penelope pulled up every article Kent Lazlo had ever written for *The Washington Post* and then did a full background search on him. When Lazlo had told her he was being groomed to take over the family business, he had meant groomed to replace Michael Walker as CEO. He'd moved steadily up the ranks, and when he resigned abruptly three years ago, around the same time his father had died, he had been in charge of Walker Industries' International Division. Most of the older and non-Walker Industries stories he filed for *The Post* would interest someone on Wall Street but to Penelope reading them was about as pleasurable as a root canal performed without Novocain. She mostly just skimmed through them quickly.

The stories from the last few weeks were different. Michael Walker was in trouble with his board of directors and his stockholders. On Monday there was going to be a vote in New York and the smart money was betting that Walker would be unemployed come Tuesday. She was just about to turn her focus toward Sal Trotta when she heard a light tap on her bedroom door.

"Come in," she said without taking her eyes off the screen. It was Ian Fleming.

"Michael Walker will be here in half an hour."

Penelope glanced at the clock in the lower right hand corner of her computer screen and cursed softly under her breath. Jumping to her feet she noted that Ian was dressed more in line for casual Friday than dinner at the best restaurant on the East Coast. "Are you going with me?"

"Yes ma'am."

"Is that what you're wearing?"

"Yes ma'am."

"Don't you think a jacket and tie would be more appropriate?" Penelope asked.

Ian shrugged. "Why would I think that?"

Penelope shook her head and sighed. "Whatever. Is Ms. Mitchell still here?"

"Yes ma'am."

"Joey!" Penelope shouted. "Help!"

Josephine glided into the room and scooted Ian out. "Right side or left?" she asked as she headed toward the walk-in closet.

"Left," Penelope answered gloomily.

"Poor baby."

"I'm going to run through the shower," Penelope said. After a quick rinse which didn't include her hair, she discovered Joey had laid out three options for her. The first one she immediately dismissed. "I'm going to a business dinner, not applying for a job as a pole dancer at a strip club," she said as she tossed the sheer, clingy dress aside.

"You're right," Josephine said as she returned the dress to the closet. "We need to save this for my party tomorrow night. Where are you going exactly?" Josephine asked as she held up the two remaining choices.

"Not sure," Penelope answered as she applied lipstick in front of the mirror on her dressing table. She sighed and shook her head. Another question she had forgotten to ask. "They just said that Trotta wanted dinner at the best restaurant on the East Coast."

"Okay," Josephine said as she handed Penelope a sleek black cocktail dress. "You can wear basic black anywhere."

A few minutes later Penelope emerged from the bedroom in her Herve Leger cocktail dress, Christian Louboutin pumps and a clutching a Bottega Veneta minaudiere. Around her throat were her grandmother's natural pearls.

"Wow! Mom!" Carrie said as she was trying to gag down some juice concoction that Sally Winters had forced on her. Before more reviews could come in, there was a light tapping on the door. Ian was already there and had his eye to the peephole. Penelope frowned in the direction of Fleming as he opened the door. Instead of being in a suit and tie as she had suggested, he was still dressed casually.

Michael Walker came in with Kent Lazlo and Lucas Haley following in his wake. The three men were all were wearing khaki slacks and three-button golf shirts. With Fleming as their fourth, they looked like a foursome that had just finished up on the 18th hole and were heading into the clubhouse for a beer. Timothy Ellison emerged from the guest bedroom, similarly attired and carrying a briefcase.

"Do you have everything?" Walker asked.

"A courier dropped them off an hour ago."

"Excellent," Michael Walker said as he patted Timothy Ellison on the shoulder. "Look, if you need to stay here…"

"No," Ellison said a bit too quickly as he shot a glance over his shoulder toward his betrothed. All of the men nodded that they understood.

Walker turned his attention in the direction of Penelope. "You look nice."

"I thought," Penelope said softly as she rubbed her forehead and tried to control her emotions, "we were going to the best restaurant on the East Coast?"

"We are," Walker said with a laugh. "No one said the most expensive."

"I need to change."

"We don't have time," Walker said as he hooked his arm under hers and led her toward the door. "Besides, you look great."

Penelope glared at Fleming as she brushed past him. "You might have given me a clue, maybe a small hint."

"Next time I'll use crayons and flashing lights," Ian answered without the slightest hint of sarcasm in his voice.

Penelope released her grip on Michael Walker's arm and wheeled on Fleming. "What does that mean?"

"Part of you knew what to wear," Ian answered.

"How do you figure that?"

Fleming held the door open. "Before you started getting dressed you saw what I had on. You even asked about it so that indicates you knew on some level there was a problem. Instead of listening to that inner voice you closed your mind, assumed I was wrong, and didn't ask the next question."

"What was the next question?"

Fleming smiled. "Why are you dressed like that?"

Penelope was fuming. "So," she said as she glared at Ian, "you knew I was making a mistake and didn't tell me?"

"I can only shine the light on the path," he answered calmly. "It's up to you to see it." Before Penelope could protest, Fleming was out the door. "Shotgun and radio!"

THE BIG ESCALADE pulled to the curb in front of a hole in the wall with a flickering neon sign that said "Ruby's BBQ." It was in a rough part of the District. Even with bodyguards among their entourage, Penelope still found herself gripping her purse tightly as her feet touched the sidewalk. Inside, the restaurant looked as if it had last been remodeled during the Roosevelt administration, Teddy not FDR. The floor was large squares of black and white marble and the ceiling was tin. The lack of acoustics made the sound of clinking glasses and forks on plates bounce and reverberate around the dimly lit room. Combined with raucous conversations in at least four different languages, it was hard to imagine a worse place for a quiet business meeting.

With the mixtures of races and nationalities in the spotlessly clean dining area, Ruby's could pass for the United Nations cafeteria. Penelope recognized a U.S. Senator, three congressmen and one cabinet member spread around the diner. As they entered, a large African-American woman with salt and pepper hair, eyes that missed nothing, and a mouth that said little was working the cash register. Seeing Michael Walker, she nodded toward a smaller room at the back. Seated by himself at a table for eight was Salvador Trotta. If central casting ever got a request for someone to play an Atlantic City pit boss or someone to explain the subtle difference between *"the juice"* and *"vigorish"*, Sal Trotta would have been their first call.

In the neighborhood of three hundred pounds with thick black hair and even thicker eyebrows, Trotta was all southern Italian. He had a napkin roughly the size of a small table cloth tucked in the collar of his shirt. All of the appetizers on the menu were spread out on the table in front of him. He nodded when he saw Walker and Lazlo but made no attempt to get up until his eye caught Penelope Spence. The presence of a lady, especially one dressed like her, caused the napkin to vanish as he instantly rose to his feet. After the introductions were made and everyone was seated, Penelope noticed that Trotta had placed the napkin in his lap and was starting to unwrap his previously ignored silverware.

Without a moment's hesitation Penelope unfastened the pearls from around her neck and dropped them in her purse. With a flourish she shook out one of the oversized cloth napkins and tucked it into the neck of her cocktail dress. All eyes at the table were on her. Preferring her fingers over her flatware, she grabbed a St. Louis style rib and began gnawing on it until it was picked clean. She tossed the bone in an empty basket and licked the sauce off of her fingers. "Not bad," Penelope shrugged, "but if you think that's the best BBQ on the East Coast, I need to get you down to Charleston."

Sal Trotta's eyes brightened as he re-tucked his napkin into his collar and pointed at Penelope before reaching for a chicken wing and dropping it on his plate. "I like you," he said with a smile. Trotta picked up a basket and held it across the table for Penelope. "Try this rib with the Memphis rub and Ruby's special sauce and let me know what you think."

Penelope grabbed a rib bone and, before Trotta could pull the basket back, twirled the meat end of the bone in bright red BBQ sauce from the bottom of the basket, then took a bite. She made a face, shrugged, and looked at the rib as if there was something missing. Holding the bone in her right hand, with her left she spun the cap off a bottle of hot sauce and put six drops on the meat before taking another bite. She nodded her approval.

Trotta roared with laughter as he nodded his approval. "That one's a keeper, Michael."

"I have to agree, Sal," Walker answered as he tucked a napkin into the front of his shirt.

Salvador Trotta's eyes moved around the table before finally coming to a stop on Michael Walker. "Let's get this over with so we can enjoy our meal." The two men locked eyes; the table fell still. "After the market closes on Monday, the board of directors is going to announce that you've been replaced as CEO of Walker Industries."

CHAPTER FIFTEEN

PENELOPE WAS HALFWAY toward reaching for a skewer of grilled jumbo shrimp when the bombshell landed. Her hand froze in midair and her eyes turned to Michael Walker, who was sitting to her immediate left. Walker took the news with his usual calm. Anyone else might have at least blinked at being told that the company he had spent his entire adult life building and which had placed him among the richest men on the planet was being taken away from him. Not Michael Walker.

"It's not personal, Michael," Trotta continued. "It's business."

"No problem, Sal," Walker answered as he accepted a frosted mug of draft beer from their waitress. "So you were able to get Gabrielle's vote?"

"Yeah. The Duchess was a no brainer. Your sister is really pissed at you," Trotta said as he grabbed a two-bone baby back off a platter in the middle of the table. When his eyes caught Penelope, his shoulders sagged. "Sorry, Ms. Spence. My wife is always on me about my language."

"Call me Ms. Spence again and your wife will be the least of your worries," she said as she wiped some sauce off of her chin. "It's a rule. Anyone who has seen me lick my fingers has to call me Penelope."

Sal Trotta roared again and wagged a finger in her direction. "You're trouble," he said as he pushed the rib platter in her direction and turned back to Michael Walker. "With what I already had and the Duchess having junior here's proxy," Trotta pointed a rib bone in Lazlo's direction, "you're done." Trotta accepted a mug of beer and winked at the young black woman who handed it to him. "Thank you." He grew serious for a moment as he turned back toward Walker. "You're not going to make this ugly, are you?"

"Absolutely not," Walker answered with a smile. "Ian." Walker said as he pointed to the far end of the table where Fleming was leaning over a plate with one of everything on it, trying to decide what to try next. Having figured his input wasn't going to be needed, Ian was so wrapped up in his own epicurean world he had completely tuned out the rest of the table. "Ian." Walker said a bit louder, shaking him back to this plane of reality.

"What?"

"Pass the cornbread."

"Sure," Fleming said cheerfully as he started the basket around the table.

Lazlo turned to Trotta. "Winslow or Cochran?" he asked as he grabbed a square of piping hot corn bread from the basket before sending it back on its way.

"Neither," Trotta answered. He took a pull from his mug and wiped the foam off his upper lip with a corner of his napkin.

"What do you mean neither?" Lazlo demanded. "Who is going to be the new CEO if it's not Cochran or Winslow?"

Trotta glanced over to Walker who was shaking his head and chuckling under his breath. "Wall Street is going to love this."

Trotta eyed the table to see what he was going to try next. "Right now what they think in Brussels is more important than Wall Street." He selected a basket of fried okra and dumped a portion onto his plate.

"No!" Kent Lazlo shouted as he rose halfway to his feet.

Trotta shrugged. "It was the only way to get your mother's vote." He grabbed a double hunk of cornbread and made a spot for it on his plate.

"Albert is a buffoon!" Lazlo shouted loud enough to turn heads in the main dining room. Realizing he was drawing attention, he lowered his voice. "My mom pays all of the bills and gives him a huge allowance and he's still always broke."

"Look, Kent," Trotta said as he brushed crumbs off his napkin. "All those contracts with the EU you negotiated before taking your little hike are up for renewal this year. Without those, Walker Industries is finished. You may not think much of Albert, but the people in Europe love him. Besides," Trotta's eyes locked on Lazlo, "if you're not willing to suit up and get in the game, you don't have the right to question the plays we call."

"What does that mean?"

Trotta didn't answer; he didn't need to. Everyone at the table, including Kent Lazlo, knew exactly what he meant. The big desk at Walker Industries had a "reserved" sign with his name on it since he was in the womb, and he had chosen to walk away. Kent Lazlo had completely lost his appetite. His elbows were on the table and his face was buried in his hands. "This is not happening," Lazlo muttered to no one in particular.

Walker motioned toward the steaming basket of fried okra. "Is that as good as it smells?"

"Betta," Trotta answered. "They make it fresh in the back and use some kind of special batter to coat it. Then they cook it tempura style instead of in a basket." Walker held up his plate and Trotta forked a portion onto it.

"Can I have some?" Ian asked. Trotta handed Fleming the basket and he dumped the rest on his plate.

Walker took a bite and made a happy face. "We're going to need more of that." Penelope had to force her mouth to stay closed. Here she was at a table where a union guy with a $200 billion dollar portfolio had just told the CEO of a Fortune 50 company that he was going to be fired on Monday, and they were discussing the breading on a deep fried vegetable.

For the next few minutes all conversation stopped and consumption began in earnest. Everyone was enjoying the meal except Kent Lazlo. He picked and poked but nothing managed to make the trip from plate to mouth. Finally he said, "What if I break my trust and throw my votes behind either Winslow or Cochran?"

"If Gabrielle loses your proxy, that might stop Albert, but it wouldn't do Cochran or Winslow any good." Trotta gave his mouth another swipe with the oversized napkin before downing the last of his mug of beer. "Unless, of course," Trotta's eyes moved from Lazlo over to Walker then back to Lazlo, "you can convince your uncle to vote with you. He's still the largest shareholder. Then if you can convince me; between the three of us, we would control fifty-eight percent of the voting stock."

Kent Lazlo's eyes brightened and he looked as if a heavy weight had just been lifted from his shoulders. "So we could put in anyone we want?"

"Nope." Trotta answered. "Having Albert as the CEO hardly makes my heart go pitty-pat, but I don't see a lot of options other than the Ninth Duke of Fantasyland."

"You wouldn't vote for either Winslow or Cochran?" Lazlo asked, horrified.

"Nope," Trotta said flatly as he eyed the other items on the table.

Kent Lazlo turned to Michael Walker. "What about you?"

"I'm with Sal. Neither Winslow nor Cochran carry any weight in Europe and without the EU renewals Walker Industries may not be able to recover. Albert would not be my first choice but he is the best option currently available."

"What if I pull my proxy from my mother? Wouldn't that stop Albert?"

"If you pull your support, then Sal will get mine," Walker said with a sigh as Trotta nodded his approval of the decision. "Walker Industries is on shaky enough footing. I won't let the board meeting on Monday turn into a food fight. I'm not going to let my company be destroyed. Sal will get my proxy and Albert will be the new CEO with you or without you."

Trotta put an arm around Michael Walker. "I love this man."

Kent Lazlo buried his face in his hands again. "There has to be another option."

"There is only one person in the world I believe can do as good or maybe even a better job of running Walker Industries than I can," Michael Walker said. "He's sitting at this table."

Lazlo leaned back in his chair and glared at Walker. "I should have seen this coming."

"Walker Industries has one hundred eighty-nine thousand employees worldwide and I haven't laid a single one of them off during this downturn. What do you think is the first thing Cochran or Winslow will do? They are good men, but they're bean counters. They don't have your vision. Plus they have next to zero international experience."

"So my only choice is Albert or me?" Lazlo paused and seemed to think deeply about it for a few moments before he turned to Trotta. "What do you think, Sal?"

The big man shrugged and reached for another rib. "You would be my first choice too, but I didn't think that was an option with the way you stormed out." Trotta shook his head. "It looks like the ball is in your court, junior. You in, or do we go with Prince Albert?"

No one at the table spoke. Penelope had to force herself to even breathe. Lazlo sat frozen in place with his eyes fixed motionless on his plate. Finally a voice almost too soft to be heard over the din in the restaurant said, "It may take some time to reclaim control of my trust."

"Actually not," Walker said brightly as he motioned to Ellison, who immediately shoved Lazlo's plate aside and put some documents in front of him.

"What's this?" Lazlo asked as he started flipping through the papers that had just materialized.

"I already had legal draw up the papers. You can have them filed first thing Monday morning and they will be certified before noon."

"My mom is going to kill me." Lazlo accepted the pen Ellison was offering and began signing and initialing the papers in front of him. "We'll need to get these notarized." Lazlo laughed when he looked up and saw that Ellison already had a notary seal in his hand. He pushed the stack of documents in Penelope's direction.

Penelope was confused. "What?" she asked.

"We need two witnesses," Lazlo answered as he pointed to a blank signature line. Neatly typed underneath the line was Penelope's name and address. Below it was Salvador Trotta's.

Penelope's eyes flew open and locked on Michael Walker.

"Welcome to my world," Lazlo said as he handed her the pen.

"Nice, Michael," Trotta said as he raised his glass in a salute. Another set of documents were placed in front of Sal Trotta.

"What's this?" Trotta asked as he reached into his front pocket for his reading glasses.

"For all parties concerned, it is probably best that I not make an appearance at the board meeting on Monday," Walker said. "This is my proxy, voting for Kent Walker Lazlo as the new CEO of Walker Industries, which is yours on one condition."

"What's that?" Lazlo and Trotta asked simultaneously.

"I want to trade my entire holdings in Walker Industries for one hundred percent ownership of the telecommunications division."

"What's the current valuation of each?" Lazlo asked. Ellison put a spreadsheet in front of him. Lazlo read then reread the document. "Uncle Mike," Lazlo said softly. "You'll lose over two hundred million dollars on this deal and that's even if you get the replacement satellite operational."

"Use the additional money to keep from laying anyone off while you're rebuilding the brand and I'll call it even." Walker motioned to Ellison, who put more documents in front of both Lazlo and Trotta.

Trotta scanned the papers in front of him. "The stock will go up at least ten percent on Monday, maybe twice that." Trotta said as he caught the eye of the waitress. "Can we get some more of that okra?"

"Also," Walker added, "Winters, Haley, Ellison and anyone else associated with the Hermes Project or my personal staff stays with me. Do we have a deal?" Michael Walker asked.

Kent Lazlo shook his head. "You're crazy, but we have a deal."

Michael Walker stood up and held his arms out. Kent Lazlo shook his head again, rose slowly to his feet and gave his uncle a bone crushing hug.

Returning to his seat, Lazlo nodded in Penelope's direction. "Looks like you got me again."

"What do you mean?" Penelope answered.

"It's the Hermes Project all over again. I can't very well write a story about myself."

Sal Trotta stopped licking his fingers and said, "Good thing you didn't write that Hermes story, kiddo."

"Why is that?"

"If you had, you'd have been tainted with the same brush as Michael, and I couldn't have supported you for CEO."

Penelope Spence and Kent Lazlo wheeled and looked knowingly at Michael Walker who was grinning from ear to ear.

MARK HATCHET TOOK the loss of his best financial reporter better than Penelope expected. It might have been the huge scoop that had landed in his lap that helped ease the pain. Plus, Mark knew a guy like Lazlo was just passing through. He was grateful for the time he'd gotten out of him. Hatchet sent a pair of staff reporters from the financial beat to Penelope's condo at the Watergate so they could interview Walker and Lazlo without tipping their hand. Sal Trotta had declined the invitation to join the party; there were a few bars he wanted to visit before he had to catch the early shuttle back to New York City the next morning. They made deadline with over half an hour to spare.

Penelope wrote the story about the sit down at 'Ruby's' but insisted that the two staff reporters get the bylines on the interviews of Walker and Lazlo. She would only take a *"Penelope Drayton Spence Contributed to this Story"* at the bottom of each. This was the kind of story which could define a career and she had stumbled into it backwards. She'd already had her fifteen minutes.

Lazlo found Spence out on the balcony and joined her. "That was a nice thing you did with the byline."

Penelope waved it off. "All I did was say 'yes' to a dinner invitation. After your little lecture in Mark's office, I was afraid to ask for anything more."

They both laughed.

"Look. About that…"

"Fuggedaboutit," Penelope said in the best impersonation of Sal Trotta she could muster. They both laughed again.

"You know Uncle Mike really likes you."

Penelope shrugged. "Did he put you up to this?"

"No," Lazlo said with a laugh, "but there is something you should know."

"What's that?"

Lazlo checked over his shoulder to be sure no one was within earshot. "I didn't mention it because he didn't mention it. He is taking a terrible risk."

Penelope turned to face Lazlo, who had concern etched on his face. "Uncle Mike has purchased the satellite division outright and it has taken all of his capital."

"Okay," Penelope said, with no idea where this conversation was headed.

"Walker Telecom has had a major satellite fail in the past year, which has really stretched the company's resources. They have been forced to buy satellite time from the competition. We have a replacement scheduled to launch next week."

"He mentioned that."

Lazlo drew in a deep breath as he glanced over his shoulder again. "The total value of this launch and the contracts it will service over the life of the satellite is very close to the Blue Book value of the Walker Telecom."

"Okay."

"Uncle Mike told me he was one hundred percent certain there would not be any problems with fulfilling all of Telecom's contracts, and he's not one for hyperbole or exaggeration."

"So what's the problem?" Penelope asked.

"Unless there is something going on I'm missing, I don't see how he can make that guarantee. With Uncle Mike refusing to let anyone see the designs of this satellite, the insurance for the launch has been cancelled." Lazlo could see from the expression on Penelope's face that she still wasn't tracking. "If there is a problem with that launch and for some reason this satellite doesn't make it into orbit, without insurance Walker Telecom wouldn't have the money to rent other satellites or rebuild the one that was lost. Since they would not be able to deliver on their contracts, their cash flow would start to dry up immediately. With all of this Hermes Project and Fourth Awakening nonsense Uncle Mike has been spouting, it would be virtually impossible for him to get the financing he'd need to keep the division afloat. Uncle Mike, other than his holdings in the Hermes project and a few stray pieces of real estate would, in effect, be bankrupt."

"What?"

"He knew I wouldn't approve launching the satellite without insurance. That's why he wanted total control of the Telecom wing."

"I had no idea," Penelope said as she blinked her eyes and shook her head.

Kent Lazlo rested his elbows on the railing. "Uncle Mike has always been a risk taker. As we both know firsthand, he always has a plan working but usually I can see his endgame. Not this time."

"I thought you needed a government license to put a satellite in space?"

"You do, and he has the license courtesy of Homeland Security."

"Let me guess," Penelope said while shaking her head again. "Noah Shepherd at the Emerging Technology Division approved it."

Lazlo nodded, but before he could answer, Michael Walker popped his head out the patio door. "Do you have a one story per day limit?"

"I can multi-task," Penelope answered with a smile. "Why?"

"Someone just blew up the Hermes Project Building."

CHAPTER SIXTEEN

"**W**AS ANYONE HURT?" Penelope asked as she headed back into the condo to get a sweater.

"I seriously doubt it," Walker answered calmly. "We'll ride over and take a look."

Kent Lazlo started to join the crowd making their way toward the door when Michael Walker stepped in front of him. "Not you."

"Why not?" Lazlo asked.

"You have more important things to do."

"Such as?"

"You're meeting with Walker Industries' EU contacts in Brussels in twelve hours. With the EU renewals on the table, a personal visit by the incoming CEO is exactly the kind of thing that flatters the egos of European bureaucrats. Besides, this is a Hermes Project problem that has no connection to Walker Industries." The two men locked eyes before breaking into broad smiles. "My plane, sorry, your plane is fueled and waiting at Reagan. All of the people you will need are either already there or on the way." Walker's face softened and the affection he had for Lazlo was obvious for all to see. "I am so grateful that you decided to take on this new challenge."

Kent Lazlo wrapped his arms around Michael Walker and gave him a hug. The changing of the guard. "I'll make you proud, Uncle Mike."

"Too late." Walker patted the younger man on the back. "You did that years ago."

BY THE TIME Walker and Spence had talked their way past the police who had cordoned off the area, all the excitement was over. The firemen were packing up their gear and getting ready for their next call, except for two men trying to water down the few remaining hot spots as they wrestled with a hose roughly the diameter of a well-fed anaconda. The building had been completely leveled and the smell of burnt plastic and carpeting, mixed with the stench of water-soaked garbage, hung heavily in the air.

Robert Smith had been rolled out of bed after only an hour's sleep and it showed. The sour mood he had been in earlier had not improved. He was on the curb in front of the carcass of the Hermes Project building, talking to the Fire Marshal. Penelope and Walker joined the conversation.

"Are you sure you didn't have anything flammable in the storage area?" the Fire Marshal asked as he scratched his head.

"This is a business office," Smith answered, "not a warehouse." Smith nodded at Walker and Spence.

"Well," the Fire Marshal motioned toward the remains. "Something sure as heck blew up inside there. It took out every piece of glass in the building. Lucky you don't have any neighbors close by or they could have gone up as well."

Spence glanced sideways in the direction of Walker who felt her eyes and shook his head that now was not the time for questions.

"The explosion came from the storage area?" Walker asked casually.

"Yes," the Fire Marshal answered. "It blew out all of the interior wall supports, and the entire building folded up like an accordion."

"Was anyone injured?" Walker asked.

"Impossible to say," the Fire Marshal said as he wiped his brow with a well-used handkerchief. "Are all of your people accounted for?"

"The building was empty," Smith answered. Smith turned his eyes to Walker. "I'm really sorry, Michael. The crate was scheduled to be picked up later this morning."

If Michael Walker was upset over the loss of his ultra-secret satellite, his body language didn't show it. Walker patted Smith on the back. "It looks like you have this under control, Robert." With a nod he motioned for Spence to follow. "Call me if you need me."

Instead of heading back to the car, they weaved their way across the street through puddles and fire hoses toward a squat building that looked as if it had been a five-store strip mall in a previous life. All of the windows were boarded up and graffiti was painted on every exposed part of the exterior. They picked their way toward a battered middle door in the rear of the building, which didn't look as if it had been used in years.

"Okay," Walker said, "a few ground rules."

"Such as?"

"You are off the record."

"If I decline?" Penelope asked.

"Then I'll have Ian take you home."

"What's in it for me?"

"An exclusive on roughly the same scale as the Fourth Awakening. Another book deal. Another movie deal. My undying gratitude."

"You really know how to sweet talk a lady," Penelope said with a laugh. "What's behind the door?"

Michael Walker smiled as he lifted the cover off of a concealed touchpad and entered a ten-digit number. With a faint 'whoosh' the door silently swung open. "Why don't you see for yourself?"

Penelope was stunned when she crossed the threshold. Michael Walker was always full of surprises, but this one would definitely make his personal top ten. Inside the decaying husk of a building was a room that rivaled what she had seen at Homeland Security, dimly lit to enhance the images on the bank of monitors along the left and right hand walls. A dozen young men and two women, including some she recognized from the original core of the Hermes Project, were sitting around waiting for their arrival. Half a dozen comfortable chairs were pointed at the front wall, which had a 120 inch plasma screen with the Walker Industries screensaver bouncing around on it.

"Did you get what we need, Stevie?" Walker asked a Nordic God with flowing blonde hair and rippling muscles who would look perfect on the cover of a romance novel. He flashed a smile that would make the average woman's knees buckle and nodded his head. "The new imaging software is cooking in the super computer right now and we should have an ID momentarily."

"What in the world is going on here?" Penelope demanded.

"You remember Stevie?"

"Hard to forget," Penelope said as she extended her hand. For a moment she thought he might kiss it. His grip was dry and firm. His eyes flashed with mischief.

"Good to see you again, Penelope." His eyes held hers for a moment longer than necessary before returning to Walker. Unlike the other members of the Hermes project, Stevie had never once called her Ms. Spence. After he released her hand, Penelope resisted the urge to use her pants leg to wipe off the testosterone. "The plan worked perfectly, boss."

"The plan? What plan?" Penelope looked around the room. "What is this place?"

"Let's take your last question first," Walker said with a smile. "This is the security control center for what's left of the building across the street."

"I saw a security room in the other building."

"True," Walker answered. "Let's just say this one is a bit more sophisticated."

There was a faint beep, like an electronic timer going off. "I've got the imaging. You ready for me to start?" Stevie asked.

"No, we're still waiting for someone," Walker answered. Walker motioned for Penelope to have a seat in one of the chairs facing the main viewing screen. "As for the plan, we're trying to narrow down the field of potential adversaries. Judging by the grin on Stevie's face we've just done that. We are also hoping to smoke out our spy from across the street."

"You mean the people working across the street in the Hermes Building didn't know this was here?"

"They had no idea."

"Including Smith?"

"Especially Smith. If they had, they may not have taken the bait."

"The bait, what bait?" Walker waited for her to process the new information. "Oh my!" Penelope's eyes flew open wide. "You knew they couldn't resist a chance to destroy your satellite."

Walker wiggled his hand. "Close, but no cigar. What they really want to do is steal the satellite, reverse engineer it, and get their own version into space before we can build another one. They would only blow it up as a last resort."

Before Penelope could formulate another question, the exterior door swooshed open.

"We can start now, Stevie," Walker shouted over his shoulder. "Our guest is here."

Penelope turned and nearly fell off of her chair when she saw Director Noah Shepherd of Homeland Security heading towards them.

"Judging by the mess across the street," Shepherd said casually, "I'm going to assume we will not be getting our equipment back." It was a statement, not a question. Despite having been roused from bed,

Shepherd was well-groomed and clean shaven. He nodded at Penelope. "In what capacity is Ms. Spence here this evening?"

"Interested spectator," Walker answered. "She understands the significance of what we're doing, so don't expect to see any surprises in the morning paper."

"Is that correct, Ms. Spence?" Shepherd asked without the slightest hint of emotion either in his voice or on his face.

"That's correct. This is off the record until I get your release."

"Then let's proceed," Shepherd said.

Walker claimed the middle of the three seats in the front row with Shepherd taking his left flank and Penelope still sitting to the right. The huge plasma screen at the front of the room sprang to life. Stevie began a narrative as they all watched near HD quality footage of a white step van, roughly the size and shape of a UPS truck except with "Walker Industries" painted on the side, back up to the rear loading dock of the Hermes Building. "They arrived at 12:31 a.m. local." On the screen six men, dressed in black with ski masks covering their faces, jumped out of the truck.

"You were right, Michael, their first intention was to steal the satellite and not destroy it," Shepherd said.

"Wait a minute," Penelope demanded. "You both knew they were coming?"

"I wouldn't say we knew. I would say we were hoping they would come."

Penelope was incredulous. "And you just let them in and allowed them to blow up your office building?"

Walker shrugged. "It wasn't much of a building, but it fit our parameters."

"Which were?" Penelope asked.

"If they did blow it up, no one would be injured and no other property would be damaged."

Penelope's mouth fell open and her eyes grew large. "You bought this building nearly a year ago." Walker nodded. "How long have you been planning all of this?"

Walker shrugged and smiled. "Why don't you hold your questions until we're finished or we'll be here all night?" Penelope didn't like it but she nodded her agreement.

On the screen, one of the men pulled out a device which looked like something from a 1950 space movie. It was shaped like an oversized handgun but had a small dish where the end of the barrel should have been. He aimed it at the camera mounted on the rear wall and the image on the screen jumped.

"That little gem produces an EM burst which will knock out the electronics of any unshielded camera," Stevie said."

"Those were decoys," Walker said before Spence asked, "and ours were hidden and shielded."

Turning her attention back to the screen, she saw the men trying the rear door, but it would not open. "They had both a swipe card and the active keypad code from today," Stevie said from somewhere behind them. "They either had world class intel or, as suspected, it is an inside job." Walker put his hand on Penelope's arm to keep her from jumping out of her seat. Her vow of silence was granted before she knew that there was a confirmed spy in the Hermes Project. "We had deactivated the door, and unless they'd brought an acetylene torch, the way we had it reinforced they weren't getting through it without making a lot of noise and taking longer than they wanted to hang around."

The image on the screen shifted to the front door. This time it was in vivid HD color and included audio. They had left two of the six to watch the truck and the remaining four were hurrying into the lobby. They moved without speaking. The image on the screen in the front of the room rolled again as one of the men fired at what they assumed were surveillance cameras. The man panned slowly, looking for more targets. He stopped when he was looking directly at the hidden video camera which was almost exactly at his eye level. Instead of shooting, he adjusted his ski mask and continued to sweep the building.

Penelope was dying to ask where the camera had been hidden. She had been in that building earlier and could only remember one thing being on the west wall. Then it hit her. She had to bite her tongue to keep from laughing out loud. She leaned into Walker. "Are the cameras behind the *feng shui* mirrors?" Walker nodded.

From behind them, Stevie began his narrative again. "Once we had them in the primary identification area, I messed with them a little to see if I could get any of them to talk," Stevie said. The next image was of the men in front of the door leading to the storage area where the satellite was stored. One of them slid the magnetic card through the scanner and entered a number on the touchpad. There was the faint sound like a door unlocking and the light on the touchpad went from "red" to "green." They tried to open the door, but it wouldn't budge. The image went into fast forward. "They were pretty disciplined. I did this a half dozen times and not a peep out of them. Finally I let them in. We captured the full body scan on all four while we had them there, Director." Shepherd nodded.

"Full body scan?" Penelope whispered. "Like they do at the airport?"

"Ours is a bit more advanced," Walker answered softy. "This is a next generation prototype that can do High Definition 3D imaging and even acquire dental records."

Before Penelope could ask another question, the screen changed to show the storage area. As soon as one of the men touched the loading bay doors, a much heavier steel barrier slammed down, kicking up a cloud of dust that coated everyone and everything. All of the lights in the storage area clicked on and a loud alarm started going off. Stevie cranked the volume down from ear piercing to merely annoying and continued his narrative. "At that point they pretty much abandoned any idea of getting out of there with the satellite."

On the screen, the four men reached into their backpacks and started placing charges around the room. They put four on the crate containing the satellite. "The way the building went up, I'm guessing it was some kind of C-4 derivative on steroids," Stevie said. "Not the kind of stuff you would pick up at your local gun swap or even from your neighborhood black market arms dealer."

"Let's just go to the ID," Walker said.

"You sure? I've got some really cool video we shot from over here of the building blowing..."

"I'm sure," Walker answered.

Stevie sighed. "If you insist." In a scene like something out of a science fiction movie, the image on the screen broke into four squares and the computer was peeling off the last of their ski masks and constructing their faces. The images were so clear and accurate they could have been used for the passport photos.

"Enlarge the face in the lower right hand corner," Shepherd said softly. As soon as the image filled the screen, Shepherd rose to his feet and muttered, "Taniel Dildabekov."

"Who is Taniel Dildabekov?" Penelope asked.

"He's a nasty piece of work," Walker answered. "He was the mastermind behind that school attack in Croatia that left over 200 children dead. He also blew up a crowded movie theater in Istanbul, among other things. He may not be as well known as some of the other high profile terrorists, but according to his Interpol file he's wanted in over fifty countries."

"Any connection to Viktor Kursolov," Penelope asked.

"If he were any more connected, they would be best men at each other's weddings," Walker answered.

"I need a secure line," Shepherd said politely. He had it in less than two seconds. "This is Noah Franklin Shepherd, Director of Emerging Technologies for Homeland Security. ID 6-7-Roger-4-9-Baker-4-2-2. Lock down the White House and get the Vice President to his bunker. We have a confirmed terrorist threat in Washington DC. I repeat. Confirmed." Shepherd pushed the button to disconnect and then dialed another number. "This is Shepherd. We have a confirmed terrorist attack in Washington DC. We're going to need to set up an emergency meeting with Homeland Security, FBI, CIA, Secret Service, Joint Chiefs and NSA. Immediately elevate the threat level from 'yellow' to 'red'." Shepherd made eye contact with Stevie who nodded that he was on the same page. "You will be receiving a file with the pictures of four known terrorists who have been confirmed to be in the District within the past hour. I want their picture on the dashboard of every law enforcement vehicle in the Eastern time zone within the next five minutes." Shepherd's voice was as matter of fact as if he were ordering takeout. "Locate the Secretary of State, we need to wake the President."

CHAPTER SEVENTEEN

SHEPHERD STRODE TO the middle of the room and looked at the screen. "Do we have eyes on them?" Before he could finish his sentence, a satellite image of Washington replaced everything on the screen.

"We gave your guys a heads up the minute the truck pulled in," Stevie said, "and they've been tracking the occupants ever since."

"Why wasn't I notified?" Shepherd asked calmly.

"I contacted Special Agent Wolfe at the time of the break in," Stevie answered. "He's been coordinating all activity since then. Until five minutes ago we were looking at a simple breaking and entering, and arson. It didn't go medieval until the super computer confirmed the ID. I've got the Twins on the com."

"Put them on speaker."

On the screen was the grotesquely enlarged face of Zach Obee, better known as Zhack. "We got 'em, boss," Obee said. "They dumped the truck and they are currently on I-95 just north of Fredericksburg. The Wolfe pack is about a mile behind them waiting to see where they're headed."

"All six of them are in the car?"

"Yes, sir." Zhack answered. "They got sprinkled with pixie dust and it's totally off the hook."

"Pixie dust?" Shepherd asked.

Walker cleared his throat. "It's a product Walker Industries developed for the Israelis to help them keep tabs on known terrorists. Once they have been dusted, or get too close to anyone who has been dusted, with the right filter combination they will glow like candles on the satellite imagery."

"Project Good Morning Sunshine?" Noah Shepherd asked. Walker nodded. "They told us they were still working on that."

Walker shrugged. "This is the prototype. We coated them when the garage door slammed down."

"Sir," Zhack's face vanished from the screen and was replaced by a satellite shot of a car driving along a nearly deserted section of interstate highway. The image on the screen panned back and there were three full sized SUVs pacing the target. "Wolfe has the Virginia Highway Patrol in position to shut down the entire interstate between their current position and Fredericksburg. He says there is a bridge ahead where he is confident they can make the take down." The satellite image zoomed out so they could see the approaching bridge.

"Get me Wolfe," Shepherd said.

"Coming online now," Stevie said.

"Director." Wolfe's voice was deep and businesslike. "We just got the BOLO and I was about to call you. We have the perfect take down spot coming up if you give me the green light. There is no civilian population, and if we block both ends, the only escape is a 200-foot drop over the side of the Rappahannock River Bridge. The Virginia highway patrol is ready to shut down the interstate and we have a pair of eighteen wheelers ready to block the south end of the bridge.

Shepherd didn't hesitate. "Go."

Everyone in the room held their breath as they watched the action unfold from 200 miles in space.

"This is Special Agent Marcus Wolfe of Homeland Security. We have a go. Close the south end of the bridge over the Rappahannock River on I-95. Do not allow anyone onto the interstate until further notice. There must be absolutely no headlights or sirens on the bridge. Let me make this clear to all parties. If they see one flashing light, the chances we all go home safe tonight goes down the tube. By now you all know who is in that car. Be stupid with these guys and someone will end up dead. Virginia Highway Patrol, no heroes and no cowboys. If I so much as see a dome light in a car in front of these guys, I will consider it as a warning signal to the terrorists and an act of treason. Is that clear? "

The bridge was now less than four miles ahead of Wolfe, and the hounds were gradually starting to close the distance between them and the fox. The third car in line pulled into the passing lane and paced the lead car, blocking the highway. All three of the SUVs turned off their headlights. Walker read the puzzled look on Penelope's face. "It's a moonless night and with black vehicles, unless their driver is very observant, they can hopefully get within a few hundred yards of the target without being seen. Then they'll hit their car with an EM pulse which will take out the entire electrical system."

"What if the driver is very observant?" Penelope asked softly.

"Let's hope that's not the case," Walker answered, never taking his eyes off the screen.

Walker's play-by-play analysis was interrupted by a scratchy voice coming over the com. "This is Sergeant Cooper of the Virginia Highway patrol. We have all access to the interstate blocked and the semis will be in position in two minutes."

"No sirens and no lights. I don't want to tip them that you're at the end of the bridge."

"I think we all got that, sir."

"Sergeant Cooper," Wolfe said. "We plan to disable their car well in front of your position. These men are armed and extremely dangerous. Break out the body armor if you've got it."

"Yes, sir," Cooper couldn't keep the quiver out of his voice.

"Cooper," Wolfe said softly.

"Yes, sir."

"That car has six known terrorists in it and they've already blown up a building tonight." There was a long pause. "If they somehow get past us, don't let any of them off that bridge."

"Understood."

Penelope could hear her heart pounding in her ears. The impression she had of Wolfe from the previous occasions their paths had crossed was of a dangerous Neanderthal. Right now she was grateful he and his men were on their side. Her eyes swept the room. The tension was so thick she could taste it. All eyes were on the screen as the seconds crawled by at glacier speed. The fox was just about to the bridge and the three chase hounds started closing the distance toward their target. Fast.

Everyone leaned forward and held their breath as if somehow the sound of their collective breathing might tip off the men in the lead car. When the road widened to three lanes on the bridge, the third car pulled up parallel to the other two. Together they would completely block the north end of the bridge in case the fox tried to double back. They were less than a hundred yards behind when the target car began to slow down.

"They just hit the car with the electromagnetic burst," Walker whispered into Penelope's ear. She barely nodded. Her eyes were fixed unblinking on the plasma screen.

As the terrorists' car rolled to a stop near the middle of the bridge, it was quickly boxed in by the three Homeland Security vehicles, all with their high beams and bright spotlights aimed inside the car, blinding the occupants. It took the iris of the satellite a few seconds to adjust and by the time it had, the Homeland Security vehicles had emptied and the eighteen men had fanned out.

They could see the silhouette of a pair of Wolfe's men firing weapons of some kind at the rear window of the car. Half a beat later a bright light exploded inside the car, followed an instant later by another.

Penelope, horror struck, turned to Walker and gripped his hand. Had she just watched six people die?

"Flash bang grenades," Walker said. "They're nonlethal but with two going off in such a confined space, they won't be able to see or hear anything for the next half hour or so."

From the bird's eye view, everyone in the command center watched as the four doors of the car were jerked open and the occupants, four shrouded with an eerie yellow glow and two that merely glittered slightly from having rubbed against the others, were sent sprawling face first on the ground. It was over in less than fifteen seconds.

A breathless Marcus Wolfe came on the com. "We have six. No shots fired."

"Do you have Taniel Dildabekov?" Shepherd asked casually.

"Hold." On the screen they could clearly see Wolfe moving from man to man. After looking at number five, his voice clicked again over the speakers. "Director, Taniel Dildabekov is in custody."

"I want them at Fort Meade before some idiot from Justice wants to read them their Miranda rights."

"Yes, sir. We already have two helicopters from Quantico coming in."

Stevie gave a high five to the tech standing next to him. "We came. We saw. We kicked their asses!"

"Well done, Marcus," Noah Shepherd said softly. "I see a Presidential commendation in your near future."

"Thank you, sir." There was a pause. "I understand this tip came from Michael Walker."

"That's correct."

There was another pause. "The next time you see him, thank him for me."

"You can thank him yourself, he's standing next to me."

There was another, even longer pause. Twice before Michael Walker had embarrassed Marcus Wolfe and his team, once when Walker had escaped from Wolfe's personal custody and once when Wolfe had fallen for a Walker trick and arrested the wrong person. "You still owe me one, Mr. Walker."

"Indeed I do," Walker said with a laugh. "Congratulations, Special Agent Wolfe. Well done."

Penelope put her hands in her lap so no one could see that she was trembling. She could still hear her heart pounding in her ears, but it was closer to the opening music of "2001, a Space Odyssey" than the 1812 Overture. She forced herself to take small breaths through her mouth to try to keep from throwing up. This had easily been the most stressful fifteen minutes of her entire life; even topping the night a year ago when her house had blown up, practically with her still inside.

Michael Walker and Noah Shepherd were both relaxed, at least outwardly. "I don't want any credit for this, Noah," Walker said. "You and your men get it all."

"In exchange for?" Shepherd asked.

"Penelope gets to write the story." Shepherd nodded as if that was a given. "I'm also going to ask for a rather large favor." Walker put his arm around Shepherd's shoulder and guided him to a quiet corner of the room. Penelope watched, but couldn't hear what Michael Walker was saying. With all of the amazing things she had experienced with Michael Walker, at 1:44 a.m. she got to see something rarer than a total eclipse of the sun over the Capitol Building. Director Noah Shepherd of Homeland Security laughing so hard he had tears in his eyes.

CHAPTER EIGHTEEN

"**A**RE YOU SURE this is what you want to say?" asked the twenty-something 'Assistant Overnight Weekend Editor'. The young woman, dressed head to toe in black, had multiple piercings and hints of tattoos peeking out from under the ends of her long sleeve shirt. Penelope had rolled into the newsroom a few minutes before two a.m. With the Saturday edition already at press, only a skeleton crew of two was working. The pair holding down the fort was a matched set. Apparently there weren't many people willing to work both third shift and the weekend, even to be able to put *The Washington Post* on their resume. The head of the coven called herself "Valdamerca" but Penelope doubted it would match the name on her driver's license. Until a few of the grownups were rolled out of bed and returned to the newsroom, the princess of darkness was in charge and she seemed inclined to make the most of her opportunity to give Penelope a hard time.

"What's the problem?" Penelope asked as she tried to suppress a yawn.

"It sounds like you're claiming you actually got to witness the capture via real-time Homeland Security satellite."

"I did."

She shook her head in disbelief and gave her an '*if you say so*' shrug. "Do you have a suggestion on how I'm supposed to fact check that claim?"

Before Penelope could respond, one of the elevators 'dinged' and its door opened. Mark Hatchet and the Metro and National Affairs editors stepped off along with three senior political correspondents. A half beat later the other elevator that serviced the floor opened and nearly a dozen of the Post's top scribes from a variety of departments got off. Valdamerca recoiled in horror as if someone had invaded her personal domain, pulled back the drapes and exposed her to direct sunlight. In a matter of moments the room had a mid-afternoon hum as Mark started barking orders.

"Get interview rooms set up," Hatchet said in a voice that carried over the building noise. "Grab any space you can. Your editors will give you your assignments, and I don't want to hear a peep from anyone. This is too big for petty ego, people." He made eye contact with Penelope. "Nellie, you'll use my office. Our guests should all be here any minute."

The elevator opened again and first off was the CEO of *The Washington Post* Group, Josephine's new hubby, Franklin Mitchell. Bunched up close behind were three men, one everyone in the room instantly recognized and two others only the hardcore political reporters knew on sight. Mitchell tried to maneuver the trio of the Secretary of Homeland Security and his new golden boys, Director Noah Shepherd and Special Agent Marcus Wolfe, in the direction of the conference room.

The Secretary was having none of it. His eyes found Penelope and he walked straight over to her and extended his hand. "It is a pleasure to finally meet you Ms. Spence. I've heard nothing but good things about you from Director Shepherd and Special Agent Wolfe."

Considering her history with Shepherd and Wolfe, she found that hard to believe.

"Thank you, Mr. Secretary."

"Please, call me George."

"Thank you, George. Please call me Penelope." Glancing over her shoulder at Valdamerca who, if it was imaginable, had gone even paler she added, "Can you help me with some fact checking?"

"I'll certainly try."

"Could you confirm, on the record, that I was in the room watching the satellite feed of the capture?"

The bullpen instantly fell silent as all the reporters moved closer and hung on every word. The Secretary of Homeland Security felt the energy in the room and was enough of a politician to recognize a captive audience when he saw one. He cleared his throat and then spoke a bit louder than necessary so that even those in the back could hear. "Yes, for the record. You were in the command center when this remarkable capture took place."

A murmur rippled through the room as Penelope sheepishly muttered, "Thank yoou." Try as she might to resist, her fourteen generations of Southern heritage forced her to add an extra 'oo' to her 'you'. She did manage to maintain enough control to resist the urge to stick her tongue out at the 'Assistant Overnight Weekend Editor.'

"In addition," the Secretary of Homeland Security paused and let the suspense build. This man really knew how to work a room. "The President has personally asked me to send his regards. He would also like to invite you and Michael Walker to the White House for a private dinner with him and the First Lady."

The elevator opened yet again and the Commandant of Marine Corps Base Quantico, the Commander of the Virginia Highway Patrol, State Trooper Francis Aloysius Cooper and a steady stream of lesser players wanting to be sure their contribution was not overlooked emerged. Early that morning Penelope learned the old proverb is true. Success has many fathers while failure is an orphan. When a government agency scores a major win, those 'unnamed high government officials,' who will usually only be willing to talk off the record, are suddenly not so reluctant to see their name in print.

"Mr. Secretary," Hatchet said as he motioned toward his office. The rest of the visitors were paired off with reporters and taken to quieter spots to be interviewed.

After an hour of near chaos, most of the outsiders had left and the room settled into an intense rhythm. Dozens of reporters were at their keyboards, notes in hand, with editors looking over their shoulders. This had been one of the best nights of Penelope's life. It was only the second time in over two decades she had gotten to work on a story elbow to elbow with a room full of kindred spirits. For the first time in a long time she felt like she was finally home. Feeding off the energy of the other reporters had replenished something that had been neglected in her soul for far too long, but after being awake and running in top gear for nearly twenty-one straight hours, her physical tank was approaching empty.

Mark Hatchet, unshaven and with blood-shot eyes, wandered past and patted Penelope on top of her head as he made his way back from the coffee machine. "You've still got it, Nellie," he said as he flopped into a chair next to her. "Your interview with the Secretary of Homeland Security was top drawer." He attempted to take a sip of coffee. It was too hot so he sat the mug down on her borrowed desk.

"I thought you had sworn off caffeine," she said as she tried, with little success, to hide a yawn behind her fist.

"I have, but I need help in trying to keep up with you."

Penelope noticed Valdamerca skulking around the edges of the room.

"What's the deal with Elvira?" Penelope asked. "See seemed like she was going out of her way to be unpleasant."

Hatchet pivoted in his seat to see who Penelope was talking about. "We're going down to a single person on the graveyard shift, so she will be out of work here shortly."

Something about the combination of Valdamerca and the graveyard shift struck Penelope as incredibly funny. She made a soft snorting sound she hoped Mark hadn't heard then pinched herself hard in the leg. Her only hope was to try to regain control of the slaphappy sillies before it was too late. They had started pawing the ground and appeared to be getting ready to stampede. Once the sillies were out of the corral they were completely beyond Penelope's control. She also knew Mark Hatchet was one of the few people who could make her giggle and when she started, especially when she was this tired, there would be no dignified end in sight. Hatchet's eyes twinkled. He could see all the telltale signs. Having shared so many long nights working on the college newspaper together, he knew she was ripe for the picking. She knew it too.

Hatchet tried his coffee again. It was still too hot. "Can you draw?"

Here it comes Penelope thought as she eyed Mark Hatchet with suspicion. She was hoping Mark was not going to blow all the street cred she had built up in the last twenty-four hours by making her laugh so hard she wet her pants in front of a bunch of kids.

"You know I can't draw?"

"Too bad. After tonight the only Pulitzer left for you will be editorial cartoons."

Penelope let out a sigh of relief as she patted his arm. He had let her off easy.

Hatchet tried his coffee again and it was still hotter than he liked, but it was tolerable. "How in the world did you talk Noah Shepherd into letting you in on this?"

This time Penelope even didn't bother to cover her yawn. She had known Mark for too long to be bound by her natural Southern courtesy. "There's a little more to the story. You can read about it in my next book."

"Oh my God!" Hatchet said loud enough that it turned heads. "What is Michael Walker up to this time?"

"I have no idea, but he is certainly entertaining to be around." Penelope folded her arms on the desktop and lowered her head. The adrenalin rush which had kept her going had completely run its course and been replaced by bone gnawing fatigue. "Wake me when it's over."

Hatchet motioned for one of his senior editors to join them. "You need her anymore?"

"Do you want to sit in on any of the interviews still in progress?" the editor asked. Penelope waved him off without even bothering to lift her head or open her eyes. "Then I would say we have everything covered. What about bylines?"

"Nellie gets top billing..."

"No," Penelope said as she cut him off. She tried to force her head up but couldn't muster the strength. "I'll take the top on the primary story and the interview I did with the Secretary of Homeland Security. Whoever does the interview gets the top byline and I'll take a 'contributed to' at the bottom."

Mark Hatchet patted her on the head again. "You just locked up Miss Congeniality." Penelope was too tired to even mount a response. He turned his focus back to his senior editor. "I'm going to check upstairs and see if we can do a sixteen-page insert for Sunday. I want the head of the advertising department here within the hour. Even those clowns should be able to sell space in that." Hatchet turned his attention back to Penelope and pointed a finger at her. "You go home and get some rest." She wasn't about to argue.

When Penelope finally stumbled out of *The Washington Post* building, the sun was just contemplating coming up but a final decision was still in committee. In the newspaper rack on the curb was the Saturday edition of *The Post* with her Walker Industries scoop as the lead story. Who would have thought the financial story of the year could be completely overshadowed and replaced with a new blockbuster while most people were asleep? Fleming held the town car's passenger door open for her and she motioned for him to join her.

"I wanted to continue our conversation," Penelope said.

Fleming's eyes lingered on the radio in the front for a moment. "That would be great," he said with little conviction.

"Explain your simplicity and complexity and ask the next question concept to me."

"Sure. Don't make life more complicated than it needs to be."

"That sounds pretty simple," Penelope said with a sigh. "How do I do that?

"Release all the stuff you don't need."

"How do I tell what I need and what I don't need?"

"Release everything and the important stuff will come back," Ian answered.

"Release everything and the important stuff will come back?"

"That's what I just said," Fleming answered with a puzzled expression on his face.

"I repeated it since it didn't make any sense to me."

"Okay. Maybe this will help. Take last night for example."

"What happened last night?" Penelope asked.

"You released your angst about your daughter's wedding."

"How do you know that?"

"The arrival of the party planners and the check to pay for everything."

"How is that related?"

Fleming looked at her with a puzzled expression on his face. "How could it not be related?"

"What does that mean?"

"Did you remember that bonus clause in your contract?" he asked.

"No."

"Do you remember anyone ever mentioning it to you?"

"Where are we headed with all of this?" Penelope asked.

"Your former husband informed you that he could not afford to pay for your daughter's wedding and it disturbed you. You were able to fully release your anger toward your ex-husband and your concern about where the money would come from for such an elaborate wedding. When you awoke, the solution was there."

"So?"

"You were able to manifest a new reality for yourself."

Penelope sighed and shook her head. "You don't put much stock in coincidences do you?"

"Nope. Besides that was a pretty easy release."

"You think having a crazy pregnant daughter, a nightmare wedding, and my ex-husband declaring bankruptcy is easy."

Fleming touched his forehead and said, "Simple." He touched Penelope's forehead and said, "Complex. It's not the size of the problem, it is how much weight you have given it and how deeply you let it affect you. You were so busy you didn't have time to dwell on it and there wasn't enough time for it to get ingrained, so it was easy to let go. It might be harder for you to release some kid who pulled your pigtails in third grade than it was to release that."

"Are you sure you're not related to Michael Walker?"

"We're all related on some level."

Penelope yawned and rubbed her eyes. "I'm too tired for this now."

"Congratulations, by the way."

"For what?"

"You found your bliss today."

"What does that mean?"

"For the first time you found exactly what will make you happy."

"Did I miss something?" Penelope asked.

"Twice today, your aura changed to silver."

"My aura?"

"Yes, ma'am."

"I'll bite. What does that mean?"

"You're getting rid of the BS in your life and starting to allow what's really important to move up to the front of the line."

"Do you have any tips or suggestions on how to speed the process along?" Penelope asked.

"Keep doing what you're doing. Once we get you completely past this wedding thing, we can work on bigger stuff."

"Bigger stuff?"

"Like releasing your feelings toward your family. And, of course the big one, Michael Walker."

"The family part I can understand, but Michael?"

"You won't find what you're looking for until you stop looking for it," Ian said.

"I'm too tired for Zen wisdom at the moment."

"I bet. Can I hook a PS3 up to your television?"

Penelope rubbed her forehead. "Where did that come from?"

"The games on my Nintendo aren't that challenging anymore and I'd like to try the Move controller."

"Sure, whatever." Penelope tried to roll the stiffness out of her neck without much success. "Can I ask you a personal question?"

"Sure."

"Don't take this the wrong way but you come across as a bit odd."

"How so?" Ian asked.

"What's the deal with you and television?"

"It's a passing phase," Ian said with a laugh.

"Most of it isn't worth watching."

"I've pretty much figured that out on my own," Ian answered.

"Then why do you watch it so much?"

"My dad was a tyrant. When I was growing up he didn't let me watch TV."

"You have a daddy issue?" Penelope asked.

"Not anymore. He's dead and I've released all of the anger from him stealing my childhood."

"Stealing your childhood?"

"I was the only child of a type "A" jerk. He wanted me to get into Harvard and I was going to get with the program whether I liked it or not." Ian pivoted in his seat to better face Penelope. "From kindergarten through grad school the only grade I ever got was an "A". For him that wasn't something to be praised, it was expected. He wanted his son to be some big James Bond kind of super spy."

"It sounds dreadful but explains the name."

"It could have been worse."

"How so?"

"My dad wanted me to be a success and he pushed me, hard," Ian said. "Some parents go to the other extreme and drive their children to failure."

"Explain," Penelope said.

"There are a lot more Archie Bunkers and Homer Simpsons out there than Ozzie and Harrietts. There are parents who belittle their kids so they are never better than they are. They minimize accomplishment and maximize failures. The only way they can feel important is by making their children a burden they have had to bear."

Penelope's mind flashed to her childhood. Her father was definitely the supportive type, not pathological like Ian's father. Her mother was, well, her mother. She wouldn't go so far as to say she had wanted Penelope to fail, but she certainly had no problem shoving her brother in front of her every chance she got. "Family dynamics can be complex."

"That's an understatement. Often kids are collateral damage to petty power plays between parents. Sadly people end up with limitations thanks to their parents without the parents even noticing because they are dealing with their own problems. Problems they inherited from their parents."

"You don't seem to have much regard for the family structure."

"It is what it is. For most people family issues are the most difficult to release because even the most minor childhood snub or slight has gained power from being carried around for a lifetime. Plus, too many parents live vicariously through their kids. They try to capture some idolized idea of the perfect childhood they feel they were denied." A smile broke across Ian's face and his eyes drifted in the direction of the rising sun. "The funny part about my dad...from listening to him I always thought he had this really cool job at the CIA. I found out after I started working for Homeland Security that all he did at Langley was sit in a cubicle and read Russian newspapers all day for twenty–five years. He didn't want me to have the same dead end job."

"What about your mom?"

"She reminds me a lot of you."

"Is that a good or a bad thing?" Penelope asked with a smile, pretty sure she already knew the answer.

"She treated me the way you appear to have treated your children. Like you, she didn't burden me with her expectations. All she ever wanted was for me to be happy and find my own bliss."

"That's sweet. Thank you."

Ian shrugged. "I just wish she would have stood up to my father more on my behalf."

"Is she still alive?"

"Very much so and she can't wait to meet you. She is a huge fan."

"Give me her address and I'll send her an autographed copy of my book."

"She doesn't read much anymore."

A puzzled expression crossed Penelope's face. "If she doesn't read much how can she be a big fan?"

"Excellent next question. When you figure it out, let me know." As the town car pulled to the curb in front of the Watergate complex, Fleming smiled and with a horrible Cuban accent said, "Lucy, we're home!" Before the car had rolled to a complete stop, he was out the door.

PENELOPE'S APARTMENT WAS dark and silent, and she didn't want to take a chance of waking Princess Carrie by continuing her conversation with Fleming. On the kitchen counter was a note from Sally Winters.

No progress on securing Drayton Hall. I know Carrie will be disappointed, but considering the time constraints, we may need to start considering a 'Plan B'. I'll stop in after lunch to discuss our options.

Sally

Penelope sighed as she read the note again and folded it up so Carrie wouldn't see what Sally had written. With a wave to Fleming, who had already plopped in front of the TV, she headed toward her bedroom, closed the door and leaned against it. Her eyes went from the bed to the bathroom then to the corner of her yoga mat which was peeking out from under the dust ruffle of her bed. For a fleeting moment, Penelope considered abandoning the last two and just flopping face-first into bed. Running her tongue across the front of her teeth and feeling the film coating them, that plan was quickly abandoned. After a cursory visit to the powder room, where only the essentials were dealt with, she looked at the bed then the mat. "Sorry, Ian," she muttered to herself. "I'm too tired." She kicked her shoes into the closet and, as she headed for her wonderful, inviting bed the air-conditioning clicked on. A small gust of wind picked Sally's note up off her dresser, and it fluttered to her feet. Shaking her head in resignation, she unrolled her mat and did a few quick stretches before sitting cross legged on it.

Whether from fatigue or her meditation, after a few moments she felt her body relax and the white noise vanish. Her mind became still before she started a new Mantra. "Carrie's wedding is going to be fine. Carrie's wedding is going to be fine."

PENELOPE DIDN'T REMEMBER rolling up her pad or climbing into bed. The clock on her night stand said it was one o'clock and the sun ringing the heavy drapes covering her window confirmed it was p.m. She could hear hushed voices in the kitchen. Forcing herself out of bed, she did a few stretches before heading to the shower and then the kitchen to explore her rehydrating and refueling options. As she opened the door of the refrigerator she heard a squeal followed by the sound of thundering feet heading in her direction. Before she could react, her eldest daughter had her engulfed in a huge hug.

"I don't know how you did it!" Carrie's eyes welled up. "Thank you, thank you, thank you."

CHAPTER NINETEEN

A BEAMING SALLY WINTERS was a few steps behind Carrie. "I got the phone call this morning."

Carrie was so excited she blurted it out, "We got Drayton Hall for the wedding!"

Ian Fleming, apparently needing more room to challenge the game console, had shoved all of the furniture in the media center against the wall. Holding something that looked like a wand with a glowing clown's nose on the end, he was playing a vigorous game of PS3 ping-pong. Without turning away from the screen, he extended his left arm and gave her thumbs up.

"What are you talking about?" Penelope asked as she tried to disengage herself from the clutches of her eldest daughter. Carrie reluctantly released her mother but was so excited she couldn't stand still.

"I don't know what strings you had to pull or favors you had to call in, but this is so..." She hugged her mother around the neck again and began to sob. "You." Sniff. "Are the best." Sniff. "Mother in the whole world." She broke away and wiped her eyes. "I'm going to go call grandma and Uncle Rob. They both just knew you could make this happen."

"I'm sure they did," Penelope said with a forced smile.

Carrie was almost to her bedroom when she circled back for a box of Kleenex she'd left on the dining room table. As she retraced the path toward her room, she took one of the tissues and blew her nose. The neighbors wouldn't have been faulted for thinking a flock of Canada geese had landed on the roof.

Sally handed Penelope a letter from the National Trust for Historic Preservation's Southern office in Charleston, confirming the dates and signed by their Executive Director, David Abernathy. "This certainly makes my job a lot easier." She waited until Penelope had finished reading the letter. "You know this guy?"

"I'm sure we've met," Penelope answered. "Charleston is not that big of a town and I've gone to a lot of fundraisers."

"So this isn't your handiwork?"

"I had nothing to do with it." Suddenly it hit her and she slapped herself in the middle of her forehead. "But I have a pretty good idea who did."

"Ah," Sally answered as she reached for her oversized purse. "That would make sense."

Penelope looked around and noticed that Winters was alone. "What happened to the rest of your entourage?"

"They are all on their way to Europe with the new CEO. I swapped jobs with the head of PR for the Telecom Group. Walker Industries' public image is her problem now."

"Really?" Penelope pulled back slightly. "That sounds like a less than lateral move to me."

"The money is better and I'm still the senior VP of a major corporation." Sally Winters shrugged. "Besides, knowing Michael, when he gets past this little bump in the road it wouldn't surprise me if the Telecom Group isn't bigger than Walker Industries in five or ten years. The man is amazing." Sally unplugged her laptop and unzipped its carrying case.

"Where are you going?" Penelope asked.

"Charleston," Sally answered as she surveyed the room to be sure she hadn't left anything behind. "Now that we have a location, we can book the bands, get a caterer and florist, stuff like that. Josephine put me in touch with a wedding planner, but it will be easier to do it from there than by long distance."

"Is Carrie going with you?"

"Absolutely. I'm taking Timmy as well." On cue Timothy Ellison emerged from the guest room with a large gym bag over his shoulder.

"Should I start packing?" Penelope asked.

"No," Sally answered absently as she flipped through her notes. "Give me a week to ten days to get the groundwork work done. We'll need you when there are final decisions to be made. Until then you would just get in the way."

"Thanks a bunch."

"That didn't come out right," Sally said with a laugh. "What I meant to say is that your daughter is a bright, headstrong young lady. Let her go down and make the preliminary decisions. There is no point in having every minor detail becoming a battle royal. We'll parachute you in when everything is pretty much decided or down to a couple of choices."

Penelope sighed as she looked at Carrie's door. "I thought the mother of the bride was supposed to handle these details."

"Please," Sally Winters said as she flipped her computer bag over her shoulder, "that's why there are ten pages of wedding planners in the Manhattan Yellow Pages." They both turned when they saw Carrie emerge from the guest room with a suitcase small enough to be a carry-on bumping along behind her. Ellison took it from her and gave her a gentle peck on the cheek. "It looks like we're about ready to roll." Winters surveyed the apartment one last time. "I'll touch base with you as needed to keep you up to speed and call if there are any disasters that need your immediate attention."

Carrie joined the conversation and gave her mother another hug. "Thanks, Mom." Her eyes started to tear. "I can't believe..."

"Hey," Penelope said. "There has always been a tradition in the Drayton family that when a daughter gets married, her father would give her a new house to live in."

"I thought Dad was..."

Penelope kissed her index finger and put it over her daughter's lips. "Whatever you don't spend from the check I gave you for the wedding will be yours to keep. Hopefully there will be enough left to buy you a nice house somewhere. Consider it the traditional Drayton family wedding gift from your father." Carrie, again, burst into tears. Unable to form words, she hugged her mother around the neck so hard Sally Winters had to step in before any permanent damage was inflicted. Penelope held her eldest at arm's length and sighed. "And now that you're spending your own money instead of mine, try to be civil with the vendors and don't beat them up too much on prices." The trio laughed as Penelope walked them to the door and watched as they headed toward the elevator.

Penelope felt her eyes starting to well up as Timothy took her daughter's hand and pulled her close. Carrie looked up at him, smiled and then rested her head on his shoulder as they waited for the elevator. One down, two to go. Timothy Ellison was every mother's dream for her daughter. Hopefully her other children's marriages would lack some of the drama of this one. Penelope stood in the corridor and waved as the elevator door closed.

She returned to her apartment, which she knew would remain blissfully quiet for the first time in two days, shut the door and leaned against it. Closing her eyes, she drew in a cleansing breath and felt the tension leaving her body. It seemed whenever she got within close proximity of Michael Walker, especially when he had a plan working, time started to slow down. The past forty-eight hours had seen more action than the previous forty-eight days combined. "Shoot," she muttered softly as she realized the next act in the Michael Walker Magical Mystical Tour, Josephine's black tie party, was only a few hours away. Keeping her eyes closed, she drew in another breath and pushed away from the door. Her heart jumped into her mouth when she nearly ran into Ian Fleming, who was standing a few feet in front of her.

"I'm going to have to put a bell on you," Penelope said as her hand flew to her throat.

"That was a very nice thing you did for your daughter."

"Oh, the money? I can afford it."

"The money was probably the least important aspect of what you did," Fleming said calmly.

"What does that mean?"

"Your releasing techniques are really improving. Because of that you are achieving an inner peace that is being reflected on those around you."

"Yeah," Penelope said as she eyed Ian with suspicion, "about that whole releasing thing. Do you really expect me to believe that I'm able to influence something that big just by putting it out of my mind?"

Fleming seemed genuinely surprised by Penelope's question. "It's not the size or complexity of the obstacle that is important. It is how much power you have given it."

Penelope shook her head and sighed. "Why is it that whenever I talk to anyone even remotely related to the Hermes Project, I start looking around for men in white jackets carrying restraints?"

Fleming winced slightly before continuing his point, which struck Penelope as odd since he hadn't previously shown any emotion. "When it comes to problems, people are like baby elephants."

"What does Dumbo have to do with any of this?"

"It's an old circus trick," Fleming answered casually. "They would put a heavy stake in the ground and attach a chain to it and then attach the chain to a bracelet around the baby elephant's ankle. The young elephant will pull on it for a few days, but because it is so small, the stake will hold. Eventually the young elephant stops trying. For the rest of its life, even after it is big enough to turn over a car or uproot a tree, because of the limitation put on it by its handler as an infant, the elephant will never pull up the stake. That's what happens to people as well. We let our experiences condition us into believing that easily solved problems are intractable. Many people spend their entire lives tethered to a stake which they can easily walk away from whenever they want."

"I don't see how any part of this applies to me?"

"Thoughts have power, and the longer and more firmly you believe something, the harder it is to release. While it may outwardly appear that your daughter's wedding was a huge issue, since you really hadn't had time to process all of the potential problems, it was fairly simple to release. Some of the others will not be nearly that easy."

"What does that mean?"

Fleming shrugged. "As I told you before, our families, friends, and the environment in which we grow up are like the elephant handlers. Those closest to us are often the ones who place the most restrictions on us. Take your brother and mother for example..."

Penelope's hand flew up like a traffic cop stopping cars. "Whoa, whoa, whoa. When did you ever meet either one of them?" she demanded.

"I didn't have to," Fleming answered calmly. "We have traveled very similar paths."

"What does that mean?"

"Twice Carrie has brought them up and I've seen the way you reacted."

"Are you just making this up as you go along?" Penelope asked.

"As far as I can tell something is," Fleming said with a laugh before turning more serious. "Stop me if I'm wrong but I'm assuming, considering the family name and history, you went to private school." Penelope nodded that he should go on. "I'm also assuming your family pushed hard for you to do well academically and attend an Ivy League college." Penelope nodded again. "I'm also going to assume that all of your classmates were under similar parental pressure."

"So?"

"The point is this, what has become of the best and brightest of your generation in Charleston?"

Penelope folded her arms across her chest and glared at Fleming. "Our generation produced a good number of doctors and lawyers, plus a fair share of college professors and business leaders."

"I didn't ask what they did. I asked what became of them?"

"I don't understand the question," Penelope answered with a growl.

"How many are divorced? How many are trapped in careers that are not making them happy?"

Penelope had never really thought about it before but the vast majority of those she went to school with were on their second or even third marriage. While outwardly there was the veneer of accomplishment and prestige, beneath the surface as a group they were miserable. "What's your point?" Penelope asked defensively.

"Where are the artists and the dreamers? Where are the philosophers and thinkers?" Fleming's eyes locked on Penelope. "Almost all of them are like the baby elephant. They were saddled with the expectations of their parents. They excelled in school and took the path that would make their parents happy, but not necessarily the path that would make them happy. Now, because of a sense of responsibility to family or an unwillingness to lower their standard of living, if you want to call it living, they're trapped."

Penelope felt her anger building. She took a moment to compose herself before she let her emotions get the better of her and snap back in defense of her family and friends. One thing Penelope had learned in the past year, Michael Walker seldom did anything without a reason and while his motives were often frustratingly opaque she had learned to value his judgment. Walker had paired her with Fleming for a reason that, so far, was unclear. She was willing to give him the benefit of the doubt, at least for the moment. Penelope cleared her throat and said with more calmness than she felt, "Those are some pretty sweeping value judgments on people you've never met."

Fleming shrugged. "I don't need to meet them, people are people." Fleming shook his head. "The saddest part is how this story keeps repeating itself, generation after generation. All of them have, on some level, done the same thing to their children."

Penelope felt her control slipping as her eyes flashed with anger. "It's called being a parent. We put up guardrails to keep our children on the right path."

"I understand," Fleming answered gently, "but you are the one who chose the path and put up the barriers that prevent your children from selecting a different path. For better or worse, your choices have a huge influence on your children's lives." The faintest flicker of a smile crossed Fleming's face as he nodded his approval. "To your great credit, you appear to have resisted your family's pressure better than most."

"What does that mean?"

"I can't imagine your family was overly delighted when you announced you wanted to be a reporter."

This comment stopped Penelope dead in her tracks as her mind flashed back to Christmas break during her sophomore year at Columbia when she announced her intentions to pursue a career in journalism. Her mother was aghast. The half-hearted defense by her father only made it worse. Her father's words were supportive, but his eyes told the real story. Penelope could see the disappointment. Her brother Rob openly mocked her. Even three years later, when she became the youngest woman to have ever received a Pulitzer for Investigative Reporting, her family still didn't embrace her choice.

Rob, the good son who had gotten his business degree at Clemson so he could run the family's multiple business interests, was still the chosen one. In the eight years since Penelope's father had died Rob had managed, or mismanaged, to slice nearly sixty percent off of a family fortune which had been accumulating since before the American Revolution. This had not diminished his stature one bit in their mother's eyes. He was still the favorite, the one who had done exactly what his mother wanted.

Maybe that was why Penelope and the free spirited Josephine Middleton had formed such a close relationship since grade school. Unlike so many in their high school and college, they had taken the path less chosen. Many of her classmates had picked the safe, well-traveled road to medical or law school. About a third ended up fat and comfortable removing gall bladders, while another third got fat and comfortable suing on behalf of people unhappy with the way their gallbladders were removed. The rest were now tenured professors writing unfathomably dense prose, or in the finance industry figuring out ways to move money from one pocket to another without actually producing anything. Sadly, as if looking for validation on the squandered promise of their own lives, they had passed the same type of expectations on to their children.

Penelope felt a great sadness welling up in her soul, and her shoulders sagged. Fleming had given her too much credit for charting her own way and resisting familial pressure. For her entire life, except for a few rare occasions, she had always let others influence her choices: first her parents and then her ex-husband. She'd wanted to be the perfect daughter and then the perfect wife. After winning the Pulitzer, she could have postponed her impending wedding to Bill Spence and taken a job with either *The New York Times* or *The Washington Post*, but she hadn't. Instead of following her dream, her bliss, she tried to be the good girl and make her parents happy. Make Bill happy. Make everyone happy except Penelope. If only she could let all of the guilt and regrets toward her family go.

Penelope closed her eyes, drew in a deep breath, held it briefly, then slowly released it. Opening her eyes, she discovered Ian was studying her intently.

"What?" Penelope asked softly.

"What were you just thinking about?"

Penelope sighed and shook her head. "My relationship with my immediate family and friends."

"Don't fight it. Surrender."

"What are you talking about?" Penelope asked.

For the first time Penelope saw Ian smile. Really smile. It was the kind of smile that every woman wanted from a man. "Release all of your angst toward your family and accept them for who they are." For the first time since they had met, Fleming touched her. As he took her hands into his she felt a familiar tingle she had only experienced once before, with Michael Walker. It was like a weak jolt of static electricity. "I can see the pain it is causing you," Fleming said, his voice barely audible. "You need to surrender so you can move on to the next stage of your life."

"What stage is that?"

"The stage where you experience infinite and total peace."

Closing her eyes Penelope drew in a deep breath. She visualized the straw she had used the night before but this time, with Ian clutching her hands, it was the size of a smokestack.

"Let it go," Fleming said softly. Or at least Penelope thought he had said it. She wasn't sure if she had heard him with her ears or on a much different, deeper, non-symbolic level where words began to lose their meaning.

Penelope felt a surge of energy building somewhere between her stomach and her heart. Tears began to flow from her eyes. Negative emotions and their memories began to bubble up. What began as a trickle soon became a torrent. Instead of pulling away, she gripped Ian's hands tighter and tried to just allow it all to pass through. Every snub and slight, real or perceived; every unkind word or petty reaction began to surface. Slowly, a warm silence enveloped her.

She was heading toward a familiar place. It was the place she had visited briefly once before in Jackson Hole a year earlier. A place with no up and no down. A place where time and space had no importance. A place of total tranquility and bliss. As she continued to let go and surrender a dam of even greater emotion and pain broke open. Her sense of peace was replaced by gripping fear as the reservoir of accumulated emotions washed out and over her. She continued to surrender and as each passed beyond the artificial barrier she had constructed to contain them, the emotion simply vanished. No trace remained. It was as if none of them had ever existed. The associated memories were still there but they'd lost their charge. An ever deepening feeling of peace settled in and she allowed herself to sink fully into it.

CHAPTER TWENTY

Penelope blinked her eyes a few times as she tried to orient herself. She was in a room with the curtains drawn. Slowly the fog began to roll out and she realized she was lying on her back in her own bed with the covers tucked neatly under her chin. As her mind began to focus, her eyes grew large. Lifting the sheets she was relieved to discover that, other than her shoes, she was still fully dressed. Penelope rubbed her temples with the heels of her hands and cleared her throat.

"Welcome back," said a soft voice from the shadows in the corner of the room. Instead of panic, a small smile broke across her face.

"What are you doing in here?" Penelope asked as she sat up in bed and turned her eyes toward the man sitting on the ladderback chair in the corner of the room.

"I didn't want to leave you alone," answered Ian Fleming.

"I appreciate that." Penelope rolled her neck as she took in a deep breath through her nose then slowly released it. As Fleming stepped out of the shadows and stood next to the bed; Penelope pointed toward something thin and white hanging from his lips. "What's that?"

Fleming pulled a bright red Tootsie Pop out of his mouth. "Who loves ya, baby?"

"We really need to find you adult supervision." Penelope shook her head and tried to frown but couldn't quite get there. Fleming's childlike enthusiasm was starting to grow on her. "What just happened?"

"Ahh, sweetheart, you've been heading down this long dark road for a long, long time." Fleming rolled the Tootsie Pop around in his mouth. "The clock was ticking and it was just a matter of time," he said as he sat down on the side of the bed.

"Enough with the Telly Savalas already," Penelope said as she scooted over to make more room.

"Did people really talk like that in the 1970s?" Ian asked.

"Only in cheap TV shows and bad movies," Penelope answered. "What just happened to me?"

"Well," Fleming said as he bit into his Tootsie Pop and a startled expression covered his face. "Did you know these things have chocolate on the inside?"

"What did you expect, it's a *Tootsie* Pop?"

"I didn't have any expectations. But I certainly didn't see that one coming." Fleming pulled the stick out of his mouth and examined it as he chewed. "Nice."

Penelope shook her head. "Can we get back to me? Should I be calling 911 or making an appointment with a neurosurgeon?"

Fleming waved her off. "I wouldn't worry about it. You just had a huge release."

"What does that mean?"

"You've been building up to it for the last few days," Fleming said as he flipped the stick into the waste basket next to Penelope's bed. "The ease with which you handled your daughter was a really good sign that you were getting your life back on track."

"My life has been a comedy of errors for the past few weeks."

"Exactly, but you didn't let it knock you off course."

"Again," Penelope said, "what does that mean?"

"By not giving any of these new assaults any power..."

"What is it with you and giving thoughts power?" Penelope asked, cutting him off.

Ian shrugged. "When you don't give things power, life becomes a lot less complicated."

"That still doesn't explain what happened to me."

"Of course it does!" Fleming said with a laugh. "Once you proved the little stuff wasn't going to bother you, you were ready to tackle the bigger stuff."

"So," Penelope said, "you're saying I've released all of my negative feeling toward my family."

"Maybe, but you may also still have some work to do," Fleming said with a smile. "I think you are going to find you will be getting along much better with your family and the people around you from now on."

"Why do you say that?"

"Ma'am, you just experienced a massive release that was so powerful it overwhelmed your body and mind. I've seen this coming for a few weeks..."

"What do you mean you've seen it coming for weeks? I just met you two days ago."

"True," Fleming said as he tried to use his tongue to pry Tootsie Roll nugget off his teeth, "but I've been following you around for over a month."

"What?!" Penelope shot up straight in bed. "Michael Walker had you following me?"

A puzzled expression covered Ian's face. "We really need to work on you releasing Michael Walker. You're starting to sound like a broken record."

"So, you're saying he didn't put you up to following me around?"

"No ma'am."

"Then why were you doing it?"

"Ah," Ian said with a smile. "Now that's the big question isn't it?"

Penelope let that one pass. "If you've been following me around, how come I didn't notice you?"

"I've been trained to be inconspicuous, and you were so focused on your own world you made it pretty easy." Ian stuck a finger in his mouth to try to get the last of the chocolate off his molar. "You didn't even notice me sublet the apartment across the hall."

Penelope's eyes flew open. "You did what?"

"I've been around you for two days and you've never asked the next question."

"I give up. What's the next question?"

"Where is my suitcase?"

"Where is my suitcase?"

"I asked you first," Fleming said with a laugh.

Penelope paused as she searched her memory.

"Am I wearing the same clothes I had on yesterday? Do I look and smell like I've been sleeping on your couch?"

Penelope closed her eyes and shook her head. He was right. Carrie and Timothy had claimed the only other bedroom and Ian had blended into the background so completely she had ignored him. She had not asked the obvious next question. Penelope felt a headache starting to build as she rubbed her forehead. "We'll come back to you and your stalking of me later. Right now tell me about this big release thingy."

"Since you have previously had a non-symbolic experience..."

"Non-symbolic experience?"

"That's what happened to you in Jackson Hole last year when you were briefly forced into a state enlightenment."

"Right," Penelope's mind flashed back to the moment she found out why the government had cancelled the Hermes Project. A group of volunteers, sent over by Homeland Security with the hope of expanding their consciousness, had been psychologically damaged by the experiment to the point that three had committed suicide and eleven others were in a near vegetative state.

When Michael Walker told her she was at the same risk, she tried to run, but he blocked her path. Turning, Penelope discovered Sally Winters standing behind her with a hypodermic needle at her throat. Feeling betrayed and unable to fight or flee, all of her internal circuit breakers started to click off and she collapsed into a similar place to the one Ian had just guided her. She would likely still be there if Michael Walker hadn't somehow been able to reach her and coax her back. Now it was Ian's turn to be her guardian angel. Penelope motioned for him to continue.

"Since you've been there before, it is usually easier to get back the next time and," Ian said with a smile, "as you've seen, the results can be dramatic."

"Should I expect more events like this?"

Ian shrugged. "Some people release things slowly over time, which gives them an adjustment period. Others get hit with a tidal wave like you just experienced." He pointed a warning finger in her direction. "I would say this was probably a onetime event unless, of course, you start to backslide and let it build up again."

For a year she had been haunted by that moment, which had been both exhilarating and terrifying. On some level she now realized the real reason she had abandoned her yoga and meditation. It wasn't her busy schedule, that was just a convenient excuse. Something about the event had triggered a reaction. Instead of embracing the moment it had reinforced her defensive shields. Despite what she had seen firsthand at the Hermes complex, she had been unable to release and understand. She'd felt manipulated. Having arrived at a similar place, willingly this time, she knew on some level that everything was about to change.

Penelope rolled the stiffness out of her neck. "Is this going to get any easier?"

"Maybe," Fleming answered. "It depends on who you listen to. If you study with the Maharishi people they'll tell you the more non-symbolic experiences you have the more you're likely to have. You kind of get into a groove until it becomes your normal way of being in the world. Then there are those who say it all just happens when it happens and practice doesn't help. Some, like your friend Josephine, even find enlightenment without even realizing what has changed."

"Josephine?" Penelope was incredulous. "Josephine Middleton Mitchell?"

"Sure," Ian said with a laugh, "she's great."

"Joey hates yoga and thinks my personal quest is a bunch of New Age nonsense."

Ian shrugged. "What does that have to do with her being enlightened? She has released all of her feeling towards her past and is living totally in the moment while experiencing bliss."

"Oh My God! Josephine's party! Penelope's head turned to the clock on her nightstand. "Michael is going to be here in less than an hour!"

As Penelope hustled Ian out of her bedroom, over his shoulder he said, "Try the right side of your closet."

"**W**ELL, LOOK AT you," Michael Walker said as Penelope made her grand entrance from her bedroom still putting in one of her earrings. In his custom-tailored and hand-made tuxedo and silk dress shirt, he looked every inch the billionaire industrialist.

"You've seen this dress before," Penelope said as she positioned herself in front of a mirror to see if any final adjustments were required.

"That wasn't what I was talking about," Walker said with a smile.

Penelope glanced over her shoulder with a puzzled look on her face. For some reason, Michael Walker's voice sounded slightly different. It was deeper and seemed to reverberate as if he were talking to her in a long, empty hallway. "What does that mean?" she asked as she turned her attention back toward the mirror. She felt Michael Walker next to her. A tingle went up her spine as his shoulder brushed against hers while he shared the mirror to adjust his tie. He looked and smelled fantastic.

"Let's just say it has been a long time since I've seen you look this radiant."

While she wasn't completely sold on the 'radiant' concept, to her absolute amazement, all of her clothes on the right side of her closet fit perfectly again and the stuff on the left was suddenly roomy. Apparently she had released more than just emotional baggage.

Penelope pulled back and studied Walker. If she didn't know better, she would swear he was flirting. While still smarting from their conversation two days ago, her attitude had softened. Because of him she had two more blockbuster stories, and she knew she would be hard pressed to ever thank him properly for what he had done for Carrie. While they may not have a future together, it was nice that some of the tension had dissipated. "Sorry," she said playfully, "you had your chance." Penelope glanced over at Ian who looked thoroughly bored, with his hands stuffed in this tuxedo pockets. "Besides, there's a new man in my life."

Walker smiled and inched away. "Really?" His blue gray eyes locked on hers and a roguish smile covered his face. "The evening is still young."

"Don't hold your breath." A hint of a grin crossed Penelope's face as she turned back to the mirror. Her eyes focused on her lipstick. "I really appreciate what you did for my daughter."

A puzzled expression covered Walker's face. "What did I do for your daughter?"

Penelope made a face in the mirror and snorted. "Right." Walker held up his hands and shook his head. Penelope's brow crinkled as she turned away from the glass and faced Walker. "I thought that was the favor you asked Director Shepherd was to have him get in touch with the National Trust and get permission for Carrie's wedding to be held at Drayton Hall."

"No," Walker said as he shook his head. "The favor I asked of Noah was just a little bit more important than securing a wedding venue."

"Really?" Penelope said as she brushed past Walker and patted him on the cheek in passing. "Wrong answer, Mr. Walker." Oddly, unlike their conversation on the flight back to Washington, this time she didn't feel any anger toward him. While he could be frustrating and annoying at times, he was what he was and she wasn't going to let it bother her. That didn't mean he had been totally forgiven. She glanced back over her shoulder at Walker as she headed toward the door. "You may want to take an overcoat, it's going to be chilly tonight."

CHAPTER TWENTY-ONE

JOSEPHINE'S NEW HOME was magnificent. It was located just off Ambassador's Row, a block from Massachusetts Avenue and about halfway between DuPont Circle and the Naval Observatory. The former embassy of a country that had lost its importance and primary source of income after the collapse of the Soviet Union, it was a massive three story mansion surrounded by a high stone wall and state-of-the-art surveillance equipment.

Penelope had wanted to continue her conversation with Ian, who was sitting facing her in the back of the limo, but she didn't want to share any additional personal information with Walker. She assumed her "good girl" posture of hands in her lap, eyes out the window and knees together but not touching the man next to her. What in the world had she seen in him? She could see that he had played her like a silly sophomore school girl with a crush on the popular guy in the senior class. From this point on, he was a source for her stories and nothing more. Both Walker and Fleming could sense her mood, and the short ride from the Watergate to Josephine's was in silence.

They had to wait for several cars in front of them to discharge their passengers before it was their turn. A man nearly the size of Lucas Haley opened the door and extended a hand to Penelope, which she accepted. He was wearing a tuxedo, had a Secret Service-style earpiece, and held a clipboard in his other hand. He quickly checked Spence, Walker and "friends" off his list and motioned for them to head toward the metal detectors. Since this was the ultimate Washington "A List" party – there were rumors that backbench congressmen and senators would swap their votes for a coveted invitation – this level of security was to be expected.

Walker hooked his arm under Penelope's, which caused her to stiffen slightly as they ascended the half-dozen marble steps leading to the ballroom. The room was massive with thirty foot ceilings and ornate chandeliers. It was divided into three sections. About two thirds of the total space was filled with the rich, powerful, and famous sipping mostly champagne and nibbling on colorful tidbits served on silver trays by attractive young men and women. There was a section with tables that seated a hundred or so. At the far end in front of a softly playing orchestra was a dance floor onto which thirty couples, if everyone knew each other well, could squeeze at the same time. As if in a scene from an old movie, a distinguished man in tails was announcing each arrival.

"Mr. Michael James Walker and Ms. Penelope Drayton Spence."

Even in a room full of jaded Washington elites, nearly every head turned. Walker took her arm a bit more firmly, and they started down the steps together but miles apart. At the bottom of the stairs, Haley appeared with two flutes of sparking liquid. "Hum, twice in two days?" Penelope whispered.

"Twice for what?"

"Last night was the first time I've ever seen you drink anything stronger than water."

"My body paid the price this morning but when in Rome. Sal Trotta hates to drink alone, and besides, this is club soda." Walker leaned in. "Don't worry, yours is champagne."

Penelope handed her glass back to Haley and said, "I'll have what he's having." Haley nodded, but before he could even turn around, Ian Fleming handed her a fresh glass.

"Thank God," said a familiar voice from across the room. Josephine Middleton Mitchell, drink in one hand and new husband in the other, glided over to greet them. "Frankie has been asking me every thirty seconds when you were going to get here." Josephine's eyes narrowed as she read her old friend's body language. She shot Penelope a "what's up?" look that was waved off with a barely perceptible head shake.

Franklin Mitchell, CEO of *The Washington Post Group*, nodded briefly toward Walker before grasping Penelope's right hand in both of his. "I've been in this business for nearly forty years and I've never seen the same reporter break two stories so big in the same day. Never! Marvelous, absolutely marvelous."

"Easy, tiger," Josephine said as she forced her husband to release his grip on Penelope.

"I understand from Mark," Mitchell continued, ignoring Josephine, "that you haven't signed your contract renewal. Is there a problem?"

"Actually," Penelope said with a sigh, "there are going to have to be a few changes."

Franklin Mitchell's face darkened and his voice turned somber. "What kind of changes?"

"Well, my office and my compensation for starters."

Mitchell was now deadly serious. "As you may be aware, we are experiencing a budget crunch, so I'm not sure how much more we can increase your salary. I suppose, based on this weekend, we can justify getting you a corner..." Mitchell stopped dead when he saw Penelope trying to keep from laughing. "I don't find any of this the least bit amusing."

"Franklin," Penelope said as she placed her hand on his arm, "you completely misunderstood what I'm asking. I don't want a corner office; I want a desk in the bullpen."

"What?" Mitchell was stunned. "Why?"

"I've seen livelier funeral parlors than the top floor. I want to be where the action is."

For a moment, The CEO of *The Washington Post Group* was speechless. Finally he blinked his eyes a few times, cleared his throat and continued. "What about your compensation package?"

"If I were to agree to be paid one dollar a year, would that leave enough money in your budget to allow you to keep all of the reporters you planned to lay off?"

"It would be close but..."

"Good, I will work for *The Washington Post* for one dollar per year for as long as you do not cut the newsroom staff." Penelope pointed a warning finger in Mitchell's direction. "My new contract will be written in such a way that, the moment you lay off any of your reporters, I instantly become a 100% free agent," Penelope said as she extended her hand. "Do we have a deal?"

Franklin Mitchell grabbed Penelope's hand. "Deal," he said enthusiastically. "One question. Why?"

"Two reasons," Penelope said as she glanced over her shoulder in the direction of Ian. "It was pointed out to me by a very wise man that the newsroom is where I find my bliss." She turned her focus toward Michael Walker. "Second, someone once told me the nice thing about having gobs of money is it allows you to do the right thing from time to time."

Mitchell's eyes moved back and forth from Josephine to Penelope. "They grow some truly remarkable women in Charleston."

"Here, here!" Michael Walker said as he raised his glass. Penelope forced a weak smile but didn't bother to touch Walker's glass with her own.

Josephine hooked her arm under Penelope's. "If you gentlemen will excuse me, there is someone here Penelope needs to meet."

Josephine pulled Penelope close so no one else could hear as they bobbed and weaved across the floor. "I haven't seen you that uncomfortable on a date since your mother made you go to senior prom with that guy you'd already broken up with."

Penelope felt the tension leave her body. "Billy Conrad. I had completely forgotten about him." The two women chuckled. "Was that just a ploy to get me away so you could abuse me for my lack of a love life?" Spence whispered in her lifelong friend's ear.

"The heck with *your* love life," Josephine answered as she rose to her full height and scanned the room. "After your little performance just now, I'm certainly glad I got a nap earlier. I have a feeling Frankie is going to be frisky tonight."

Josephine tugged Penelope's arm. "There they are." A puzzled expression covered Penelope's face as Josephine guided her toward a couple that looked familiar but severely out of place. "I'm sure you remember David Abernathy and his lovely wife Brenda," Josephine said as she presented Penelope to the couple. "David, Penelope was just telling me how pleased she was that the National Trust had been so kind as to allow her daughter to get married at Drayton Hall on such short notice. She wanted to thank you personally."

"Oh no," Abernathy sputtered, "we need to thank you, Mrs. Mitchell."

"David," Josephine said as she batted her eyes, "we've known each other for over twenty years. If you call me Mrs. Mitchell again, I just might need to have a chat with your mother."

"I'm sorry, Josephine. I, we," Abernathy nodded toward his wife, "can't believe you actually invited us to your wonderful party."

"She even sent a private jet to bring us up here," squeaked Brenda Abernathy. "My word."

Josephine whispered in Penelope's ear. "That was when Frankie was afraid you were about to jump ship. I think I could have gotten him to streak this party if I had told him it would have helped get your signature on a new contract." Josephine nodded toward an open door leading outside. "Meet me on the veranda in five minutes." With a wave, she left and started working the room.

"You made my daughter very happy, David," Penelope said warmly.

"For all the Drayton family has done for the National..." Abernathy stopped short and his eyes grew large. "Is that who I think it is?" he whispered as a middle-aged man, flanked by two aides, headed in their direction.

Penelope glanced over her shoulder and smiled warmly. "Mr. Vice President, I would like you to meet dear friends of mine, David Abernathy and his wife Brenda. David is the Executive Director of the National Trust of Historic Sites. He flew up from Charleston to be here."

David and Brenda Abernathy nearly fainted. A photographer appeared out of nowhere and snapped a quick picture of the four of them. "It was nice meeting you, folks." As fast as he had appeared, he just as quickly vanished into the crowd. Penelope resisted the urge to put her finger under Brenda's chin and push her mouth closed. The Vice President was followed by one of the senators from South Carolina, a television network news anchor, and a male movie star everyone in the room except Penelope seemed to recognize on sight. After about ten minutes, Penelope was finally able to pull away and make her way to the veranda.

Josephine had just bummed a cigarette from one of the busboys and was spinning the wheel on her gold lighter with no success. "How are the Abernathys?"

"Right now I think I could even get permission for William's wedding." They both laughed. "I owe you a big one."

"Please," Josephine said as she tried the lighter one more time. "I won't live long enough to pay you back for all the things you've done for me. Besides, this one was more for Carrie than you."

"Speaking of Charleston, Ian said something that struck me as odd. He said most of the people we grew up with had their spiritual growth stifled by their parents and their education."

"Makes sense to me."

"Wait a minute," Penelope said as she pulled back in amazement. "You agree with Ian?"

"Sure. Look at the number of them that are miserable. They're in unhappy marriages and careers they hate that were picked out for them by mommy and daddy. We were lucky to finally escape."

"That's exactly what Ian said."

"You know, you have another daughter that's marrying age."

"What does that mean?" Before Josephine could answer, Penelope's eyes grew large. "Kelly and Ian?"

"She could do worse. We certainly did."

"What in the world does that mean?"

"The best thing to ever happen to us was to have our worthless husbands walk out on us." Josephine shook her head. "It was liberating when I finally figured out it was my life and that my family would just have to live with the shame of having a divorced Middleton woman wandering around the streets of Charleston unattended. When I let that go, I started being happy for the first time in my life."

Penelope's mind flashed back to what Ian had said about Joey being enlightened and not realizing it. Was it possible? "So you released your negative feelings toward your family."

"Released?" Josephine shook her head. "If you call kicking Ronald Rickman's sorry ass to the curb and telling my family to kiss mine releasing, then I released."

"Interesting," Penelope said as she pondered Josephine's answer. "That's what Ian said I needed to do. How did you do it?"

"No idea," Josephine answered. "One day I just decided it wasn't important anymore. Once that happened, Frankie magically appeared and life has been good ever since."

"Let me ask you something."

"Sure."

"I'm getting mixed signals from Walker."

"Walker, huh?" Josephine said with a laugh.

"What does that mean?"

"Before you were all Michael said this and Michael did that."

Penelope rolled her eyes and shook her head. "Two days ago he directly told me I wasn't enlightened enough for him, but then tonight I thought for a second he was going to jump my bones in front of Ian and Lucas."

"Ah, just as I thought. You have your Mojo back."

"What do you mean?" Penelope asked.

"My lighter has quit working again. That's always a sure sign you're making progress in one of your 'quest for enlightenment' phases. Boring," she said as she continued to spin the wheel on the lighter to no effect. Josephine glared first at Penelope then at the lighter. "See?"

Penelope looked at Josephine's body-hugging dress and then sideways at her old friend. "Since you don't seem to have a purse, exactly where were you carrying that lighter?"

"Don't ask," Josephine answered with a laugh. "Frankie doesn't like me smoking, so I have to be resourceful. Let's leave it at that."

"Gladly," Penelope answered with a shiver. "So you think Walker is heating up again because I've been getting back into my meditation?"

"You know I don't buy a word of that stuff. I think he's warming up because you're not so needy anymore."

"Needy?"

"Pumpkin," Josephine said as she patted Penelope's arm. "He is the first man I've ever seen intimidate you. For a year you've walked around like some star struck groupie backstage at a Bon Jovi concert."

"What?"

"To his great credit, he didn't take advantage of you."

"Take advantage of me," Penelope sputtered, "how could he have taken advantage of me?"

"Gee," Josephine said with a sigh, "where to start. He is rich and yummy and you were still a basket case after your divorce. You've been a hopeless romantic since elementary school and he looked perfectly cast for the role of Prince Charming. Throw in the fact you hadn't gotten any for a long, long, long, long..."

"Okay, okay," Penelope said shaking her head, "point taken."

"Something has really changed about you in the past few days, and if I've noticed, then I'm sure he has too."

"How so?"

"Let's see...where to start? You didn't flip out when Carrie showed up unexpected but expecting. The mention of your brother and mother didn't send you screaming over the edge. Your ex-husband filing for bankruptcy didn't even seem to register. Your little performance with Frankie and your new contract did more for him than a bottle of Viagra. Thanks, by the way."

"Glad to help."

"Plus," Josephine held Penelope at arm's length and studied her closely, "you look different."

"What do you mean I look different?"

"You look more radiant and alive."

"Hum."

"Hum, what?" Josephine asked.

"Walker said I look radiant tonight as well."

"You're not pregnant are you?"

"Ah, no. I'm missing an intermediary step so unless it is an immaculate conception . . ."

"Too bad," Josephine said with a laugh. "It would explain the glow."

"Remember when I told you about my experience in Jackson Hole a year ago."

"I still say someone slipped you a roofie and you blacked out."

Penelope ignored the comment. "I had another one earlier today."

"Ahh," Josephine said.

"Ahh what."

"Obviously Michael Walker is working his voodoo on you again."

"I wasn't with Walker, I was with Ian."

Josephine snuggled in closer and gripped Penelope's arm. "I didn't realize you had that much cougar in you. Tell me all the details."

"Is that all you ever think about?"

"Pretty much. Ever since my doctor prescribed some estrogen for me..." Josephine eyes danced. "You know, maybe there is a way to get Michael Walker even more interested."

"I don't like that look." Penelope said.

"We could use Ian to make him jealous."

"That would never work. He knows I would never go for Ian. He's younger than my kids. Plus, Walker is not the jealous type."

"Oh, sweetie," Josephine said with a mischievous smile and a shake of her head, "have you learned nothing being around me for all these years? All men are the jealous type, and jealousy is the most powerful weapon in the bag. Have you noticed that as you've cooled off, he's warmed up?"

Penelope thought about it for a moment, drew in a deep breath, and nodded.

"There you go."

"There I go where?"

"When you want to drive a man crazy, play hard to get." Josephine craned her neck looking for the busboy she had gotten the cigarette from figuring he had to be good with fire, but he had vanished. "Flirt with someone else and watch what happens. The big green monster will jump up and bite Walker in the butt."

"If you say so," Penelope answered.

"We'd better get back in there," Josephine said as she hid the cigarette in one of the oversized planters lining the edge of the patio. "Frankie gets nervous if I'm out of eyeshot for too long."

"Smart man," Penelope answered.

They returned to the main ballroom just as a late arrival was being announced.

"Mr. Viktor Kursolov and Ms. Natasha Kirov."

CHAPTER TWENTY-TWO

"THAT'S QUITE AN entrance," Josephine said. Nearly every man was staring slack-jawed at Natasha Kirov as she glided down the steps toward the ballroom on the arm of Viktor Kursolov. These same men were all receiving cold glares from the women at their sides, but if they noticed they didn't seem to care. "A bunch of rich and powerful men are going to be lonely tonight," Josephine added.

Natasha Kirov was easily the most strikingly beautiful woman Penelope had ever seen in person. In her early twenties, if that, she had flawless milk-white skin, raven black hair, and fierce green eyes. In her heels, she was a bit over six feet tall, and from across the room it appeared she hadn't needed nor bothered with any make-up. She was wearing a shimmering emerald green form-hugging floor length dress and, from the lack of bumps, ridges or wrinkles, apparently nothing underneath. The silk dress was slit up her right thigh to nearly her waist. Each step offered a glimpse of her amazing legs and hinted at her forty-inch-plus inseam.

"I had better go find Frankie before he has a heart attack," Josephine whispered to Penelope before heading across the room.

Penelope sized up the pair. Natasha Kirov was the ultimate rich man's trophy, and the contrast between her and the man on her arm was jarring. Where she was long and lean, he was thick and square. She radiated youth and vitality while Penelope wasn't sure exactly how to describe what Viktor Kursolov radiated. Kursolov was a full six inches shorter and three times the age of the beauty at his side. He looked, at best, as if he was escorting his granddaughter into the ballroom and, at worst, as if he had forked over a great deal of cash for the company of an expensive call girl to try to impress friends at his high school reunion.

Penelope hadn't known what to expect, but after the big build up from Michael Walker the squat little man across the room was a bit disappointing. Kursolov was secretive and press-shy to the point that she hadn't even been able to locate a photograph of him. Seeing him in person, it was easy to understand why. There was no camera angle or lens combination that would ever be flattering for him. Despite her best efforts, all she could find were a few articles in which he was mentioned briefly in passing. There was a short *Wikipedia* bio which, considering the glowing tone, his staff had likely written to defend against someone posting something less flattering. All she knew for sure was that his father was Russian and his mother was Mongolian. His father had been a rocket scientist at the Baikonur Cosmodrome in Kazakhstan, the massive complex where first the Soviets and then the Russians launched all of the rockets for their space program. While the Russians still had long term leases on the facility, Kursolov now had it under his direct control.

According to *Wikipedia*, Kursolov's mother was a direct descendent of Genghis Khan. Since it was unverified, and considering the inaccuracy of much of the material on the internet, Penelope would require several grains of salt before she would swallow that tidbit. Seeing him in the flesh she decided that, except for his father's fair skin and sandy-colored hair, his mother had obviously provided the bulk of his genes. With a few trips to the tanning bed, a bottle of black hair dye and a change of clothes, he could walk unnoticed down the streets of any city or town in Central Asia.

Michael Walker caught Penelope's eye and motioned for her to join him near the dance floor. He nodded toward the couple working the room. "Viktor Kursolov," he said flatly, with even less emotion than usual.

"That is some date," Penelope said shaking her head.

Walker shrugged. "Top five maybe, but I thought the last one was prettier."

Penelope looked first at the woman on Kursolov's arm then back toward Walker. She found it difficult to imagine anyone more attractive than her. "Excuse me? Top five?"

"Kursolov is a collector," Walker said with a sigh, "and one of the things he collects is beautiful women. They usually only have a shelf life of a year or two before they're replaced with someone younger."

Penelope's immediate reaction was to be horrified, but then her reporter's instincts started to kick in and she asked the next question. "Women who look like that don't grow on trees. Where does he find them?"

"I imagine, like all of the others, he found her in an orphanage when she was five or six, and she was raised to be one of his concubines."

"You're kidding?" Penelope said as she continued to study the woman. "Who does he think he is, Louis the Fourteenth?"

"No," Walker answered, never taking his eyes off of Kursolov. "French kings were generally buffoonish figureheads while Kursolov may be the most powerful person on earth. He is certainly the wealthiest."

"Seriously?" Penelope looked at Kursolov with new eyes. "I don't remember ever seeing his name on any of the *Forbes* lists."

"That's because most things involving Western culture hold no interest for him, and he understands it is not important to own something as long as you control it. Since the collapse of the Soviet Union he has quietly built a massive power base by flying under the radar and avoiding publicity. Despite his country being between China and Russia, he has brilliantly managed to remain neutral and make friends on both sides. Then there is the mineral wealth. Kazakhstan has proven oil reserves greater than those of the United States and China combined. And that's just what he is willing to admit. I've seen data speculating that he may be sitting on more oil than Saudi Arabia in a country roughly the same size as Western Europe. In addition to massive reserves of petroleum and natural gas, Kazakhstan is among the world's leading producers of uranium, manganese, chrome ore, nickel, cobalt, copper, and many other materials needed to keep the developed world running. On top of that, he endeared himself with the West by being the first former Soviet satellite country to repay all of its International Monetary Fund loans. The EU bankers love him."

"Interesting," Penelope said.

"What?" Walker asked without taking his eyes off of Kursolov.

"It sounds like he has taken a page from the Michael Walker playbook."

"How so?"

"Build a powerbase behind the scenes with a variety of countries while keeping a low profile."

"That's one way to look at it," Walker answered without much conviction. Obviously his mind was in a different place. Penelope had never seen him so pensive. Normally, he was unflappable, but there was something about Viktor Kursolov that was making him uncomfortable and it was starting to rub off on her. Walker seemed to be entranced by Kursolov and unable to take his eyes off of him.

"What's wrong?" Penelope said as she touched his arm. The contact of her hand seemed to break the spell and the old Michael Walker reappeared.

"Have you ever heard of Ponerology?"

"Are you making up words again?"

"When did I ever make up words?"

"When you were trying to explain the Fourth Awakening to me and you kept talking about '*non-symbolic*' something or the other."

"When you have emerging science," Walker answered with a laugh, "you have to call it something. A hundred years ago automobile and airplane would have qualified under your definition of made up words. Besides, I'm not the one who made this one up. The credit goes to a Polish psychiatrist named Andrzej Lobaczewski. He has written an important book, *Political Ponerology: A Science on the Nature of Evil Adjusted for Political Purposes.*"

"Ahh," Penelope's eyes brightened, "from the Greek *poneros*?" Walker nodded. "Sounds like a real page turner."

"The writing is a bit dense but the message is important. Remember when I told you that with each new awakening there is always a group that will exploit it for their own gain?"

"Yes."

"Lobaczewski brilliantly explains the pathology of the kind of people who commit genocide and ethnic cleansing, and build police states."

"Sounds like an uplifting read."

Walker continued. "There is another important book you should read, *The Sociopath Next Door,* written by clinical psychologist Dr. Martha Stout. Her basic theory is that one in twenty-five people in the world are sociopaths completely devoid of a conscience. They do not understand guilt or shame and believe the world is their plaything."

"That's rather frightening."

"The frightening part," Walker said with a sigh, "is how many of these lost souls are attracted to politics." Walker nodded in the direction of Viktor Kursolov. "I just look at him and realize how grateful I am."

"Grateful for what?"

"Grateful for you, the Hermes Project, and others who have kept me on the right path. It would be so easy to lose my humanity." Michael Walker drew in a breath, blinked a few times and lowered his eyes. Gathering his thoughts, he locked his eyes back on Penelope's. "As you pointed out, in many ways Viktor Kursolov and I are very much alike. That is true in many more ways than you realize. Each of us managed to ascend to financial heights few men ever dream of, much less reach in a single lifetime. More importantly, we both became aware of the emerging Fourth Awakening at around the same time." Walker's eyes drifted away from Penelope and found Kursolov near the middle of the room. "But for the grace of God, I could be exactly like him."

Penelope wasn't sure what to make of Walker's baring of his soul to her. Normally he was guarded and in total control. Now that she had pretty much written him off as a lost cause in terms of being a potential love interest, he seemed different. For some inexplicable reason, as she started releasing him, he had moved closer instead of further away. She made a mental note to ask Ian about this, although she knew from experience his answer would probably not make much sense.

Penelope turned her attention back to the task at hand and followed Walker's eyes across the room. From a distance Victor Kursolov had been merely unattractive. As he had gotten closer, she felt an uncomfortable feeling building in the pit of her stomach that went beyond just the effect of his physical appearance. Her eyes moved to the woman on his arm. She wondered if he treated all women as if they were baseball prospects, and if he had scouts visiting orphanages looking for those who could be groomed to someday make it to the big leagues. She wondered if there wasn't a twelve year old little girl somewhere on the bench waiting for her turn to walk down the stairs on Kursolov's arm after time and gravity had made Natasha Kirov merely beautiful instead of spectacular. It took all of Penelope's will power to keep the disgust off her face.

Walker leaned in and whispered in Spence's ear as he saw the pair approaching. "This should be an interesting conversation."

CHAPTER TWENTY-THREE

KURSOLOV EXTENDED HIS right hand. "Michael," Kursolov said with an accent Penelope could not place, "it has been too long." He put his left hand in the small of Natasha Kirov's back and urged her forward as if he were displaying a prized head of livestock at a 4H competition. As Penelope had suspected, Natasha did not have on any makeup. It would have been like spray painting graffiti on the Mona Lisa. "I don't believe you've met Natasha. Natasha Kirov, Michael Walker."

"Это - человек, о котором Вы говорили?" Natasha Kirov asked Kursolov.

Before the thickset little man could answer, Michael Walker bowed slightly and said, "Я надеюсь, что он говорил хорошо."

Natasha Kirov's eyes brightened as she kissed Michael Walker gently on both cheeks. "You speak excellent Russian," she said with a slight British accent.

"Yes," Walker answered warmly, "but please don't tell anyone. It is a requirement for all of my senior staff and security personnel. Pretending we don't understand a language has been helpful in negotiations."

Natasha waved her finger in Michael Walker's direction and a radiant smile broke across her face. "Viktor was right," she said in a steamy low voice which suited her perfectly. "You are trouble."

"Viktor, Natasha, allow me to present Penelope Drayton Spence."

Viktor Kursolov's eyes locked on Penelope. They were like black stones submerged in shallow water. Penelope forced a smile but felt like a sheep being sized up by a wolf. "It is an honor." Always a bit put-off by the European tendency to kiss cheeks instead of shaking hands, Penelope stood stiffly as first Kursolov and then his elegant companion embraced her. Where Natasha's kiss had been light, dry and almost surreal; Viktor's had been heavy, damp, and a bit creepy. Penelope intertwined her hands in front of herself so she didn't offend Viktor by inadvertently wiping her face.

A waiter arrived with a tray containing four drinks. There were two glasses of club soda for Walker and Spence, champagne for Kirov, and a small glass with a deep amber liquid in a heavy leaded crystal highball glass. A quizzical smile crossed Kursolov's face as he lifted the glass, smelling the contents as he swirled the liquid around before taking a sip. The moment it touched his lips, Kursolov eyes grew wide. "No!" Walker smiled and nodded. "Macallan 1926?" Walker nodded again. "Where in the world did you get this?"

"I have three bottles in my private stock," Walker answered.

"I would very much like to buy one of them, Michael."

"I'm sorry, they are not for sale."

"But you don't even drink, Michael."

"As usual," Walker said, "you are very well informed, Viktor."

"Perhaps, but we were not aware you and your people were fluent in Russian. We will have to be more careful about what we say in front of you in the future." Kursolov took another sip of the scotch as his eyes locked on Penelope and his face twisted into what generously might be called a grin. "Having a bottle of Macallan and not drinking is like having a beautiful woman and never making love to her."

Penelope felt her cheeks flush slightly. If Kursolov knew Walker was a teetotaler, what else did he know? Did he have a dossier on her? Wanting to change the subject, she asked, "Excuse me, but what is Macallan 1926?"

"It is a single malt whisky," Walker answered without taking his eyes off of Kursolov.

Kursolov made a noise that sounded like he was clearing his throat. Penelope assumed it was his version of laughter. "That would be like saying Natasha is pleasant looking or Penelope is a good reporter." Kursolov focused his attention on Spence. "Macallan 1926 is merely the rarest and finest single malt scotch whiskey in the world. Men like Michael and me only want the very best."

"I was surprised when you were outbid for that bottle in 2007," Walker said.

Kursolov shrugged. "I was tied up and had foolishly placed a $100,000 limit on my bid. They were unable to reach me to raise it, so I missed the opportunity."

Penelope blinked as the number finally registered. "You bid $100,000 for a bottle of whiskey and lost?"

"Yes," Kursolov said with a laugh. "The previous bottle had only sold for $58,000, so I thought I was safe."

"I'm sure that will not happen a second time," Walker said warmly.

Kursolov's eyes narrowed but the smile was unchanged. "I seldom make the same mistake twice, Michael. Are you sure I cannot convince you to part with one?" Kursolov's eyes danced from Walker to Natasha who immediately touched Michael's arm and moved to his side where she curled against him like a house cat. She flashed Walker a knowing smile that spoke volumes. "I can be most generous," Kursolov said. "Name your price."

Penelope felt like she was watching a pimp negotiate with a John. In her eyes, Kursolov had no redeeming qualities. How could Michael Walker, even for a fleeting moment, compare himself to this slimy slug?

"I won't sell you a bottle," Walker said, "but I might be willing to give you one." Walker patted Natasha's hand and made no attempt to put any space between them. Despite her best efforts to convince herself she didn't still have feelings for Michael, Penelope started to do a slow boil.

"What would I need to do to earn such a generous gift?"

"Stop trying to develop a portable version of my Hermes Project, and it is yours."

The two men's eyes locked; neither blinked. With a barely perceivable nod of his head, no more than an eighth of an inch, Kursolov signaled Natasha to untangle from Walker and return to his side. "What if I told you I have no interest in developing any mechanical devices along the lines of your famous Hermes Project?"

"Convince me and the bottle is yours."

"You know it is impossible to prove a negative, my friend."

"Indeed. But a few days ago someone shot a crude electro-magnetic burst at my Wyoming compound."

"Crude?"

"Yes, Viktor, from the satellite photos and what we measured on our instruments, it was at least a year behind our current working model." Both men's lips were curved upward in smiles, but their eyes told a different story.

"I can assure you, Michael, I had absolutely nothing to do with the development of this... what did you call it? This crude weapon that was fired at your facility." Kursolov took another sip of the Macallan. "I had assumed, from reading Penelope's online article, that your current working model was destroyed last night." Kursolov nodded politely toward Spence who was stone-faced bordering on contemptuous.

Kursolov couldn't resist the chance to show off in front of her and, by extension, Walker. "That is a great loss since I understand it was scheduled to be moved this morning." Walker's shoulders sagged slightly and a wry smile covered Kursolov's face. "These things happen, Michael. There is no reason to be upset."

"As usual, you are extremely well-informed, Viktor," Walker answered with a slight bow that broadened the smile on Kursolov's face.

"It is such an embarrassment that the men who blew up your satellite were my countrymen."

"I can see how distraught you are." Walker's eyes twinkled. "You misread my body language, Victor. I was a bit disappointed by something you've told me, but no harm was done and we learned a great deal."

The smile vanished from Kursolov's face. "What do you mean?"

"It was a trap. We lured *your countrymen* into the building so we could identify them and track them down."

Kursolov's eyes stayed locked on Walker as he took another sip of the single malt. "Then I can assume the Hermes satellite was not actually in the building which was destroyed?"

"No," Walker answered calmly. Penelope started to protest since that would have been helpful information to share before she wrote her story, but Michael Walker's hand on her arm stopped her short. "It has never been within 3,000 miles of Washington."

"May I ask where it is now?"

"It is safely on the deck of the Boeing Sea Launch platform *Odyssey* which has already arrived at the equator."

"Very interesting, Michael," Kursolov said softly. "You know, of course, that many of my people work on the Boeing launch ship?"

Walker nodded toward Kursolov with a mischievous gleam in his eye. "Yes. With all of these terrorists running around trying to steal or destroy it, thank your people for guarding it so well for me."

Penelope's hand shot to her mouth as she tried to keep from laughing. Walker had not lost his touch. Penelope's reaction caused a smile to flicker for the briefest moment across Natasha's face. Neither reaction escaped Viktor. Obviously not used to being out maneuvered by anyone, Kursolov's eyes narrowed further and his voice was barely audible.

"So," Kursolov said softly as he struggled to maintain his composure, "the entire episode with NASA and your performance on television was some sort of a Kabuki dance?"

"We looked at it as an opportunity," Walker answered.

"An opportunity?"

"Yes," Walker's eyes brightened, "in the past 24 hours we have learned who we should be keeping our eyes on, and now, thanks to you, I've learned who the spy is in my organization." Walker held up his glass in a mock toast. "Thank you, Viktor. This has been a very profitable evening for me."

"So you are saying I am the one who revealed these things to you?"

"Yes," Walker answered with a Cheshire cat grin. "We shall be eternally grateful for your help."

Viktor Kursolov smiled. "Many things can still go wrong."

"True," Walker answered with a smile as he glanced at Lucas Haley, who nodded. "Just so you know, while I appreciate the security onboard the facility, a group of former Navy SEALs has arrived at the Boeing launch platform to guard my satellite until it is launched. Also, I requested and received a small favor from Homeland Security." Walker's smile vanished. "The *USS Ronald Reagan* Strike Group has been diverted from training exercises near San Diego to the area to observe the launch."

"Ah," Kursolov nodded. "So that is why the *Ronald Reagan* has changed course?"

"Yes," Walker answered calmly.

"Interesting," Kursolov said as he took another sip of his whiskey. "I had the impression that your influence in Washington had been greatly diminished. It would appear that I was ill informed, yes?"

"It would appear you have been misinformed about a great many things recently," Walker answered with a smile. "Considering four of the world's most-wanted terrorists have already attempted to destroy it, my friends in Washington consider this launch as one of their highest priorities. Any ship or plane which attempts to get within 250 miles of the Boeing site will be stopped."

Penelope was unable to keep her mouth from falling open. So that was the favor Walker had asked of Noah Shepherd. He was right. It was a bit bigger than asking for help opening up a historic site for a short notice weekend wedding.

"Those are International waters, Michael. Your government is willing to provoke an incident to protect your launch?"

"Provoke whom, Viktor? The major powers with blue water navies have all agreed to keep their ships out of the area. Any other vessels will be considered rogue and hostile, and treated accordingly." Walker's eyes narrowed. "That would include all of the trawler and fishing vessels you own that seem to only fish around US Naval Attack Groups."

Viktor Kursolov raised his glass in Walker's direction but said nothing.

"There is no reason we should be enemies, Viktor," Walker said softly. "Once my satellite is in orbit..."

"I agree, Michael." Kursolov finished his drink and motioned for a waiter to take his empty glass. "Let's have this conversation *if* you manage to get your satellite into orbit. Many things can still happen." Kursolov turned his attention toward Spence. "I understand you are a remarkable dancer, Penelope." Changing his glance to Walker, Kursolov continued. "You do not mind, Michael, if I ask this lovely lady for a dance?"

"Of course not," Walker answered warmly. If there was any jealousy in Walker, Penelope couldn't see it in his eyes.

Penelope was trapped. While she found Viktor Kursolov repulsive, to refuse such a dance request would violate a lifetime of congenial Southern upbringing.

"If you would not mind keeping Natasha amused then?" Kursolov asked. Walker nodded. "Excellent." Kursolov extended his hand to Spence who accepted it with a forced smile as he led her to the empty dance floor. "Maestro, if you please. A TANGO!" Kursolov said loudly enough to make every head in the room turn and all conversations stop.

Kursolov roughly grabbed Penelope and pulled her close. Their eyes locked. The music began to play. Viktor Kursolov was neither as graceful nor as disciplined as Michael Walker on the dance floor, and certainly not nearly as gentle. While his movements were crisp and precise, they lacked Walker's zeal. As he held her close and then tossed her away Penelope could sense that, like Walker, he had a raw animal power churning just under the surface. To Walker, a tango was lovemaking on the dance floor, to Kursolov it was rough sex in the back seat of a car. As the music played, more and more people began to line the edge of the dance floor, but Penelope didn't see them. Her eyes were locked on Kursolov's. As the music ended, there was a loud round of applause, and a few shouted

"Bravo" and "Magnifico" across the hall.

Before Penelope could bow, she saw the look on Kursolov's face and froze. For the first time Penelope noticed that people were not looking at her and Viktor, but rather at the other end of the dance floor. Natasha Kirov was sprawled panting at Michael Walker's feet. Walker's left arm was raised in tribute to his dance partner. Natasha, with Walker's help, regained her feet, and both bowed deeply to the applause. Natasha held Michael Walker's face in both her hands then, and between bursts of rapid-fire Russian, she kissed him on both cheeks before flinging her arms around him. Joey was right, jealousy is a powerful emotion.

Penelope turned back to Kursolov but she had been completely forgotten by the stocky little man. He had motioned for one of his aides to join him. Without ever taking his eyes off of Michael Walker, he hissed rapid fire instructions before storming off the dance floor.

CHAPTER TWENTY-FOUR

"Y OU ARE A fool," Natasha Kirov said as she fluffed her hair in the mirror and decided that was all the freshening up she was going to need. She turned and leaned on the sink next to Penelope. "He loves you."

"Who? Michael?" she asked with a sigh. "Why do you think he loves me?"

"When I threw myself at him, he didn't react."

"Really?" Penelope swallowed a smile and glanced sideways at Natasha as she continued to check her hair. "I didn't notice." While Penelope wasn't buying a word of what Natasha was selling, she still liked the way it sounded. "What about you and Viktor?"

A wry smile broke across the exotic woman's face and her eyes appeared to be focusing on something far away. "I am the luckiest woman in the world."

"Seriously?"

"Let me ask you this," Natasha said as she inched closer and leaned in so no one else could hear. "Have you ever been hungry or cold? I mean the kind of hunger and cold that makes you afraid you may not survive till morning?"

Penelope stopped her grooming and turned to study the face of Natasha. "No," she answered weakly.

"Is it safe to assume that you've never had to hide in a rat-infested sewer for a night to avoid being gang raped?" Penelope was stunned and shook her head. "Until Viktor found me, I was just one of thousands, maybe millions, of throwaway children in the old Soviet bloc. He took me in, gave me the best of everything and saved me. In exchange, I give him a few years of my youth and beauty. I would say I got the better end of the deal, no?"

"That depends," Penelope said as she turned back for a final check of the mirror. "What will happen when he gets tired of you?"

Kirov shrugged. "He will go his way and I will go my way." Natasha's eye twinkled as she laughed at the horror on Penelope's face. "Viktor has bought me a villa in the south of France and I have twenty-five million Euros in an account in Switzerland."

"Really?" Penelope's mind rapidly processed this new bit of information. "There is more to him than I thought."

Natasha's face grew dark. "You have no idea."

"What does that mean?" Penelope asked, but Natasha shook her head, indicating she had said too much already.

"You know your Michael and my Viktor are mortal enemies? Yes?"

"I've pretty much figured that out."

"Tonight your Michael humiliated my Viktor. You need to be very careful." Natasha Kirov leaned in close and whispered. "He is a very dangerous man."

"Viktor or Michael?"

Natasha laughed as she straightened to her full height, towering six inches over Penelope. "Probably both."

"After meeting Viktor I would agree, but why would you include Walker?"

"Michael Walker already has, what do you call it? A God complex. If he gets his satellite into space, there will be no stopping him."

"Stopping him from what?"

"Who knows?" Natasha said softly as she brushed a stray hair of Penelope's bangs into place. Her fingertips were soft and warm. "My Viktor is going to do everything within his power to stop your Michael."

'First off," Penelope said as she dropped her lipstick into her clutch and glanced sideways at Kirov. "He is not my Michael."

"Then you are bigger fool than I thought," Natasha said as she gave her mane a final shake.

Penelope ignored the jab and continued. "As your Viktor already discovered this evening, Walker can be quite resourceful."

"The same can be said for Viktor." Natasha Kirov grabbed Penelope's arm as she started to turn away from the mirror. Their eyes locked. Kirov's voice was deep and husky. "Be very careful. There is much more going on here than you can ever imagine, and your Michael will soon discover he is not nearly as clever as he thinks."

"What does that mean?" Penelope asked.

Kirov started to speak but stopped short when the door opened and an aristocratic elderly woman shuffled in and eyed the two with suspicion. Natasha released her grip on Penelope's arm and they headed toward the door. "You will know soon enough," the young woman whispered in Penelope's ear.

Natasha Kirov and Penelope Spence emerged from the powder room and scanned the hall for their dates. Natasha spotted them having an animated conversation on the other side of the room. Lacking Kirov's height, Penelope heard them before she saw them. If they were mortal enemies it would have been hard to imagine considering the rowdy laughter coming from the pair. Before the two women arrived, a buzz started around the perimeter of the ballroom. Panicked young men and women were talking into cell phones while scurrying in search of their bosses. Messages were whispered into important ears, causing eyebrows to rise and rapid-fire orders to be issued. Immediately the crowd began to thin. As the women finally worked their way back to the men, Penelope asked, "What's going on?"

Viktor Kursolov hooked his arm under Natasha's and motioned for his aides to get their car. "If I had to guess," he said confidently, "I would say that someone just launched an attack on Las Vegas using the technology Walker Industries had developed." He turned his full attention toward Michael Walker. "Interesting choice don't you think, attacking possibly the most decadent city on earth?" A cold smile covered Kursolov's face. "It will be interesting to see how much world support your satellite launch still has when news of this gets out." With a slight nod of their heads, Viktor Kursolov and Natasha Kirov turned as a unit and headed for the main exit.

The instant they were out of sight, Lucas Haley appeared and pointed to the kitchen. "It's a zoo out front. The car's out back."

"Where are we going?"

Walker laughed and winked at her, "You heard the man, Vegas, baby!"

SINCE IT WAS after 10 p.m. traffic was light on the Interstate and Lucas Haley had the Escalade approaching 90 mph as it blew past the exit for Reagan airport. Before Penelope could ask Walker finished his conversation with whomever he was speaking to on his cell, clicked it closed and said, "Kent has my jet. We're going to hitch a ride over at Andrews." Walker leaned back in his seat and smiled at Spence. As usual, he was unflappable. Less than an hour earlier, and for the second time in two days, she had been ready to claw his eyes out. First his dismissive attitude on the flight from New York and then his upstaging her with his little tango stunt with Natasha. Now, with all of Washington swirling in crisis mode, sitting next to him felt like the calm eye of a massive storm.

"We're going to have to take Sally Winters back for a few days. She could handle the spin control of the breakup of Walker Industries from Charleston but I'm going to need her on the ground in Las Vegas."

"Carrie's a big girl. She'll be fine." As Penelope nodded her head, she caught a flash of light out of the corner of her eye. An unmarked Crown Victoria with emergency lights flashing in its grill was closing the distance between them. Fast. "It looks like you might be a bit late for your flight." The words were barely out of her mouth when the car blew past them on the right and settled in front of Escalade. She felt the heavy vehicle accelerate.

"After the PR they got last night," Walker said with a laugh, "I doubt anyone from Walker Industries will be getting a ticket in Washington anytime soon."

Penelope shook her head. Had it really been less than twenty-four hours? She had noticed this pattern before. Whenever she was around Michael time seemed to move differently, slower, and there was an intensity level she had never felt before. It was exhilarating and unnerving at the same time. He tried to explain it to her, but his explanation was always a bit hard to swallow. He claimed those on the path to enlightenment often found their journey accelerating merely by being in his presence. Before she got to know him and the people responsible for the Hermes Project, she thought it was just his ego talking. The longer she chewed on it, the better his explanation tasted.

She felt the Escalade slowing as it approached the gate of Andrews Air Force Base. Apparently someone had phoned ahead and they were expected. All other traffic had been moved to the side, and they were waved through without having to stop. Haley hit a pair of speed bumps hard enough to cause the undercarriage to scrape the pavement. He mumbled a weak "Sorry."

The unmarked car peeled off at the gate and now Haley was following an Air Force Jeep. The Escalade accelerated again and weaved its way to the tarmac where a sleek Gulfstream G550 with an American flag on the tail was waiting with its stairs down. Pulling to a stop, Ian and Haley jumped out, opened the door for Walker and Spence, and immediately went to the rear of the heavy eight-passenger vehicle to open the tailgate.

As Penelope watched, Haley and Fleming began unloading luggage. Penelope's shoulders sagged and her head dropped when she recognized one of the suitcases as hers. Next to it was her laptop case.

"Have you been looting my house again?" Penelope asked Walker.

"Not me this time," Walker answered with a nod toward Ian.

The first day Penelope had met Michael Walker, he had somehow managed to get into her house unnoticed and make off with half her closet and her laptop while she was sleeping a few feet away. Penelope's eyes flew wide open. She grabbed Michael Walker's arm and spun him around to face her. "You were expecting this?"

Walker shrugged. "It was one of the contingencies."

Spence shook her head in disbelief. "You're telling me you expected Viktor Kursolov to use your technology to attack a major American city."

"It's not just 'my' technology anymore. We're just a bit further along than everyone else. Besides, I doubt he would have taken the bait without you."

"Me!" Penelope protested. "What in the world did I do?"

Walker hooked his arm under Spence's and started her moving again. He let Penelope go first up the ten steps into the Gulfstream before motioning toward the last two seats in the rear of the plane. "I doubt I could have provoked him tonight without you," Walker said calmly.

"What do you mean provoke him?"

"While I'm confident that attacking an American city was the last thing on his mind when the evening started, several things happened that changed everything."

"Such as?"

"He knew there was always a risk that his terrorist cell might be captured alive and I'm sure he factored in that possibility. That pretty much pulled back the drapes and left him with limited deniability. He should have left the country immediately after they were arrested but he couldn't resist the urge to rub my nose in the fact that he had destroyed the Hermes satellite. When I told him his men had walked into a trap and had not only been captured but also failed to destroy the satellite he knew his plan was unraveling fast. When he learned that the Hermes Project satellite had been unguarded and in the possession of a company that he effectively controls, and that he could have destroyed it at his leisure anytime for the past month, he knew he had to come up with something very different and fast."

"I still don't see how I played any part in this?"

"People such as Viktor have a very small peer group. My dance with Natasha would have been meaningless if you hadn't been there. While Kursolov has the ability to completely detach himself from people and emotions, upstaging him in front of some of the most powerful people in the world merited a response. He made a bad decision."

"You set me up?"

"No," Walker said with a laugh, "we set Viktor up."

Penelope folded her arms across her chest and looked out the porthole window. "You could have told me."

"Not likely," Walker said. "You have easily the worst poker face I've ever seen."

"I do not!" Penelope barked defensively but without conviction. She knew he was right. If he had given her a head's up she would have been so nervous that Viktor would have avoided the trap. Penelope decided to change the subject.

"I don't see how that could have provoked him to attack Las Vegas."

"He made a political calculation. Since Noah Shepherd had hustled the terrorists off to Fort Meade and declared them enemy combatants before the Justice Department even knew they were in custody, he figured it was only a matter of time before Homeland Security broke one of the men involved. He obviously has friends and spies in high places in our government, but a terrorist attack on the Hermes Building was an overt act of war on American soil by anyone's definition. I'm sure all of his bought-and-paid-for friends in Washington are already starting to get nervous and are weighing their options. As the news starts to leak out, they will abandon him in droves."

"I still don't see how that provoked an attack."

"In for a dime, in for a dollar. His influence in Washington will be gone before the fog dissipates on the Potomac tomorrow morning. He is finished in the United States and he knows it. At this point, he had nothing to lose by launching the attack and possibly something to gain."

"What could he possibly gain?"

"It was a Hail Mary attempt to discredit me. However, he made a quick decision under severe pressure, which soon he'll realize was a mistake."

"Why was it a mistake?"

Walker barked at Haley, "Lucas, what's the status?" Haley, his ear pressed to his cell phone, didn't answer but gave a thumbs up. "Excellent," Walker said as he turned his attention back to Spence. "A team from the Hermes Project has arrived in Las Vegas and things are already returning to normal."

"What!" Penelope shook her head in disbelief. "You had a team in Las Vegas waiting for this to happen."

"No," Walker answered casually. "We had them on standby halfway between Las Vegas and Salt Lake City."

"Why?"

"We made a few assumptions," Walker answered.

"You know what happens when you assume?" Penelope asked.

"Yes," Walker answered. "In this case it was necessary to make some assumptions to prepare contingencies."

"Okay, let's hear them."

"The burst that hit the Jackson Hole facility was older technology which, because of its bulk, would take time to mount on an aircraft. So we concluded that limited them to the same land-based delivery system they used on Hermes. If that assumption was correct, then they would need an elevated position to shoot down from."

"Okay," Spence said half-heartedly, "I guess that makes sense."

"Next, because we believed they were still in a truck, we assumed they really didn't want to drive very far and run the risk of being seen or captured." Walker read the puzzled expression on Penelope's face and answered the question before it was asked. "With every national security agency in the country looking for them, they wanted to get off the road and away from potential satellite detection." Penelope nodded she understood. "That meant the most likely target would be Salt Lake City, which is only a five-hour drive from Jackson. Next would be Las Vegas, or possibly Phoenix or even Los Angeles if they were willing to risk that much time in the open."

"You did all of this assuming in the three days since the attack in Jackson?"

"This was only one of several contingencies we had in place," Walker answered with a smile. "Salt Lake City was closest and had the lowest risk factor but we figured Kursolov would be unable to resist hitting Las Vegas. We hedged our bet, split the distance and had the equipment mounted on a helicopter at a private airstrip outside of Cedar City, Utah."

"What equipment?"

"Remember what happened to Mark Hatchet?"

"A bit hard to forget," Penelope answered with a shiver. In the controlled environment of the Hermes Project, Mark was hit with an EM burst that briefly turned him into a paranoid maniac. After a few minor adjustments to the setting, he was hit with another which returned him to his normal self.

"That's pretty much what happened to the entire city of Las Vegas," Walker said with a smile. "Viktor hit them with a negative burst and we hit them with a positive one," Walker drew in a sharp breath through his nose and slowly released it between his lips, "I just hope not too positive."

"What on earth does that mean?"

Walker waved it off. "It's not important. What is important is that Viktor Kursolov is probably getting reports of what's happening right now in Las Vegas and he is starting to grasp the size of his mistake."

"What exactly did he grasp?"

Walker smiled and gave her a moment to work it out for herself. Depending on her mood, Penelope either hated or loved these little challenges Walker liked to throw in her path. In the past few days she seemed to be knocking the rust off her reporting skills, so this one was welcomed.

"Let's see," she said with a sigh, "he uses a Hermes Project style EM burst as a weapon and you quickly nullified it...OH! MY! GOD!" Both of Penelope's hands flew to her mouth. "He just made your case for you on the importance of being able to nullify the effects when it is used as a weapon by an unfriendly force. And with you being able to nullify the effects so quickly, you proved it will work. Brilliant!" Walker bowed slightly which prompted Penelope to playfully slug him in the arm. "What do you think Kursolov's next move will be?"

"Right now we have Kursolov back on his heels," Walker said as he turned serious again. "This will make him even more dangerous. When he thought he had destroyed my satellite, he got overconfident and made a mistake. He confirmed the identity of the spy within the Hermes Project, and I didn't..."

"What in the world are you talking about?" Penelope demanded, cutting Walker off in mid-sentence. "Did this happen while I was in the lady's room with Natasha?"

"No, you were standing right there."

Penelope was mentally replaying the conversation in her mind when her eyes flew open and an audible gasp escaped her lips. "Nooo. He thought the satellite was being shipped today."

Walker tapped the end of his nose. "I gave everyone different shipping days. Robert Smith was the only one who thought the satellite was going to be picked up this morning. When Kursolov said he thought it was this morning as well, it could have only come from you or Robert. Wait a minute...it wasn't you was it?"

"Very funny." Penelope slumped back in her chair and shook her head. "Wow. That's hard to believe. Robert Smith a spy."

"Why? You were the one who pointed him out."

"Me? What did I do?"

"When you quiet your mind you're very intuitive. You told me the first time you met Smith you didn't trust him. When I get messages like that, I pay attention. After that I didn't trust him either."

"Are you going to have Smith arrested or something?"

Walker shrugged. "Robert Smith and his family are probably already out of the country, or at least on their way."

Penelope's mouth fell open. "Aren't you going to try to stop him?"

"No," Walker answered flatly. When he saw that wasn't going to be enough to appease Spence he continued, "For years I've been astounded by Smith's ability to resist my influence. Thanks to you, now it all makes sense."

"How do I keep getting involved in this?"

Walker laughed and shook his head. "After you told me you didn't trust him, we rechecked Smith's background. For over a year he was stationed as liaison officer at the Baikonur Cosmodrome where..."

"He met Viktor Kursolov."

"Exactly," Walker said as he nodded his approval. "It is just a guess but Smith may have bonded with Kursolov before he ever met me..."

"So that is why he is immune to your charms."

"I don't think I would describe it quite like that," Walker said with a laugh, "but essentially, yes."

"That doesn't explain why you don't want him arrested."

"Well," Walker said with a shrug, "I don't think Robert Smith and I have seen the last of each other."

Penelope folded her arms across her chest and thought about this development for a moment. As usual, Walker didn't intrude. While not overly satisfied with his answer about Smith, she couldn't think of any more questions so she returned to original subject. "It looks to me like you've outsmarted Kursolov at every turn."

"So far that is true," he said with a shrug. "But the game is not over yet and I'm sure he has more cards up his sleeve. He must have given the order for the attack on Las Vegas while we were still at the party. To execute a project of that complexity with less than an hour's notice is impressive."

"Impressive!" Penelope looked at Walker in open-mouthed wonder. "A man just attacked a major American city and you're impressed?"

"It's going to be much ado about nothing in Las Vegas," Walker said with a wave of his hand as his face brightened. "There is going to be a great deal of noise and light and probably some property damage but limited personal injuries. I'll be surprised if there is a single fatality."

"Why?"

"Because," Walker said with a laugh, "that's the way I would do it."

"What do you mean, that's the way you would do it?"

"In many ways Viktor Kursolov and I are very much alike. Okay," Walker said with a laugh when he saw the amazed look on Penelope's face, "I would never do anything like that, but I understand his thinking. He wanted to embarrass me and put me on the defensive. If a lot of people were killed or injured, he would immediately become the target instead of me. At this point, there was nothing for him to lose by attacking Las Vegas, and he hopes it causes enough embarrassment to stop my launch."

"What are the odds of that?"

"Near zero. It's a weekend and it is going to take the people who oppose me a few days to muster their forces and regroup. Sally should be able to muddy the water enough to give us the time we need."

"Time for what?"

"We moved the launch time up to tomorrow afternoon. That means the next twenty-four hours will tell the tale. "

Before Penelope could formulate a response, Special Agent Marcus Wolfe came through the door followed by Director Noah Shepherd of Homeland Security. Penelope leaned in and asked, "What are they doing here?"

"It's their airplane."

CHAPTER TWENTY-FIVE

PENELOPE WAS GRUMPY. On an intellectual level it all made perfect sense but it didn't mean she had to be happy about it. She had not expected to be invited to participate in any of the confabs at the "adult" table in the front of the Homeland Security jet and had not protested when she was relegated to the "kid" table at the back of the plane. While she understood Homeland Security's reluctance to let a credentialed reporter be privy to their conversations, she felt the decision not to let her use the jet's Wi-Fi was arbitrary. With a huge story unfolding, she needed her digital fix.

Upfront, Walker and Noah Shepherd were doing the same thing they had been doing for the past two hours, huddling with other people from Homeland Security Penelope had never seen before. There was a muted buzz of phone calls, guarded conversations, and the occasional hum of a printer spewing out the latest update. As for Penelope, she was stuck in the rear of the plane with nothing to do except stare out into darkness. She was starting to get fidgety. The first hour wasn't so bad as she'd kept herself busy entering her impressions from the evening with Viktor Kursolov into her laptop. She doubted any of it would ever be allowed in *The Washington Post,* but it might make her next book and she wanted to get it down while it was still fresh. That task was finished before they had cleared the Mississippi River.

"They should at least let me on the internet," Penelope said impatiently.

"This aircraft's link is behind the Homeland Security firewall, ma'am," Ian answered calmly. "They're not going to give you access."

"I got that much after the first three times I heard it." Penelope shook her head and closed the cover on her laptop. She hadn't realized what an internet junkie she had become. Without her constant stream of news and email, she felt as if she had been transported back in time all the way to the dark ages of the 1990s before she had first discovered the addictive online wonderland. She closed her eyes and tried without success to work the knot out of her neck. Withdrawal was no fun, but at least she was comfortable.

Even before the "Fasten Seatbelt" light had clicked off, Ian had handed Penelope a change of clothes. It was quite a step down from her designer evening gown to denim jeans, a short-sleeved pullover knit shirt, and running shoes but she didn't feel underdressed. Walker, Ian and Haley had each taken a turn in the cramped galley to make a wardrobe change, and all were now dressed the same way, more or less.

Her sulking was interrupted by the sound of Ian Fleming's voice. "You should try to get some rest."

Without opening her eyes she continued rolling her neck from side to side. "I'm too keyed up and, besides, I slept until the middle of the afternoon."

"Try this." Fleming handed Penelope a small box. "It came this morning while you were sleeping. I think it's a book."

"Really?" Penelope said shaking her head as she examined the package. "What was your first clue?"

"It has an *Amazon.com* return address and..."

Penelope held up her hand to stop him. "That was a rhetorical question."

Fleming eyed Spence with concern. "When was the last time you had anything to eat?" he asked.

Penelope had the package about half way open when she turned toward Ian and narrowed her eyes. "Where did that come from?"

"You're obviously agitated. Since I've seen you in more stressful situations than this in the past few days during which you didn't descend to this level..."

"Descend?" Penelope's eyes flashed with anger as she cut him off in mid-sentence.

"Many people, when they get tired or hungry, get a bit cranky."

Penelope drew back her index finger, loaded it up, and was just about to point it at Fleming to open fire when her stomach began to growl. With her finger still cocked she closed her eyes, drew in a deep breath, and thought about it. The last real food she had eaten had been in the restaurant with Trotta, Walker, and Lazlo over 24 hours ago. Fleming was right, she was famished. Plus, for the past three days her sleep cycle had been dumped on its head. That was always a bad combination. She opened her eyes and saw him staring at her with the innocence of a newborn. "I am a bit hungry."

"I'll see what they have in the galley." In the blink of an eye, Fleming was gone.

Penelope continued her assault on the Amazon box as she muttered to herself, "*Sometimes I think he knows me better than I do.*" The glue finally gave on the cardboard and the latest Sue Grafton novel plopped into her lap. Penelope's eyes grew large. She wasn't sure if it was the prospect of food in her immediate future or the latest book from her favorite author, but she involuntarily found herself licking her lips.

Fleming returned from foraging with a limited selection. All he had was an eight-ounce plastic bottle of orange juice. Penelope accepted it. "Better than nothing," she said with a weak smile. She broke the seal on the OJ and gulped about half down in a single swallow. If she had thought some juice would calm her, she was badly mistaken. The fresh calories hitting her system woke her stomach up with a vengeance. Instead of satisfying her hunger it only whetted her appetite. "Are there any more of these?" she asked.

"No ma'am," Fleming answered. "That was the last one."

"Wonderful."

The two sat in silence as Spence fought her primal urge to gulp down the last of her juice and then start foraging for something with a bit more substance. She was so hungry that for a brief moment she considered gnawing on the box her book had arrived in, but decided it was too high in fiber. Plus, she doubted the glue was organic.

Sitting next to her, Ian had turned his attention back to the Nintendo DS he was holding. He had white ear buds in place and his thumbs were flying across the control buttons as he stared unblinking at the small screen. He was an odd bird, Penelope thought to herself.

"Excellent," Fleming muttered as he clearly had gotten the better of the game. Before he could hit restart, Penelope touched his arm. He dropped his earphones into his lap and turned his full attention toward Penelope. "Yes ma'am."

"I want to ask you what happened this afternoon."

"Which part?" Fleming answered innocently.

"The part where you slipped me a spiritual roofie." For the first time since she had met him, Ian Fleming laughed. It wasn't the "fill the room" laugh of Michael Walker. It was quiet, self-contained and more personal. "Oh, that."

"Yeah. That."

"I didn't have anything to do with that. It was all you."

"Excuse me?" Penelope said as she gave Fleming a sideways glance. "For the second time in a year, while holding the hands of someone from the Hermes Project, I lost touch with reality and ended up some place else."

"Okay, okay," Fleming said, smiling so broadly his eyes narrowed. "I might have played a small part."

"Seriously," Penelope said curtly, "that's the best answer you've got?"

"What answer are you looking for?"

"Should I expect more of these episodes?"

"That's hard to say," Fleming said with a shrug. "You did a lovely spring cleaning today, but there is still something that has been bugging you for awhile. You'd be better off dealing with it sooner than later."

"What would that be?" Penelope asked absently as she read the dust jacket of her book.

Fleming nodded toward Michael Walker.

"You can't be serious," Penelope said while shaking her head. "I'm moving on."

"Really?" Ian said with a grin. "How do you look at Michael Walker right now?"

Penelope shrugged. "He's a source that gets me interesting stories."

"There is no attraction?"

Penelope shrugged but couldn't hold eye contact.

"That's what I thought," Ian said.

"Meaning what?" Penelope demanded.

"You've started to release your feelings toward Michael Walker but you still have work left to do."

"What the heck does that mean?"

"I'd tell you but..."

Penelope cut across him with fire in her eyes. "If you say I'm not ready for your answer you had better have a parachute handy."

Ian pulled back and laughed. "What I was going to say was that you don't like it when I go all Zen on you."

"Oh," Penelope said, a bit embarrassed by her outburst, "that's different. What were you going to say?"

"To seek is to suffer. To seek nothing is peace. When you seek nothing, you're on the Path."

"You're right," Penelope said with a pained expression on her face. "I don't like it when you go all Zen on me."

Now it was Ian's turn to shrug.

"I give up," Penelope said as she opened the novel in her lap.

Ian didn't take the hint and continued talking. "I thought it was interesting that you released a lifetime of issues with your family before you tried to release Michael Walker."

"What's the significance of that?" Penelope asked as she continued to focus on her new novel.

"You tell me," Fleming answered with a laugh. "Since you have only been carrying him around for a year I would have thought you might have tried to completely release him before tackling your family."

For about ten seconds Penelope stared open-mouthed at Fleming as she searched his face. Was it possible she still had feelings toward Michael Walker? After a year of being taken for granted and manipulated then summarily dismissed, it was hardly likely. She shot Ian a cold stare but to her surprise Fleming still didn't take the hint and continued talking.

"Now that we've got some of these issues out the way," Ian said, "we can start working on other things you need to release."

"We?" Penelope said a bit more harshly than she had intended. Fleming didn't seem to notice or, if he did, care.

"I want to help if you'll let me."

Penelope's reporter early warning signal was starting to ring. She leaned back in her seat and studied Fleming closely. A dozen questions flashed through her mind. What was in this for him? Why had he volunteered to watch over her? What did Homeland Security have to do with all of this? With only forty or so people directly associated with the Hermes Project, how was it possible she had never stumbled across him? She knew it was pointless to ask any direct questions since he had been hiding behind his "*it's classified*" since they'd met.

"How exactly will you help me?"

This time Ian detected the tone and body language that came with it. "Maybe we should talk about this later," Fleming offered.

Penelope took a moment and gathered herself. She knew she was being defensive, but the recent direction of their conversation had ruffled her feathers. Then an odd thing happened. The mere acknowledgement that the problem was hers and had nothing to do with Ian caused her body to relax. "I'm sorry," she said softly. "What exactly do you have in mind?"

"I can show you some different meditation and releasing techniques."

"Will it get any easier?"

Fleming shrugged. "That's pretty much up to you."

"What does that mean?"

"You still have a lot of work to do, but you can determine how fast you release these things. As you have already seen, a massive release can take a physical toll. Some people like to just get it over with the way you did today, while others prefer to take it slower."

"How long will it take?"

Fleming shrugged.

Penelope shook her head. Her stomach grumbled again. "You're starting to get as annoying as Michael Walker."

"Did I hear my name?" Michael Walker asked as he joined the conversation.

Penelope's hand instinctively moved to her hair and she glanced up at Walker. "I was just commenting that your little mini-me here is perfecting the same annoying habit you have of not giving a straight answer to a direct question."

"Ian," Walker said sternly.

"Yes sir."

"Play nicely with Penelope."

"Yes sir," he answered quickly as he swallowed his grin.

Penelope held up her hand with her thumb and index finger about a half inch apart. "You were that close to getting back into my good graces."

"What penitence is required?" Walker asked.

"You could get me online."

"This is a Homeland Security jet, not Starbucks."

Penelope glared at Walker and moved her fingers further apart. She broke eye contact with Walker, folded her arms across her chest and shook her head. "I'm bored out of my skull and there is nothing to eat."

"We'll be on the ground in a few minutes and we can get you something when we land. Here," Walker said as he dropped a folder in her lap.

Penelope's eyes grew large as she saw the Homeland Security logo and "Top Secret" stamp on the front. "You really know the way to a girl's heart," she said as she started to open the file folder.

"Don't get your hopes up," Walker said with a playful twinkle in his eyes she hadn't seen, or maybe just hadn't noticed, in awhile. "That was the only file folder they had handy." Penelope's shoulders slumped when she saw the contents. It was printouts of pages from various news websites. "Since they won't let you online, I thought the least I could do is keep you updated as best I could." Walker twisted his head slightly and read the top sheet. "It doesn't look like anyone has scooped you yet."

Penelope flipped quickly through the pages and had to agree. "What's going on in Las Vegas right now?"

"They've located and deactivated the device Kursolov's people used, and my people are sweeping the city. Things are starting to return to normal, but we'll know more when we land."

"When will that be?" Penelope asked.

As if on cue the "Fasten Seatbelt" light clicked on and the pilot's voice came over the intercom. "Everyone please return to your seats. We will be landing at Nellis Air Force Base in just a few minutes."

Walker returned to the front of the plane. Penelope watched as he made his way up the aisle. She felt an involuntary smile cross her face. It was nice to have the old playful relationship back with Michael Walker. It was like when they had first met a year ago, good-natured verbal jabs and counterpunches, with none of the sexual tension that had marked their relationship in recent months. As she watched him buckle himself into the seat next to Noah Shepherd, it occurred to her that she was being childish. Walker had never once given the slightest indication that he was looking for more from Penelope than someone to write favorable stories for him. He had never made a pass at her. He had never stumbled drunk down from the penthouse above her apartment to tap on her door late at night, hoping to charm his way in. He had always been a perfect gentleman. "*Too perfect,*" she thought as she closed her eyes and braced herself for another landing.

After the Homeland Security jet touched down and taxied to a hangar, Penelope saw four people in flight suits striding across the tarmac looking in their direction. To her surprise, she recognized two of them.

"That was better than sex!" Sally Winters' cheeks were flushed and her eyes were wide. As she unzipped her Air Force-issued flight suit, she handed her helmet to one of the ground crew. "Penelope, you have got to try that. Unbelievable!" Standing behind her, similarly dressed, Timothy

Ellison was white as a ghost. "To get here faster, Rascal looped us down to the Gulf of Mexico so he could open this baby up." Winters grabbed the smirking pilot of one of the F/A-18F Super Hornets parked a few hundred yards away and pushed him forward. "This is 'Rascal' and I'm 'Snowflake'. Winters, Snowflake. Get it?" Walker and Spence exchanged bemused glances as they let her ramble. "How fast were we going, Rascal?"

"We topped out at Mach 1.8, ma'am." The pilot was tall and lean with a ready smile and mischievous blue eyes.

"Mach 1.8," Sally repeated excitedly. "That's faster than the speed of sound!"

"We know," Michael Walker said. "What's wrong with Timothy?"

Winters leaned in and whispered, "After we landed to refuel at Lackland Air Force Base in Texas, they started calling him B. B.," she leaned in even closer, "Barf Bag."

THE DEVICE HAD been set up in much the same manner as when it was fired at the Hermes complex in Jackson Hole two days earlier. The "Walker Industries" van was parked on a turn out along highway 141 on a ridge near the top of Frenchman Mountain with a perfect sightline to the entire Las Vegas metro area. The rear door was open, and no attempt had been made to conceal its location.

Walker and Spence followed in the wake of Special Agent Marcus Wolfe who didn't even break stride as he weaved his way through the layers of security surrounding the truck. Penelope could see the concern etched on Walker's face as they ducked under the "police line" tape and headed toward the step van. As he rounded the corner to where he was able to see into the rear of the van, he came to such an abrupt stop she nearly walked up his back.

"Now that's funny," Walker said as he shook his head and laughed out loud.

"What?" Penelope demanded as she stepped around Walker to see what was in the rear of the step van. Near the back of the van was a small generator and, even after an hour of airing out, the interior still reeked of diesel fumes. In front of the generator was an ugly box of a device roughly the size of a refrigerator lying on its side. Attached to the end was what appeared to be some kind of dish or antenna aimed at Las Vegas.

Turning the corner, Noah Shepherd let out an audible gasp when he saw the contents in the rear of the van. He exchanged worried glances with Walker as he turned away and reached for his cell phone.

"What's wrong?" Penelope demanded.

"Apparently I may not be as clever as I thought."

"Why do you say that?"

"Kursolov didn't build this device."

"Who did?" asked Penelope.

"Me."

CHAPTER TWENTY-SIX

"HOLD ON," PENELOPE said as her head snapped in Walker's direction. "What do you mean you built it?"

Michael Walker shook his head. "This was one of our early prototypes from back in the days when Homeland Security was still funding the Hermes Project. Their lead scientists all thought the power of the Electro-Magnetic burst might be more important than the tuning of the frequencies. They insisted we build this monstrosity against our advice. After the first time it was used on their volunteers, they quickly abandoned this type of brute force and went to our more finely-tuned and less power-intensive technology."

It took a moment for Walker's words to sink in. Penelope's eyes and mouth flew open and she pointed to the device in the back of the truck. "This isn't..."

"Yes," Walker answered with a sigh, "this is the actual prototype that injured the Homeland Security volunteers."

"How did it get here?"

"I'm sure Noah Shepherd is asking that very question as we speak." Walker nodded toward the Director of Emerging Technology, who was speaking softly into his encrypted cell phone.

"So," Penelope said as her eyes flittered back and forth between the device and Walker while she considered the implications, "this was stolen from Homeland Security and not Walker Industries?"

"Yes," Walker answered absently. "This was constructed during the period when we were working under their authority, so it technically belonged to them and not us."

"This is a pretty valuable piece of technology, right?" Penelope asked.

"Indeed," he answered as he rubbed his chin. While Michael Walker was answering all of her questions, she could see in his eyes that his mind was elsewhere and moving fast.

"Why would they leave it behind?"

"Another excellent question," Walker sighed as he walked away from the rear of the van and stood by the edge of the sheer drop-off with the stunning view of Las Vegas. Casino row was brightly lit and, other than a few random fires and the abundance of emergency vehicle lights on the streets, from this height there was no outward indication the attack had ever occurred. "I wonder what Kursolov is up to?" Walker asked to no one in particular.

Their conversation stopped as a harried State Trooper with a sun-baked, cracked-leather face and at least one wrinkle for every one of his sixty years approached. He touched the brim of his Smokey the Bear hat and nodded at Spence. "Ma'am."

Penelope did her best to smile back. That was fast becoming her least favorite word.

"I'm Colonel Nobles of the Nevada Highway Patrol. Are you Michael Walker?"

"Yes."

"We've got a problem down there." Nobles nodded toward the dark city below.

"I'm aware of that, Colonel," Walker answered.

"No. It's a different problem." Colonel Nobles' eyes danced nervously at Spence, and she could sense that something about her being there was making him uncomfortable. "I understand your people have been shooting some kind of ray gun at the folks down there to calm them down."

"That's correct."

Colonel Nobles sighed. "Do you think you can turn it off?"

"Of course," Walker's eyes twinkled, "I was afraid of this."

Panic hit Penelope in the pit of her stomach. A year earlier she had seen the downside potential of the Hermes Project when a few seconds of exposure had turned Mark Hatchet into a frothing-at-the-mouth lunatic. Penelope cut into the conversation. "What's wrong?"

"Well, ma'am," Nobles was unable to make eye contact with her, and his gaze locked on his feet, "that ray gun thingy seems to be working a bit too good."

"What does that mean?" Penelope demanded.

"We're getting a lot of reports of public indecency down there."

"Public indecency?"

Michael Walker starting laughing. To save the thoroughly embarrassed straight-laced Colonel any further embarrassment, he leaned in and whispered in her ear, "Sex."

"Oh," Penelope said softly, but as the word and the implications sank in, her eyes grew bigger. "OH!"

"I'll get it turned off immediately," Walker said as he motioned for Timothy Ellison, pulled him aside, and gave him the instructions.

"Thank you." Nobles shook his head. "Worse than a gall-darned New Year's Eve down there."

She wasn't sure if it was fatigue or lack of food, but Penelope felt a giggle fit coming on and she was helpless to stop it. This was suddenly the funniest thing she had ever heard in her life. Terrorists attack a major American city, and thanks to Michael Walker the biggest problem will be a shortage of maternity beds in nine months. She put her hand on her forehead to shield her eyes and her entire body began to shake with laughter. Wiping the tears from her cheeks, she looked up at Walker. He must have been reading her mind because he had a mischievous grin on his face.

"We really need to get some food in you," Walker said.

Just as suddenly as the bout of giggles had arrived, they were gone, and Penelope's eyes narrowed. "Why is everyone so concerned with my eating habits?"

Timothy Ellison returned and started to rejoin the conversation but stopped dead in his tracks when he saw the look on Penelope's face. "Whoa," he said, directing his comment toward Walker. "I've seen that look before." Ellison shook his head and moved a step further away from Spence. "If she is anything like her daughter, we need to get her something to eat."

"She's starting to get slap happy," Walker said to Ellison as if Spence wasn't even there.

Penelope threw her hands in the air and shook her head in disgust. "What is it with you people tonight?"

Walker ignored her and continued with his instructions for Ellison. "Has the helicopter been recalled?" Ellison nodded. "Then," Walker said as he pointed a finger in Ellison's direction, "get her some food, ASAP." Ellison made a weak attempt at a salute and walked away. Walker grabbed Ellison's arm to stop him. "Take Ian with you." Ellison's gaze fell on the device in the rear of the van. He nodded that he understood.

"What's going on?" Sally Winters said as she approached the couple with her iPhone in hand.

"We're just discussing the care and feeding of Penelope Drayton Spence," Walker answered with a laugh. The aforementioned Ms. Spence folded her arms across her chest and glared at Walker.

"Yes, I'm hungry, but that is not the only thing that can make me grumpy," Penelope said with a snort.

Winters rolled her eyes and said, "Whatever." She spun her iPhone around so the screen faced Walker and Spence. "You need to see this. It went up on *YouTube* about half an hour ago."

On the screen was the image of the truck they were standing next to with "Walker Industries" clearly visible on the side. The lights of Las Vegas were in the background. The image on the screen glitched and rolled as the initial EM blast was launched. In the valley below, the lights of Las Vegas flickered for a moment but only a few went out. This was followed by stock footage of people screaming and looting, along with a remarkably unflattering picture of Michael Walker cut between pictures of Hitler and Stalin. Finally it went black, and a message in bold white letters began to scroll.

"This is the technology Michael Walker and Homeland Security are planning to launch into space in the next few days. Star Wars has arrived. Stop them before it is too late!"

As the video ended, Walker muttered, "Lovely. Is there any way to get this off of the internet?"

"Too late, the damage is done." Winters shook her head. "They were very smart. They made it a short enough video that a compressed version could be easily attached to an email. I've already had dozens of calls. Every news organization in the world has it."

"How are you going to spin it?" Walker asked calmly.

Winters had clearly already plotted her strategy. "For the second time in less than forty-eight hours terrorists have struck at targets on American soil, blah, blah. Thanks to the efforts of Walker Industries and in conjunction with Homeland Security, the damage was minimal, blah, blah. This type of terrorist attack confirms the need for this technology, blah, blah. Many of those responsible for this outrageous attack are already in custody and more arrests are eminent, blah, blah, blah."

"You think you can sell that?" Walker asked.

"Having six terrorists cooling their heels in maximum security won't hurt. Plus Stevie has a really impressive video of the Hermes building being leveled. We'll be fine."

"Okay," Walker said, "will you need me for a press conference?"

Winters shook her head. "No. We want Taniel Dildabekov and his buddies to be the face of this and not you."

"Good," Walker answered.

Winters wheeled around to leave but pulled up short when, for the first time, she saw what was in the back of the van. "Is that what I think it is?"

"Yes," Walker answered softly, concern etched on his face.

Winters drew in a breath of air and her cheeks puffed out as she slowly released it. "That's a scenario we hadn't considered. Any idea what this means?"

"We'll need to think about this one for a while," Walker answered. Penelope was seeing a different person than the one she had gotten to know in the past year. Clearly this development had given him some pause. Had Michael James Walker finally met his match in Viktor Kursolov?

"Well," Winters said as she shook her head, "We knew Kursolov was resourceful but this is a masterstroke." As Walker nodded his agreement, Noah Shepherd rejoined the group. His expression was grim, even by his standards. "Director," Winters said, "we're going to need a senior Homeland Security press liaison to co-ordinate on how we're going to explain this."

"Already on the way," Shepherd said calmly as he handed his cell phone to an aide lurking a few steps behind him.

"O'Reilly or Watson?" Winter asked.

"Both," Shepherd answered flatly.

Sally Winters glanced up at Walker and nodded her approval. "They are excellent. We'll be fine."

"We have a bigger issue than this," Shepherd said without the slightest hint of emotion in his voice.

"Really?" Walker said with a bemused look on his face.

"Yes," Shepherd answered. "Another prototype is missing."

"I don't remember sending any other prototypes into storage except..." Michael Walker's eyes grew large. "No," Walker said as he struggled to keep the smile off his face, "Big Bertha?" Shepherd's head moved up and down, at most an eighth of an inch. Michael Walker started laughing so loud all work within thirty yards of the van ceased. "Well, you have to give Kursolov style points if nothing else."

"What's Big Bertha?" Penelope asked.

When it was clear that Shepherd was in no mood for further explanations, Michael Walker took over. "An EM burst of sufficient size can blow out pretty much anything with electronic components, including the power grid. The same applies if a tactical nuclear device is exploded in the atmosphere. Toward the end of the Cold War, the biggest threat to the world was Soviet tanks rumbling across Eastern Europe on their way to Paris. Obviously, NATO was looking for something to discourage this without resorting to nukes. Someone at the Pentagon came up with the idea to use an EM burst and they decided to try to build a field unit that could disable Soviet tanks without leaving the major cities of Europe glowing in the dark. That was the genesis of Big Bertha."

"I don't see the problem."

"Like so many weapons systems that are clearly bad ideas," Walker said, "this one took on a life of its own. It was being built in a district with a powerful congressman who kept the funding alive, and it kept popping up in the Defense budget year after year. With normal delays and typical cost over runs by the time Bertha was ready the Soviet Empire had collapsed, which meant the threat was greatly diminished. At the insistence of its congressional benefactor, the Pentagon was forced to field test their new weapon during a joint operation with NATO. They borrowed a few old Soviet-era tanks from the Polish government and the rest was, shall we say, military history."

Noah Shepherd let out a faint sigh and turned his gaze toward Las Vegas. Penelope could see this was dredging up bad memories the Director would just as soon forget. She turned her focus back to Walker. "I'm guessing from your tone it didn't work."

"Actually, it exceeded all expectations," Walker said with a laugh. "When it was fired, it blew out every circuit board and transistor within a five-mile radius. This included several dozen NATO vehicles and six Bradley tanks. It destroyed two NATO command and control centers. It fried pretty much everything. "

"Not everything," Shepherd added while shaking his head.

"Right." Walker said laughing again. "Apparently the wiring in the Polish tanks was from around the Second World War era and was mostly analogue. This meant there weren't many sophisticated components to damage. Combined with the fact that the old Soviet tanks had been painted and repainted dozens of times with lead based paint, it turned out they only had minor damage. A few of the ones in the back row, where they were shielded by the other tanks, actually kept running."

"I'm guessing a weapons system that does more damage to your own equipment than the enemy's loses its funding pretty quickly," Penelope said while shaking her head.

"You would think so but we're talking Washington here," Walker answered. "The congressman who was pushing Big Bertha found out we were using EM bursts and had it shipped over to us. The fact that we were trying to miniaturize Hermes, and that Bertha was thousands of times more powerful than we could ever use didn't seem to matter. We had it for less than a day before we boxed it back up and sent it to storage in a restricted section of Ft. Meade."

"How did they manage to steal something like this from a high security facility?" Penelope asked.

"It wasn't stolen," Noah Shepherd sighed. "They drove into the complex in the middle of the day, and our people loaded it onto a truck for them."

"What?!" Penelope's head whipped back and forth between Walker and Shepherd. "How could that have happened?" she demanded.

"We're still off the record, Ms. Spence," Shepherd said and then waited for her acknowledgement, which she gave with a quick nod. Shepherd sighed again. "All of the paperwork was in order and verified multiple times."

"Who would have that kind of authority?" Penelope knew she wouldn't need all of the fingers of one hand to name the people with the ability to pull a truck into possibly the most secure Homeland Security storage facility and leave unchallenged with top secret material, without setting off any bells and whistles. Penelope's eyes grew large. "Oh My!"

CHAPTER TWENTY-SEVEN

P ENELOPE WHEELED TO face Walker. "Did you know about this?"

"That he had been stealing classified material from Homeland Security, no," Michael Walker said with a shrug. "I had my suspicions he was a mole but I didn't have proof positive until tonight when Kursolov confirmed it at the dance."

"You might have given me a heads up," Shepherd said as he motioned to his aide for his phone and began dialing a number. "I'll have him picked up."

"I'm pretty sure Smith and his family are on the plane with Kursolov," Walker said while motioning toward the rear of the van. "Seeing this, I'm now convinced Kursolov didn't make a mistake in revealing Smith was a spy. He was just toying with me. He realized I was onto Smith, and with his men in custody the clock was ticking for him in America."

"But why take Smith with him?" Shepherd asked.

"It's good business. Kursolov knows that for the right price he can buy loyalty," Walker answered. "Just because someone is exposed as secretly working for him doesn't mean he just casts them aside. Besides," Walker continued, "Robert had a high security clearance and had worked for Homeland Security for years before he started working for me. He would still have a great deal of value to a man like Kursolov. "

Penelope's mind flashed back to her conversation with Natasha about her villa and the Swiss bank account. Clearly, while the weapon used in this attack had knocked Walker off balance for a few moments, he still had a good measure of what made Kursolov tick.

Walker continued. "If he left Robert here to rot in jail, the word would get around. That would up the market price for loyalty and increase his overhead. It was nothing more than a smart business decision."

"The minute he sets foot in a country with an extradition treaty, I'll have him picked up."

"I wouldn't bother," Walker answered. "It would embarrass both of us and create more problems than it would be worth. Besides, Kursolov knows I managed to get my satellite to Boeing without Robert's knowledge. Since Smith's primary job was to keep tabs on the progress of the satellite and he failed miserably, Kursolov is not going to give much weight to anything he might tell him."

Director Shepherd eyed Walker more closely. "You hired him away from Homeland Security even though you thought he was a spy?"

"Keep your friends close and your enemies closer. Besides, I did you a favor," Walker said. "He could have done much more damage at Homeland Security than he ever did at Hermes. He has been out of the loop at your division for over a year and as fast as things there move, much of what he does have is hopelessly dated. Besides, having him focus all of his efforts on getting NASA to approve our launch took him out of our inner circle as well."

Shepherd nodded his agreement. "We should obviously release the video we took when the terrorists were inside the Hermes Building."

"What's so obvious about that?" Penelope asked as she reached into her purse for a pen and notepad.

Walker ran his fingers through his closely cropped hair and sighed. "It will further undermine Smith's credibility with Kursolov."

"Plus," Shepherd said, "I've seen the footage your team captured of the Hermes building actually being destroyed. It's pretty spectacular."

"Sally said the same thing," Walker answered.

"With no compelling videos from Las Vegas, it will be the lead of every TV news story in the country for twenty-four hours after we release it. We'll own the news cycle and get the focus back on the terrorists, and since there is no lasting damage here, Las Vegas will be page fourteen by Tuesday."

Timothy Ellison rejoined the group and handed Penelope a plastic bag with an Albertson's grocery logo on it. "The deli was closed so this was the best I could do." Penelope peered inside the bag and saw a selection of fresh fruits and granola bars. Before she could thank her future son-in-law, his phone began to vibrate and he immediately answered it. The conversation took less than five seconds before he hung up and turned to Walker. "Our ride is here."

"Excellent." Walker motioned in the direction of Shepherd and Winters. "Either one of you need me anymore?" They both shook their heads. "Great!" Walker said, "Let's round up Ian and get going." He hooked his arm under Penelope's. She went rigid.

"Go where?" Penelope demanded.

"The Galapagos Islands."

T HE SMELL OF fresh brewing coffee excited Penelope's nose and taste buds. The private-sector Walker Industries 737, unlike the public-sector Homeland Security Gulf stream, had a well stocked galley, a chef and two flight attendants. Since it was stationed in Los Angeles, the food was fresh and organic; a major step up from the assortment of cellophane wrapped items Timothy Ellison had managed to glean for her from the all night grocery store. Penelope was surprised that the crew was available and the galley was so well supplied on such short notice, but wasn't complaining. It was almost as if they had expected to be summoned but were stocked for a much larger passenger list. After a delightful western omelet and a perfectly toasted sesame bagel with cream cheese, washed down with fresh squeezed orange juice and a second cup of coffee, she sighed as she leaned back in her seat.

While her stomach had stopped growling and such an injection of calories into her system would normally improve her mood, it wasn't nearly enough this time. For three days her sleeping and eating routine had been disrupted, and now she got to throw in jet lag. She couldn't remember ever feeling this tired and grumpy. In her heart she knew none of those minor annoyances were the real reason she was getting so touchy. The culprit was lying on the small table in front of her. It was the Sunday edition of *The Washington Post*.

Penelope had been in journalism long enough to know that yesterday's news was old news. The copy of the Bulldog edition of *The Post* they had been able to grab on their way through McCarran Airport to the 737 nagged at her. While the Walker Industries story was still the lead on the business page, it was no longer on the front page or even worthy of a mention in the "A" section. The timing of her story about the capture of the terrorists was unfortunate. While her pair of internet stories had nearly crashed the Post's servers, the terrorist story had broken after all of the morning papers had already gone to bed. By time the news cycle had ticked around again for a new print edition, it had been replaced above the fold by the Las Vegas story. What had looked like the story of the decade twenty-four hours ago, the one that had made her the belle of the ball, now wasn't even the top story for the weekend.

The capture took up most of the bottom half of the front page with a note to check inside. The bulk of the copy she had written twelve hours earlier was now relegated to pages "A4" and "A5". In the age of instant communication, a printed newspaper was already obsolete before it hit the street. A day-old newspaper was only good for wrapping fish, lining a canary's cage, or training a new puppy. Knowing this and understanding it didn't make her feel any better.

She was first and foremost a newspaper reporter. The internet was fine, but she liked to be able to hold a print edition in her hands and get a smudge of ink on her fingers. It was real. It was tangible. It was something she could throw in the bottom of a box that, when rediscovered years later, would generate a smile. With the news industry moving relentlessly toward the internet and cable, physical copies of newspapers were fast becoming quaint novelties that older people liked to read. Now, instead of the morning paper spread out on the kitchen table the younger generation was getting their news on their cell phones, while listening to music through ear buds and ignoring the rest of the world. Penelope shook her head and sighed.

Out the window, the sun was coming up in the East over what she could only assume was Mexico. She had never been to the Galapagos Islands, but it was on her "bucket list." Walker had hurriedly explained that they were going to land at Baltra Airport and immediately board a helicopter to be transported to the Boeing launch site. She felt Walker had been curt and dismissive when he explained their itinerary, but she knew the problem had likely been with her perception and not actually him. With what was at stake with Kursolov, the proper care and feeding of Penelope Drayton Spence was currently low on Michael Walker's priority list.

"You need to let it go," Fleming said softly.

"Let what go?" Penelope asked with a sigh and a patronizing shake of her head.

"It."

"I'm not in the mood for guessing games, Ian."

"Exactly. That is why this is the perfect time to let it go."

Tired to her core and in a sour mood, Penelope had nearly reached the end of her patience with Hermes Project double talk in general, and Ian Fleming in particular. His childlike enthusiasm, while momentarily endearing, was growing tiresome. She was starting to feel like a babysitter for a pesky adolescent that she kept finding going through her drawers or reading her diary. Why had Michael Walker paired them? Penelope closed her eyes and shook her head. She drew in a deep breath of air through her nose, let it descend, held it for a moment, and then released it slowly through her mouth. She felt the tension and fatigue leaving her body. When she opened her eyes again, she saw Fleming smiling at her.

"Excellent start, ma'am."

"What does that mean?"

"We won't be landing for a few more hours," Fleming answered. "Why don't you try meditating?"

Penelope shook her head and sighed. "I'm not dressed for it, I don't have my mat,..." The look on Fleming's face stopped her in mid-sentence. "What?" she snapped, making no effort to keep the annoyance out of her tone of voice or off the expression on her face.

"Seriously?" he asked, his eyes wide with wonder. "You actually think you need a costume and a special place to sit to meditate?" Without breaking eye contact, he leaned back in his seat. "Wow! That certainly explains a lot."

"Define 'a lot' for me."

Fleming propped his elbow on the armrest separating them and leaned in closer. "Remember the baby elephant?" Penelope nodded. "You're a very remarkable and gifted woman, and generally very impressive to watch in action. But sometimes, out of nowhere, nonsense like that comes falling out of your mouth."

"Toes are touching the line," Penelope hissed as she wagged a warning finger in his direction. "Be very careful about the next sentence to come out of your mouth."

"No offense intended," Fleming said with a smile. "Mr. Walker told me you were an enigma, advanced in so many ways but almost childlike in others. Now I understand what he meant."

"Enlighten me."

"Like the baby elephant, you have a few preconceived notions that will hold you back until you release them. That's fairly common since we are all the sum of our experiences. Then I see you do something like what you did a few seconds ago."

"What happened a few seconds ago?"

Fleming said softly, "You really don't know do you?"

"Know what?" Penelope's fingers began tapping impatiently on the arm rest that separated them.

"With a single breath, you did an amazing release. Mr. Walker told me you did it the first time you met him."

Penelope's mind raced back to her first meeting with Michael Walker. He was sitting in an interrogation room at the Charleston Naval Station Brig, dressed in an orange prisoner's uniform and handcuffed to a table. She had just witnessed Walker turning one of the most powerful senators in the country, Clayton Horn, into a puddle of goo. Having negotiated the right to speak privately to Walker after the senator was finished, she had found herself alone with Walker for the first time.

At that point, the jury was still out on whether he was crazy enough to have killed thirty people, and she was leaning toward somewhere between him being a cold blooded mass murderer or simply criminally insane. It was the most unnerving fifteen minutes of her life. In an attempt to control her shaking, she had taken a relaxing cleansing breath. When she opened her eyes, Walker had a look on his face similar to the one she had just seen on Ian's. Walker wanted to know who her meditation instructor was. When she told him she was self-taught, Walker looked as if he was going to say something but thought better of it. With all of the odd things that happened since, she had pretty much forgotten that moment.

"It is a simple breathing exercise," Penelope said.

"Simple?" Ian Fleming started laughing so hard he couldn't maintain eye contact.

"I've been doing it for years," Penelope said meekly. "What's the big deal?"

"There are holy men who have spent a lifetime in quiet mediation who can't quiet their minds like that. Give them an hour, maybe a week, and they could match you."

"Quiet their minds?"

"Yes," Ian answered. "Do you know how difficult it is to understand that it is not just thinking about nothing?"

Penelope shrugged. "I never really thought about it."

"Excellent," Fleming said. "Meditate with me."

"What? Here? Now?"

"Sure, everyone else is." Fleming nodded toward the front of the plane where Michael Walker, Timothy Ellison and Lucas Haley all appeared to be napping in their seats. She hadn't noticed it before, but they were all sitting awfully erect to be sleeping. "We've got two hours before we land. What else do you have to do?"

Penelope let out a deep sigh and shifted in her seat. "This just seems weird."

"We can sit cross legged in the aisle and chant if it would make you more comfortable," Fleming said with a smirk. "No one will mind."

Penelope's eyes twinkled as she fought back a smile and swallowed the urge to stick her tongue out at Fleming. He was so sweet and sincere in his childlike way. Just being around him made her feel younger and more alive. There, trapped in his eye, she was wondering how it was possible she had ever had a negative thought about him. She found a comfortable spot in the thick seat and let her body relax.

Fleming released his seat belt and turned as far as he could. He was nearly facing Spence. "I want you to close your eyes and do what you normally do, but this time I'm going to touch you softly in the middle of your forehead. If you feel something don't worry, that's normal."

"If you say so."

Penelope closed her eyes and started to draw in a deep breath through her nose. Just as the energy of the air hit her sinuses, Fleming gently touched the center of her forehead with the middle finger of his right hand. She was glad he had given her a warning, it felt like a mild electric spark hit her squarely between the eyes. Instead of dissipating it traveled down through her and seemed to settle just below her belly button. As the air followed the charge downward, she felt herself falling. She started to tense before hearing Ian's voice. He only said one word, "Surrender."

She did.

CHAPTER TWENTY-EIGHT

THE GRIND OF the landing gear lowering jolted Penelope back into reality. She had the oddest sensation. It was almost as if she had just awoken from a dream where she had been the guest on the old 1970's TV show, "This is Your Life." As Ralph Edwards read off the events from her personal history and brought nearly forgotten guests from her past up on stage, for the first time she had viewed herself as just a character in a story. "Where did that come from?" she wondered. Then, with her eyes still closed, she noticed someone was holding her hand. Ian. She really needed to find him a new activity other than television. It was starting to rub off on her.

Forcing her eyes to open she was pleasantly surprised to find Michael Walker sitting next to her and his, not Fleming's, hand clutching hers.

"How are you feeling?" Walker asked with an unusual softness to his voice that sounded somehow different than normal.

"Surprisingly good." Penelope could feel the 737 losing altitude but when she glanced out the window she saw the endless azure blue of the Pacific Ocean. There was nothing which resembled land anywhere in her line of sight. "I hope your pilot knows what he's doing."

"Don't worry we've landed here many times before, though never in a plane this big."

Penelope looked around the spacious full-sized jet. "This is extravagant even by your standards," she said. "With the size of Walker Industries West Coast operation, I find it hard to believe this was the only plane available."

"What exactly do you know about our West Coast operations?"

"Well," Penelope said, "I know Walker Telecom is based in Los Angeles and that you are the eighth largest private employer in the State. Not only do you have assembly divisions and R&D in Southern California, approximately twenty miles outside of downtown Los Angeles in the San

Gabriel Mountains you have a state of the art satellite tracking facility..."

"Enough." A bemused look covered Michael Walker's face. "When did you become an expert on our West Coast operations?"

"After being embarrassed by not knowing that Kent Lazlo was your nephew."

Walker nodded and then shifted in his seat as far as the seatbelt would allow, turning to face her. "Tell me about what just happened."

Penelope shook her head. "At first I was doing my usual relaxing technique, then suddenly my mind went totally blank. There were no thoughts intruding."

"Think carefully," Walker said. "Was it really no thought at all?"

"Yes," Penelope answered as she checked the window again. "It was weird. It was as if I no longer existed but had become a part of something bigger than me. Penelope was completely gone."

Michael Walker's eyed bored into her. "How long did that last?"

Penelope thought about it for a moment. "I have no idea," she answered with a laugh. "It could have been half of a second or half an hour or half a day."

Walker nodded his approval.

"Look, Michael," Penelope said as she gave his hand a squeeze, "in the past few days I've given our time together a great deal of thought. I realized you have always been professional and honest with me, and it was unfair of me to have expectations beyond our working relationship." Penelope lowered her eyes. "I've been out of the dating pool for the better part of three decades, and if I mistook your attention and good manners for more than you intended. I apologize."

"If anyone should apologize, it is me," Walker said with a nod. "Do you remember the first time you started grilling me with questions and I said there were some I couldn't answer yet because you weren't ready?"

"Hard to forget," Penelope said with a sigh. "Until a few days ago I considered it the single most insulting thing anyone ever said to me."

"And your new number one is our conversation on the flight from New York to Washington?"

"That would be the one," Penelope said with a smirk.

"Is there any way I can make it up to you?"

Penelope studied Michael Walker and realized any harsh feelings she'd felt toward him were gone. She had released him. Completely. She noted his body language was different as well. He was more open and his eyes were more playful than normal. Also, their conversation didn't have an awkward edge anymore. It was almost as if she was talking to an old friend like Josephine instead of a potential love interest that was running off course and heading toward the rocks. Her eyes twinkled as she said, "Admitting you were a condescending pig in the first case and a world class jerk in the other would be a start."

Michael Walker cleared his throat. "I was a condescending pig when I told you there were things I couldn't tell you because you weren't ready and I was a world class jerk for implying you weren't enlightened enough to date me. Is there anything else I need to apologize for?"

Penelope thought about it for a moment. "Upstaging me at Joey's party with a woman a fourth your age would be another."

"Natasha?" Walker pulled back. "I'm not even three times as old as she is."

"Oh. I'm sorry. That makes it so much better." The engines of the 737 began to scream as the luxurious business jet with first class seating for 30 got lower and lower with still no landfall in sight. "If you subtracted her age from your age, you'd still be old enough to be her father."

Walker did the math in his head and realized Penelope was right. "In my defense, it was my intention to upstage Kursolov and not you. You were just collateral damage."

Penelope shook her head and sighed. "You don't have a lot of experience groveling, do you?"

"Not really," Walker answered. "Most women find me charming."

Penelope batted her eyes at Walker. "How many would think you were charming if you were flat broke?"

"We may find out soon enough." The old twinkle returned to Walker's eyes. "If we lose the satellite launch, I may be looking for a shipping crate and a bridge to live under." Walker propped his elbow on the arm rest and placed his chin on the palm of his hand. "Would it help if I told you I think you're ready..." The narrowing of Penelope's eyes and the flaring of her nose caused Walker to stop and rephrase his thought. "What if I told you I've been a fool and I'm ready to answer all of your questions about me and the Hermes Project fully and completely? I also humbly and sincerely apologize for holding out on you. Would that help?"

"At least your groveling is improving." Penelope motioned for Walker to continue.

"You are clearly a beautiful and remarkable woman, and I would be honored if you'd have dinner with me after all this is over."

Penelope batted her eyes in Walker's direction again. "I'll think about it." Penelope shrugged and turned toward the window. The familiar pre-landing knot in her stomach was starting to form. It appeared the tips of the wings of the jet were about to touch water and she gripped the armrest tight. Finally, she saw land, followed almost instantly by a runaway mere seconds before the wheels slammed onto the tarmac.

The full-size jet needed nearly the entire length of the runway to slow itself before rolling to a remote spot where a large Sikorsky twelve-passenger helicopter with a Boeing Sea Launch logo was waiting. Penelope wasn't sure what she had expected from her visit to the Galapagos Islands, but her first impression was a huge let down. The Baltra airport was on a flat rock that, if the "experts" were right about global warming and the rising of the ocean, would be under water by next weekend. At first glance it appeared to be flora and fauna free, the only sign of life was a few multicolored iguanas recharging their solar batteries on Eastern exposures of dirt and gravel. The sun had been up for less than an hour, but with no shade, the heat was already starting to build. Walker read Penelope's disappointment.

"The national park is on a different island. This airstrip was built during World War II to protect the Panama Canal."

Penelope eyed the low windswept airport and doubted it had indoor plumbing facilities she would be willing to use in anything short of an emergency, much less a decent restaurant. "Lovely." She watched as a plump man, probably in his early forties, dressed in khaki shorts and a white golf shirt approached. She noticed he had the same logo on his shirt pocket as the one on the side of the helicopter.

He extended his hand toward Michael Walker. "Good to see you again."

Walker nodded toward Penelope. "Bill Grayson, this is Penelope Drayton Spence."

"Oh my," Grayson said as he quickly slid his right hand down the side of his shorts before offering it to Penelope. It was mostly dry and the grip was what Penelope would expect from a desk jockey. With his left hand, Grayson tried to flatten down his comb-over but the prevailing breeze off the Pacific wasn't helpful. It was like trying to cover ten acres of ground with two acres of grass. There were a few thick places, but mostly it was gaps and bare spots. "This is such an honor. I really enjoyed your book." He motioned toward the helicopter as the pilot fired up the turbines and the blades began to slowly spin.

Walker leaned in and whispered into Spence's ear, "He's the Launch Liaison."

"What does that mean?" she asked.

"His job is to keep the VIPs happy."

She nodded that she understood.

"**W**E SHOULD BE there in a few more minutes," Grayson said loudly enough to be heard over the thump-thump of the engines. While the Sikorsky was quieter than most helicopters, it was still noisy enough to discourage casual conversation. Grayson pointed over the pilot's shoulder through the windshield. In the distance loomed a lump which appeared to be a small island with a cell phone tower in the center. "There's your bird, Mr. Walker. The lifting crane already has it in place," Grayson said with the pride of a new papa. As they got closer, the shape and size of the superstructure became clear. It was massive. "Launch Platform '*Odyssey*' used to be a deep sea drilling platform out in the North Sea," Grayson added.

"It's huge!" Penelope exclaimed as she ducked down and leaned forward for a better look.

"It is 436 feet long by 220 feet wide," Grayson said as he turned his head so he could be heard by everyone in the cabin. "It has a submerged draft displacement of 50,000 tons."

Penelope had no idea what 'submerged draft displacement' meant, but it was too noisy in the helicopter for a lengthy explanation. "Is that where we're landing?" Spence asked.

Grayson shook his head and pointed in the direction of boat about two miles from the launch platform that was the size and shape of a small cruise ship. "That's the Sea Launch *Commander*. In addition to our launch control center, it has first class accommodations and," Grayson smiled as he added, "a Four Star chef."

As the Sikorsky banked over the launch platform they could see a long white vertical cylinder with "Walker Telecom" painted on its side.

"We've started the propellant cool-down," Grayson shouted.

Walker read the confusion on Penelope's face. "For obvious safety reasons the last step to a launch is fueling the boosters. Once a satellite goes vertical and has had the tanks filled, it has to be launched within thirty-six hours. If we miss that window we have to drain the tanks, lay it back down, and take it back to Long Beach to have the fuel tanks retested."

Penelope leaned in and cupped her hand over Walker's ear so she didn't have to shout, and to also keep others from hearing, "How long would that take?"

"I don't even want to think about it," Walker answered. "With the other launches they have scheduled and the fact that it is getting close to typhoon season, it could be as long as six to eight months."

The pilot of the Sikorsky centered the wheels perfectly in the bright red landing pad on the deck of the Sea Launch *Commander* and cut the engines. The ambient noise level began to immediately drop. A small party of three middle-aged men and one very severe looking woman was waiting on deck to greet them. The woman's hair was in a bun so tight it stretched the skin on her forehead, giving the illusion of a facelift. Walker opened his arms and headed straight toward the woman. "Natalie," he said as they kissed each other's cheeks, "there is someone I want you to meet." He guided the woman in Penelope's direction. "Natalie Seleznyov, this is Penelope Drayton Spence."

Penelope froze when the woman, who was at least eight inches taller than her, kissed her on both cheeks. "I have heard many good things about you from Mikhail," she said in a deep voice, thick with an Eastern European accent. She wagged a warning finger in Walker's direction. "But you are a bad boy, Mikhail. You did not tell me she vas so beautiful. You break Natalie's heart." She motioned for everyone to follow her. "You must be tired. Your rooms are ready. Why don't you freshen up and ve vill meet in the control room in, how you say? Half hour?"

Walker glanced at Penelope who pointed her index finger in the direction of her mouth. The food on the jet had been great but that was nearly four hours ago, and she felt her hunger growing again.

"Natalie," Walker said, "how about some breakfast first?"

"Say no more." Natalie Seleznyov barked a quick set of instructions in the direction of the three men, and one of them scurried away. "Instead of the control room we vill meet in the dining room. I vill have Jean Luc make you breakfast you vill never forget."

"Eggs Benedict?" Walker asked as he glanced over his shoulder at Penelope. "As you wish."

Penelope hooked Walker's arm and leaned in as they followed Natalie toward their staterooms. "Is she Russian?"

"Yes," Walker answered with a laugh. "Nearly all of the technical staff, if not Russian, are at least holdovers from the old Soviet Union days. What were you expecting?"

"With the Boeing name plastered everywhere, a bunch of people from Seattle," Penelope said with a laugh. "Maybe a Starbucks."

"If you think this is bad, you should see the Boeing land launch division in Kazakhstan."

Penelope stopped dead in her tracks and spun Walker around. "The same Kazakhstan that Viktor Kursolov is from?"

CHAPTER TWENTY-NINE

W ALKER WAS SMILING from ear to ear as he nodded. "I told you Kursolov was guarding my satellite for me."

"True," Penelope said, "but this is Boeing we're talking about here."

"Kursolov has controlling interest in both the land based and sea launch companies," Walker said. "Despite Boeing only holding a 40% stake in the company they retained the Boeing name, but Kursolov calls all the shots - no pun intended."

"Ah," Penelope said as she started to figure it out. "Keeping the Boeing name would be more palatable for xenophobic members of Congress by at least giving the illusion our space program hadn't been outsourced overseas."

"Exactly," Walker said with an approving nod. "We dropped the satellite off at the Boeing Los Angeles pre-launch facility over a month ago so it could be properly packed and mounted to fit in the nosecone."

"How many people did you have guarding it?"

Walker shrugged. "None."

"You left it there completely unprotected?"

"Correct," Walker answered. "Because of Robert Smith, Kursolov didn't even know the satellite was completed, and we didn't want to tip our hand."

""Unbelievable."

"See," Walker said as they caught up with Natalie Seleznyov just as she was opening a stateroom door. "I told you this was going to be fun."

Penelope Spence had been on her fair share of cruise ships, but she had never seen anything like the stateroom Boeing provided for her on the Sea Launch *Commander*. Instead of being cramped and stuffy with low ceilings that induced claustrophobia, the space was huge with vaulted ceilings, a sitting room, and a separate bedroom complete with a king-sized bed and whirlpool tub. After ten minutes under the pulsating spray in the world class shower next to the tub, with the temperature just a few degrees short of scalding, she was starting to feel better. Wrapped in a towel, Penelope was delighted to discover her suitcase open on her bed. She really didn't want to put the same clothes back on.

As she buttoned her last button she knew her thirty minutes were about up, so she wasn't surprised when she heard a soft tapping on the door. She checked her hair as she walked past the mirror and decided it was fine. Opening the door she found Michael Walker with his elbows on the guard rail staring out across the glass smooth Pacific at the Sea Launch platform. The white cylinder gleamed in the sunlight against the deep blue of the Pacific. Penelope joined him. When his eyes did not leave the rocket, she gave him a bump with her shoulder.

"Hey there."

"Hey there yourself," Walker answered with a smile. "They've started the fueling." Walker glanced over his shoulder at Penelope. "Game on."

"What does that mean?"

"It means the next 12 hours are going to be very interesting." Walker pointed to some dots on the horizon. "There's the *Gipper.*"

"*Gipper?*"

"The *USS Ronald Reagan* and its Strike Group. It's the most advanced and expensive naval vessel of all time." Walker sighed and shook his head.

"What?"

"You know what military planners call aircraft carriers these days?" He didn't wait for her to answer. "Targets. It cost over four billion dollars to build the *Reagan*, to say nothing of the support ships, and it can be taken out with a single missile."

"Really?"

"There are probably a half dozen submarines from a variety of countries within firing range right now. If war were to break out in earnest between the major powers, every aircraft carrier in the world would be at the bottom of the ocean in the first six hours."

"Then why build them?" Penelope asked.

"The projection of power may be able to stop or control some of the smaller wars, and they can be used as a mobile military base against rogue states."

Penelope went to her tip toes to try to get a better view. She saw a flash of light which looked like flames erupt from the deck of the Reagan and Penelope grabbed Walker's arm. "What was that?'

"Wait for it," Walker answered softly. A half beat later there was the unmistakable roar of a jet engine. "A plane just took off."

"I'd really like to see that up close."

Walker made a funny face and smiled. "Be careful what you wish for."

"What does that mean?"

Before he could answer, a pair of men speaking a Slavic language and smoking unfiltered cigarettes approached them. They nodded as they passed, but Walker waited until they were well out of earshot before leaning in close. "I know I promised to stop being evasive, but I need you to do me a favor for the rest of the day. No questions." He glanced at the men again. "We don't know who might be listening." Penelope nodded that she understood.

"I never had a chance with you, did I?" Penelope asked.

"Why do you say that?"

"You obviously go for the tall Eastern European type."

"You mean Natalie?" Walker asked.

"And Natasha," Penelope said with a playful smile as she let the South slip into her speaking pattern. "Obviously a delicate little Southern flower like me simply can't compete with those exotic women from the steppes."

"Delicate?" Walker asked as he turned to face her grinning broadly. "Seriously? You're going to go with that?"

"Why, I have no idea what you mean, Mr. Walker," she said as she started fanning herself.

Walker smiled as he took Penelope's arm and directed her toward the rear of the ship. "We obviously need to get more food into you."

"Isn't your lady friend going to join us?"

"I left Natalie in the control room. When they're fueling the boosters, they don't need any distractions."

"Is it dangerous?" Penelope asked, her Southern accent vanishing as quickly as it had arrived.

"It can be. This division nearly went under when a Hughes Telecom satellite was destroyed on the launch pad a few years ago."

"Okay. No distractions. So what's our plan?"

"We're going to get you some breakfast, and then we'll get Hermes safely into space."

Penelope noted immediately that Michael Walker had obviously been on the Sea Launch *Commander* before. She couldn't have found the ship's main dining room without a map and a compass. Walker not only knew its location, he knew the most direct route. The inside looked like a mid-town New York Five Star restaurant with white linen tablecloths, bone china, and heavy silver flatware. There were fresh-cut flowers in the middle of each of the dozen round eight-person tables. An efficient staff had finished cleaning up from breakfast and was getting ready for lunch. A man with a towel over his arm motioned for them to join Ian, who was already seated. Walker helped Penelope with her chair.

Before she even had her napkin unfolded, a tall glass of fresh-squeezed orange juice, a full water glass, and a steaming cup of coffee materialized in front of her. She looked over her shoulder to thank her waiter but he had already vanished and been replaced by an approaching willowy African-American woman with interesting eyes and a friendly smile. In her hand, wrapped in a gingham towel, was a basket of blueberry muffins that couldn't have been out of the oven for more than a minute. Penelope wiped her napkin across her mouth just in case she was drooling.

As she broke open her first muffin, steam escaped and the aroma hit her nose, causing her to close her eyes and melt. The delightful smell triggered an immediate urge to cram the entire pastry in her mouth but fourteen generations of Southern manners kept the assault to a single, polite, bite. Despite it's larger than average size, the muffin didn't put up much of a fight and lasted less than a minute. She was contemplating a second when Eggs Benedict appeared in front of her along with a side of cheesy grits. Her eyes twinkled in Michael Walker's direction. From the grin on his face, it was clear the grits must have been his idea.

They needed salt, a common Yankee mistake, but otherwise the food was as good as she'd ever eaten. The eggs had been poached to perfection and the hollandaise had just the right amount of lemon juice zing. For nearly ten minutes the three ate in silence. It hadn't occurred to her until she watched her guardian angels cleaning their plates, but both Walker and Ian had been on the same schedule as her for the last seventy-two hours. *They obviously handle starvation and sleep deprivation better,* she thought. Finally feeling the gauge in her stomach move from "empty" to "full", she pushed a few inches away from the table and ran up the white flag at her attentive waiter.

"More coffee, Madame?" he asked.

Penelope waved him off. As she did, her eye caught Timothy Ellison in the doorway. Her future son-in-law's eyes met Walker's and his head gave a barely perceptible nod. Remembering Walker's earlier request, Penelope swallowed the urge to ask what was going on.

Bill Grayson maneuvered past Ellison in the doorway, smiling from ear to ear, and approached the table. "The clock has started. If there are no problems we should launch in a bit over three hours."

"Excellent," Michael Walker said as he motioned for Grayson to join them.

"What happens in the next three hours?" Penelope asked.

Grayson was a natural schmoozer and Penelope's question was his cue. "For the past hour and a half, we have been cooling the propellant. At L-2.5, sorry, at Launch in two hours and thirty minutes, if there are no problems, we start to fill the tanks. Once the tanks are starting to be filled, all of the crew on the launch pad will transfer over here to the command center and everything on the launch pad will be automated. We go through a series of check lists and tests, and if we have the green light at launch minus seventeen minutes the erector arm is lowered and we begin the final countdown."

"It sounds simple enough," Penelope said.

"It usually is," Grayson answered, "but we do have some built-in automatic countdown pauses."

"What does that mean?" Penelope asked.

"We have sensors all over the booster and launch pad. Any one of them can delay the flight if it sends up a warning message. That's why we have the 36-hour launch window after fueling. Usually it is something simple. There is no reason to reschedule a multi-million dollar launch because a ten dollar sensor failed. The window gives us time to save the launch."

"What about after it is launched?" Penelope asked.

"Once it is airborne, the rocket will receive a series of confirmations from the launch center: booster ignition, first stage separation, second booster ignition, things like that."

"Tell her what happens if it doesn't get the confirmation," Walker said.

Bill Grayson's salesman's smile vanished as he glanced at Michael Walker. He cleared his throat. "If the launch vessel fails to get a confirmation command from the ground control center at certain key points, then an auto-destruct sequence will begin."

Walker smiled at Penelope. "It wouldn't be nice to have a four ton satellite come dropping out of the sky."

A deep frown covered Penelope's face. She was dying to ask Michael Walker exactly why he had gone out of his way to be sure she had that depressing nugget of information. Was he signaling to her that it was where he thought Kursolov would strike? Was that the weak point in Walker's master plan? Glancing in Walker's direction, she saw his self-satisfied smile and it took all of her will power to keep from strangling him.

The smile returned to Grayson's lips. "We have never lost a satellite after the initial booster separation and we don't plan to start now." Grayson pulled himself to his feet and motioned toward the door. "Let me show you the ship and then take you to the command center."

PENELOPE WAS QUICKLY losing her tolerance for Bill Grayson. He was starting to remind her of another 'Bill', her ex-husband, Bill Spence. Obviously, neither had ever found a silent moment he felt wouldn't be enhanced by the sound of his own voice. Grayson prattled on and on about things that held no interest for her but fascinated him. Walker was no help. Whenever Grayson would stop for a breath Walker would ask him to explain another element of the Boeing Sea Launch program, which would set him off again. Penelope was relieved when they finally arrived at the control room.

Natalie Seleznyov was obviously the queen bee, and she ran a tight hive. Penelope counted twenty-four work stations, most with multiple flat screen monitors, facing a display screen the size one would expect to find at an NFL football stadium. About half the seats in the command center were occupied, and Seleznyov was barking a steady stream of orders in a variety of languages. The scowl covering her face vanished and was replaced with a smile when she saw Michael Walker enter. Penelope noted that Seleznyov managed to completely avoid eye contact with her and acted as if she were the only female in the room.

"Mikhal!" she said with forced surprise. "The fueling couplings are in place and the *Odyssey* crew is on their way over now." She glanced in the direction of an older man who was carefully watching his screen. "Ivan!" she barked.

The man with thinning white hair and a weather-worn complexion did not look up from his screen. "Pressure is holding."

"Excellent," Seleznyov returned her attention to Michael Walker. "We can launch in bit over two hours..." She stopped short when she saw Lucas Haley, wet and in a bathing suit, burst into her command center. Penelope had never seen Lucas with his shirt off before, but she wasn't surprised that he looked harder than granite. Despite his size, he likely had a body fat total that would be the envy of a collegiate wrestler. Haley was followed by two of the men Penelope recognized from her bodyguard detail a few days earlier in New York City. They were also in swimming suits and dripping slightly. One had something heavy and black in his hands about the size and shape of a deflated basketball.

"What is the meaning of this?" Natalie Seleznyov demanded.

Haley ignored her and headed straight toward Walker. "Boss, we've got a problem."

"What?" Walker answered calmly.

"We've had people in the water for the past 24 hours keeping an eye on the launch pad and this boat." Haley motioned toward one of his ex-Navy SEAL friends, who handed Walker the device. "This is a contact mine, we found six of them on the hull of the command ship." The entire room fell silent. "They weren't there an hour ago."

"Chinese-made," Walker said calmly as he examined the explosive. "How do you think it got there?"

"Since we were the only ones in the water, if I had to guess, I would say someone dropped them over the handrails and the magnets on the bottom caused them to attach to the hull."

Walker shrugged. "These are simple enough to disarm, gather all of the men..."

"Finding them and disarming them is simple enough, but that's not the problem."

"What is?"

"They are all on timers." Haley said.

"When are they set to go off?"

Before Haley could answer there was a muffled rumble and the entire ship shook. This was followed in quick succession by two more muted thuds and the massive ship groaned and began to list slightly to starboard. A few seconds later an explosion that clearly originated in the bowels of the ship several decks below, and not from the outside, rattled the control room. The display screen at the front of the room went blank and an ear splitting siren began to scream. The main lighting flickered and then went out and was replaced with a weird glow as the emergency lights clicked on. There was the faint smell of burnt plastic as smoke began to seep into the room.

Before Penelope or anyone else in the control room could react, Ian Fleming had her by the waist and heading toward the door. "Grab my belt and don't let go." Penelope gripped the back of Ian's pants as he plowed over a pair of white coated technicians blocking the exit. They burst through the door and into the fresh air with Walker and Ellison less than half a step behind. An instant later, Lucas Haley followed with Natalie Seleznyov in tow. They headed straight for the Sikorsky business helicopter where one of the work-for-hire ex-SEALs was behind the controls with the turbine engines starting to whine.

"Where are we going?" Penelope demanded as Ian roughly shoved her into a seat and fastened her seat belt.

"Well," Walker said as he helped Seleznyov secure herself in, "you said you wanted a closer look at the *USS Ronald Reagan*. It looks like your wish has come true."

As the helicopter lifted off, Penelope heard a panicked voice blaring over the Public Address system, "Attention all hands, this is Captain Morris. Fire suppression teams report to the engine room immediately!"

As the helicopter gained altitude, Penelope could see thick black smoke billowing from the center of the ship. Lifeboats were being filled with the technical crew from the control room and launched over the side. The command ship was clearly listing a few degrees to the starboard and starting to sink.

CHAPTER THIRTY

"**P**LEASE BE SURE that your seatbelt harness is properly secured," barked a young Navy ensign in a bright yellow long-sleeved sweatshirt as he walked up the narrow aisle. He eyed the 24 people with their backs facing the cockpit and their faces toward the extended loading ramp. Penelope, sitting next to Michael Walker, found it unnerving to be turned 180 degrees away from the direction she would normally face during a takeoff on a commercial flight. The fact that the aircraft still had its wings twisted and folded backwards as she was scrambling onboard had not been reassuring either. While she had confidence the US Navy would get her safely to where she was supposed to be, right now her biggest concern was what she might look like upon arrival. She knew it was silly but she wondered what affect the helmet, ear protection, and goggles they forced her to wear would have on her hair. As if this flight wasn't torture enough, now she had to worry about a severe case of hat hair.

Across the aisle in the front -- or was it the back? -- were Ian Fleming and Timothy Ellison. Behind her were Natalie Seleznyov, Bill Grayson and the other vital members of the Boeing Sea Launch team. Ellison, after his last experience with a military aircraft, looked nervous and apprehensive. Fleming was talking to him, but between the ambient noise and her ear protection Penelope could only make out one word: *release*.

All of the key personnel needed to continue the launch had been picked up from their lifeboats and shuttled to the *USS Ronald Reagan*. Penelope wasn't privy to the entire conversation which followed. But, it was clear from their shouting that Seleznyov and Grayson wanted to scrub the mission and Walker had insisted that the launch crew be relocated to the Boeing back-up facility in Long Beach so it could proceed. To Michael Walker's thinking, the rocket's tanks were filled, everything on the *Odyssey* launch platform was fully automated, they were still well within their 36 hour window, and the rocket didn't care if the commands came from a ship a few miles away or a facility near Los Angeles.

"I can't believe that after what happened they are going to let you continue with this launch," Penelope shouted into Michael Walker's ear.

"I didn't give them a choice," Walker answered. Penelope shrugged that she didn't understand. "Since we suspected Viktor Kursolov, I had a sabotage provision put in the contract. If they don't move the launch to Long Beach they are in immediate breach of our contract with a substantial penalty."

"Why would they agree to something like that?"

"In exchange, we gave Boeing a waiver absolving them from any responsibility for a launch failure and agreed to compensate them if there was any damage to the launch pad if we were forced to use their back-up facility. I had them in a box. They could either proceed with the launch with zero risk or write me a check for money that they don't have."

"So you thought Kursolov would sabotage the command ship?"

Walker smiled. "Let's just say I was one hundred percent certain something like this was going to happen."

Before Spence could quiz Walker further the Ensign in yellow, apparently satisfied with everyone's safety harnesses, addressed his charges. "You are onboard a United States Navy C-2A Greyhound personnel transport. This aircraft is attached to the primary catapult on the flight deck of the *USS Ronald Reagan*. When the catapult engages, this aircraft will accelerate from zero to one hundred and sixty miles per hour in less than two seconds. For your personal safety, please tuck your elbows in, press your chin to your chest and firmly grab your seatbelt harness with both hands. Are there any questions?"

"Why are we facing this direction?" Penelope asked.

"This C-2A Greyhound personnel transport is designed to also land on the flight deck of an aircraft carrier. Landings are more severe than take-offs. Once the tail hook engages you will go from an air speed in excess of one hundred and fifty miles per hour to a full stop in less than two hundred feet. For the protection of passengers and crew, the C-2A Greyhound personnel transport seat configuration is arranged in this manner so the seats will absorb most of the G force, thereby minimizing any injuries that can and do occur during landing." The humorless Ensign stared blankly at Penelope before continuing his monotone recitation of the obviously memorized instructions. "Do you have any additional questions, ma'am?"

Penelope had many. What kinds of injures were minimized? How well were these seats bolted to the floor? When was the last time anyone checked this catapult thing? But she held her tongue. Less than an hour earlier she had been eating breakfast on fine linen and now she was strapped backwards in a military transport getting instructions from a man a zombie would find dull. Life around Michael Walker could never be classified as boring. She tried to shift to a more comfortable position with no luck. The sailor who had checked her harness tightened the straps to the point where it wasn't a question whether she would move during the takeoff but rather whether she would be able to inhale enough oxygen to remain conscious.

"Is this really necessary?" Penelope asked Walker.

"Tick tock," Walker said. "This is the fastest way to get the launch team to the Baltra airport where our 737 is already fueled and waiting."

The Ensign in yellow started his monotone again. "For those of you who have never experienced a sea launch from an aircraft carrier, it can be a shock to your system. You will experience G-force which can and will unsettle your stomach." The ensign nodded towards a sailor in a green long sleeved sweatshirt who started down the aisle handing each person a small plastic lined bag. "Seaman Franklin will now distribute air sickness bags for each of you." As Seaman Franklin reached Penelope she noticed the sailor looked too young to shave. Ellison asked for, and received, a second bag.

"Your flight time to the Baltra Airport will be forty-three minutes." The Ensign eyed the motley crew of scientists and civilians and shook his head. "Thank you for flying Air Gipper, I hope you enjoy your flight." After he exited via the rear loading ramp, which was slightly larger than the average residential garage door, powerful hydraulics engaged and the ramp began to rise. As the size of the opening decreased, the interior of the transport began to take on an eerie darkness. Penelope's eyes attempted to adjust to the change but couldn't keep up. When the combination loading gate/door had locked in place, Penelope could hear and feel the twin turboprop engines beginning to rev. The entire plane shook in anticipation. A warning buzzer sounded and Penelope, always the perfect student, tucked her chin to her chest, closed her eyes and held her breath. Suddenly, her entire body was thrown forward as the massive cargo plane was rumbling down the flight deck of the *USS Ronald Reagan* like a marble fired from a slingshot. In less than two seconds, the noise level dropped as the wheels of the C-2A lost contact with the flight deck and the lumbering cargo plane began to gain altitude.

Penelope was panting and her cheeks were flushed. She had never felt so alive in her entire life. "Sally was right."

Michael Walker smiled as he leaned over and loosened her harness. "If you think that's exciting, you should try landing on an aircraft carrier in one of these." Walker's smile broadened as he nodded toward Timothy Ellison who was sitting to Penelope's left. He was white as a sheet "B.B."

AFTER THE SHORT hop in the backward-facing, rigid bright blue and steel seats of the military transport, the thick leather comfort of Walker's 737 seemed like a weekend at the *Four Seasons*. The takeoff in the C-2A from the flight deck of the *USS Ronald Reagan* had been exhilarating, mostly because it had been over so quickly. The landing was another matter entirely. It seemed a lifetime passed from the time the pilot told everyone to fasten their seatbelts to when the plane actually touched down. Facing the wrong direction in a dimly lit aluminum tube with no windows or frame of reference, Penelope felt like she was riding on a terrifying backward version of Space Mountain. Any desire to land in a winged aircraft on the deck of an aircraft carrier was dropped into the mental folder marked "Bad Ideas" alongside bungee jumping off of a high bridge and wearing white shoes after Labor Day.

Penelope's head turned when she heard laughter from the rear of the plane where a group of Boeing techs were obviously enjoying the transportation upgrade as much as she was. As the engines began to rev, a voice came over the public address system and requested everyone to find a seat. For a moment, when she saw Michael Walker sitting six rows back with Natalie Seleznyov, she thought she might have to sit alone for the four-hour flight to Los Angeles. As she twisted the cap off her water she heard the oddly girlish giggle of Natalie Seleznyov. Penelope resisted the urge to look behind her and forced her eyes to stay forward. This had all the makings of a long flight.

She had mixed feelings when Ian Fleming slid past her to the window seat and reached for his seatbelt. While she appreciated the company, she would have preferred Walker or even Ellison. She had a mental list of questions about what had happened on the launch command ship and was certain Fleming would not have any answers.

As if reading her mind, Fleming said, "Mr. Walker asked me to tell you to be patient and let you know that all of your questions will be answered in a few hours." Ian reached under his seat, pulled out a medium sized box, and handed it to Penelope.

"What's this?"

"Mr. Walker thought you might want all of this." Penelope lifted the lid on the box. Inside was her laptop and an iPhone with a bow on it. "He thought you might want to call your editor and maybe write a story or two."

Penelope turned in her seat, held up the iPhone and smiled at Walker who smiled back when she mouthed a silent "thank you."

Talking to Mark had left even more questions unanswered but at least she was able to bring him up to date on her activities since she had left the newsroom the day before. He'd grabbed a reporter who did an on the fly interview with her so they could post something on *The Post's* webpage. It read like the middle of a mystery novel in which no one had a clue where the story was headed or how it would end. Still, that was the best she had to offer. She had hung up with a promise to try to get back to them before deadline, but could make no guarantees. That had taken up the first two hours of the four-hour flight.

Leaning back in the comfortable chair, she closed her eyes. The multiple shots of adrenaline were starting to wear off, but her mind still raced as it tried to make sense of what had happened and what might happen next. Walker had said he was one hundred percent sure the launch command ship would be attacked. What did he know that she didn't? Was it a coincidence the plane that seemed too large when Walker Industries had sent it to pick them up in Las Vegas was now the perfect size to ferry the Boeing launch coordinator and her team to Los Angeles? Not likely. Michael Walker never left anything to chance.

Instead of worrying about things beyond her control and understanding, she started to release them. Walker, Kursolov, rocket launches, and the Hermes project began to shrink in size and importance.

All of the random conversations swirling around her melted away. The din of the jet engines fell silent. Her mind was blissfully still.

I T WASN'T UNTIL the third nudge that Penelope's eyes fluttered open. All of the members of Natalie Seleznyov's team were in a queue in the aisle of the Walker Industries 737 and slowly making their way toward the exit. Penelope was shocked, even the safe landing of an aluminum tube hurling through the air at 500 miles per hour and landing on a strip of concrete no wider than the average interstate highway had not been enough to wake her.

"How do you feel?" Ian asked as he reached to help her unbuckle her seatbelt.

Penelope slapped his hands away and pondered the question for a moment. "I don't think I've felt better in my entire life."

"Excellent," Fleming said as he waited for her to get to her feet and join the line of people exiting the plane.

On the tarmac at Los Angeles International, the 737 was stopped in front of a huge private hangar that held a collection of nearly a dozen Walker Industries light aircraft, including a pair of Gulfstream G650s and several older private jets. A few hundred feet away, the Boeing team was being loaded onto a trio of business helicopters, all with the Walker Industries logo on the side.

Penelope knew Michael Walker was wealthy. Previously, at least on an intellectual level, the intangible terms of millions and billions had meaning, but this was the first time she had gotten a glimpse of the hard assets this income level could afford. While LA was the home base for Walker Telecom and, in total employment, the second largest of their bases of operation she could only imagine the size of the fleet based in the hangar at their World Headquarters in Miami.

Ian pointed Penelope in the direction of the smallest of the three helicopters, a Mercedes-Benz EC145. Already seated inside the ultra luxurious helicopter were Walker and Seleznyov.

In many ways, the back-up facility at the Boeing site was nicer than the control center on the Sea Launch *Commander*. The room itself was nearly double the size and the ceiling was ten feet higher. Instead of being crammed together like sardines, each of the techs had a much larger work space and instead of chairs bolted to the deck, each had a high backed Herman Miller mesh chair.

The skeleton crew which had been manning the back-up Long Beach site when the launch had been aborted at sea had been busy. They were already well along in getting this command and control center fully functional and ready to take control of the mission. The moment the primary launch crew entered the room, Natalie Seleznyov began barking orders and people began to scramble.

"Mikhail," she said. "Ve vill need to recalibrate our equipment and make sure the launch vessel is still viable. If yes, then ve can resume the countdown." A large clock in the front of the room clicked to life. It said "01:47:04" Flashing in red underneath was the word "HOLDING". An overweight silver-haired man, who looked like he had to be pushing the mandatory retirement age, handed Natasha a printout. "Excellent. Resume the countdown," she said to him as she read the document before turning toward Walker and Spence. "All sensors are functioning properly. As long as the support arm retracts at the seventeen-minute mark, we should be able to launch."

On the big board in the front of the room, the "HOLDING" light went out. "01:47:03... 01:47:02"

"**Y**OU LOOK LIKE you are about to burst," Michael Walker said casually as he approached Penelope where she stood on the end of the Boeing Sea Launch facility pier.

"I think I liked it better when you thought I wasn't ready to hear something than now, when I am ready but you can't tell me. At least I had my righteous indignation to keep my mind occupied."

"One way or another, this will be over soon."

Penelope sighed. "I'm just not geared for these long periods of doing nothing. Especially when I have a few hundred questions I would like to ask."

They both noticed Timothy Ellison approaching at about the same moment. "They are getting ready to lower the erector arm."

"Get Lucas and his men out of the water," Walker said, which caused Ellison to immediately reach for his cell phone. A puzzled expression covered Penelope's face. She had noticed Walker's bodyguard hadn't been on the flight with them to Los Angeles but with so much else going on it hadn't dawned on her to ask where he had disappeared to. Walker read her face and added, "While we were in transit, Lucas stayed behind and he and his team have been guarding the legs of the launch platform."

"You don't leave much to chance, do you?"

"Not if I can help it." Michael Walker hooked his arm under Penelope's. "Show time."

WHILE NATALIE SELEZNYOV was clearly in charge of the techs, Bill Grayson was in charge of customer relations. "I always prefer a night launch," Grayson said as he motioned toward the big screen at the front of the room. The screen was mostly dark, with ill-defined shadows. "The damage has been contained and we still have a live video feed from the Sea Launch *Commander* so we will be able to watch the lift off."

At the top of the screen the countdown continued. "00:04:07... 00:04:06... 00:04:05."

As the clock clicked to under four minutes, Natalie Seleznyov looked at the panel in front of her. It was covered with a series of green lights. "Begin zee final checklist," she barked. There was a rapid fire of Russian from each of the techs and Seleznyov. As the countdown approached the final sixty seconds, she glanced over her shoulder at Walker and nodded.

Penelope stared transfixed at the massive screen in the front of the room. As the countdown reached ten seconds, somewhere far away she heard Natalie Seleznyov say, "Begin ignition sequence." The tail of the rocket began to glow and vapor could now be seen billowing out of the launch vessel.

"Ve have ignition."

The base of the launch vessel was now bright red, and suddenly the rocket began to lift off the pad. The change in light was so dramatic the iris of the camera lens took a moment to adjust. Penelope's mouth was open; her breathing stopped. She didn't blink. The camera followed the rocket skyward.

"Ve have lift-off."

"So far, so good," Michael Walker whispered. Penelope jumped slightly at the sound of his voice. She had been focusing so intently on the screen that she had forgotten he was at her elbow.

For the next several minutes the command center had a quiet but efficient hum as all of the techs concentrated on the screens in front of them. "Telemetry is within parameters," barked a man with a thick accent.

Natalie Seleznyov nodded that she understood. "Authorize zee stage one separation."

"Looking good," Bill Grayson said, a salesman's smile on his face. "We should have booster separation..." he stopped short when the lights in the control room began to flicker.

CHAPTER THIRTY-ONE

A THIN BEAD OF sweat immediately formed on Bill Grayson's upper lip, and his fleshy face turned pink. He cast a panicked look in the direction of Natalie Seleznyov, who just shrugged. The screen in the front of the room and the overhead lights all clicked off and were replaced by the dim glow of the emergency exit lighting. A terrified young woman approached Grayson and whispered something in his ear. He nodded that he understood. Clearing his throat, he said, "Apparently this section of the City of Los Angeles has experienced a power outage."

"Big Bertha," Penelope muttered as she glanced at Michael Walker. He nodded that he had already come to the same conclusion.

"Natalie?" Walker said softly.

"It has already received the command for the stage one booster to separate which was successful."

"How long before you will need to give the stage two separation command? Walker asked.

"Soon," Seleznyov answered evenly.

"Will that be a problem, Natalie?"

"Difficult to say," she answered. "Ve have redundancies built into the system, but ve used up many of our options when ve lost the primary launch command center. If ve have a prolonged power failure here at the backup command..."

As quickly as the lights had gone out, they began to come back on. The main screen in the front of the room took the longest to reboot. "There is nothing to worry about," Bill Grayson said with as much confidence as he could muster. "As you can see, the Boeing Launch Facility has its own back-up generator."

"What if the generator were to also fail?" Michael Walker asked calmly.

"We have a minimum of 20 minutes of battery backup on all of the critical components."

"Twenty minutes. Will that be long enough?" Walker made eye contact with Seleznyov who shook her head.

Bill Grayson's face turned a brighter pink as he ran a handkerchief across his forehead. "We've tested the system several times but have never actually been in a complete power loss situation at the primary and secondary command centers during a launch before."

"Where do we stand, Natalie?" Walker asked.

Seleznyov held up a finger as her full attention turned to the panel in front of her. "Sergei?" she said to the man at her immediate right.

"We have the second stage separation authorization request," said a gruff elderly man with a gravelly voice. She nodded.

For the next ten seconds no one in the room breathed until Seleznyov broke the silence. "Ve have second stage separation and the board is still green for now." Her eyes locked on Walker's.

"For now?" Walker repeated.

"If ve lose the backup generator ve may lose contact with the rocket."

"Where is our vulnerability?" Walker asked.

"Ve still have to give the command for the third stage positioning block separation," Seleznyov answered. "Once the satellite has separated from the final stage it vill be in high enough orbit that it would disintegrate on reentry and the auto-destruct vill permanently disengage. At that point ve can use positioning thrusters to maneuver it at our leisure and the launch vill be successful."

"How long before you give the final command?"

"If the generator stays on for five more minutes then ve are safe. If ve have to go to battery backup then there vill be an enhanced risk of failure."

"Well," Walker said as he nodded toward the door to the control room, "it's a good thing we posted guards around your generator."

Special Agent Marcus Wolfe of Homeland Security entered the control room dressed in camouflage clothing. "The SWAT team captured an eight-man assault team trying to take out the backup generator," Wolfe said. "They walked right into our trap and not a shot was fired."

"Excellent, Special Agent Wolfe," Walker said. "I guess that makes us even?"

"I guess it does, sir," Wolfe said. All heads turned when two exceedingly large men dressed similarly to Wolfe entered the control room. They were holding one of the Boeing techs by the scruff of the neck. "Does this one belong to you?"

"Yuri?" Seleznyov said in disbelief as her eyes danced back and forth between Walker and her co-worker. "Mikhail, I am so sorry. I've worked with Yuri for over twenty-five years."

Seleznyov began berating the man in rapid fire Russian, and he replied with a shrug and no hint of regret. "I did it for the money."

"How much?" Walker asked with an amused expression on his face.

"Five million Euros to destroy your satellite," Yuri said defiantly. He surveyed the room and shouted, "Five million Euros to anyone who destroys that..." a massive hand was clamped over his mouth as the two Homeland Security men began dragging him out. At the door, Yuri shook free briefly and shouted again, "Five million Euros!"

The seventeen men still manning their consoles eyed each other with suspicion. All were seasoned veterans of the Soviet space program. The youngest man in the room was in his mid-fifties with the oldest approaching seventy. With the Russian retirement plan a sad joke, all were still working because they had to, not because they wanted to. Natalie Seleznyov eyed the rest of her staff to see if anyone was going to take the offer.

"Third stage block separation is required in thirty seconds," said a man with a thick accent in the front row.

"Excellent. In thirty seconds it von't matter if the generator fails." As Natalie Seleznyov turned her attention back to her board; she caught sudden movement out of the corner of her eye. "Sergei, NO!"

At the desk next to hers, Seleznyov's most trusted assistant flipped up the protective cover on a red button and slammed it with the palm of his hand. In less than a heartbeat he was knocked face first to the floor by Special Agent Marcus Wolfe and held there by a knee in the back.

"What just happened?" Penelope demanded.

"Natalie?" Walker said softly.

Natalie Seleznyov had relieved one of the techs of his head set and was holding it to her ear. "Ve have confirmation, Mikhail." The scientist who was harder than nails had tears welling up in her eyes. "One of our people on the USS Ronald Reagan has confirmed a visible explosion in the night sky." A single tear rolled down her cheek. "I am so sorry."

Michael Walker kissed her on both cheeks and then gave her a weak hug. "It wasn't your fault, Natalie." He patted her on the back and said again, "It wasn't your fault."

"Mr. Walker," Grayson said breaking the heavy silence that had settled over the room, "while this is regrettable, by the terms of our contract we have no liability here."

"What!" Penelope shouted as Michael Walker put his arm in front of her to restrain her. "One of your people just intentionally blew up his satellite!"

"While that may be true," Grayson said as he wiped his face again, "by invoking the 'must launch' provision of its contract, Walker Industries assumed all responsibility for any and all eventualities including the launch being sabotaged. Therefore..."

"Shut up, Bill," Penelope said as flames erupted from her eyes. "He knew the risk." Grayson opened his mouth as if to speak, but the expression on Penelope's face made him reconsider.

Walker turned and headed slowly toward the exit.

P ENELOPE HOOKED HER arm under Walker's as they strolled along Boeing's Long Beach pier in the cool night air. At some distant point in her past Penelope may have imagined a romantic midnight stroll along the ocean with Michael Walker, but this was not the way she would have visualized it. Being a working harbor and not a weekender's marina, even on a Sunday night the port was bustling. Under the glare of floodlights a slow moving freighter with shipping containers stacked six high on its deck was inching past. Somewhere in the distance was the sound of heavy machinery, and instead of bracing salt water air there was the faint smell of diesel engines. Despite being called "The Green Port," the three quarter moon reflecting across the water highlighted a collection of small blue and green iridescent petroleum slicks and the occasional floating plastic bottle.

"What happens now?" Penelope asked.

"What do you mean?"

Penelope lowered her eyes, "Is Kent Lazlo really going to hold you to your agreement?"

"Of course," Walker said with a laugh. "Why wouldn't he?"

"He and I had a little chat on my balcony, and he thought this launch was for a replacement for a major satellite that had malfunctioned."

"That was what we wanted everyone to believe."

"If he had known this was for the Hermes Project launch, I doubt he would have taken the deal."

"Why?"

"He wouldn't have let you commit financial suicide."

"Financial suicide?" Walker asked. "Kent said that?"

"No," Penelope answered flatly, "I did. He told me the health of Walker Telecom depended on getting the replacement satellite in orbit and if this launched failed then the division might go bankrupt."

"Again," Walker answered, "that is what we wanted everyone to believe."

"Look," Penelope said as she stopped and turned to face Michael Walker. "I admire the daylights out of what you've done here today. You put the Hermes Project ahead of your own personal wealth, and not many would have your strength of conviction. But if all of the financial stories I've read are right, without a fully functioning communications satellite you are going to be bankrupt."

"Well," Walker said with the familiar gleam in his eyes. "I guess we'll find out if you were right."

"Right about what?" Penelope asked as she rested her head on his shoulder.

"If I'm broke, will the ladies still find me as charming?"

"Can you be serious just once Michael?"

A broad smile broke across his face. "I'm back to Michael. Does that mean you forgive me?"

Penelope shrugged. "I think we've both moved well past the point of needing forgiveness from each other. You are what you are and I am what I am. If we were meant to be..." Before she could finish her thought, Michael Walker swept her into his arms and kissed her.

CHAPTER THIRTY-TWO

"**I** HADN'T ENVISIONED YOU as a screamer," Michael Walker said softly as he stroked Penelope's hair.

Penelope, panting and tucked into the crook of his arm with her head resting on his chest felt her cheeks darken. "Me either."

While Penelope hadn't "gotten around" in high school and college like Josephine, she had never considered herself a prude. Though she had always enjoyed sex, it was never the center of her universe and had always seemed a bit overrated. Joey's wild tales of her philandering ex-husband's natural endowment and bedroom prowess as the reason she hadn't kicked him to the curb years earlier always rang hollow. The idea of mind-blowing, curl-your-toes, eyes-rolled-up-in-the-back-of-your-head, primal-scream sex that lasted for hours had always seemed a figment of her best friend's overly active imagination. Until tonight. Now, on the finest Egyptian cotton sheets at the Beverly Wilshire, for the first time in her life Penelope found out what all the fuss was about.

Round one had been frantic with few preliminaries and a sense of urgency to confirm what was happening was real before either of them woke up. A year of questions were asked and answered in a blur of pent up passion and release. Like a super nova it had burnt out quickly.

Round two was very different. After catching their breath and collecting clothing that had been tossed aside in haste, they sat on the end of the bed in thick terrycloth robes, laughed, talked, and shared the strawberries dipped in the fabulous dark chocolate that room service had delivered. As the conversation began to lag, Walker took her into his arms and showed her the difference between passion and love making. He took his time. Just when she thought she had reached the pinnacle of pleasure, she discovered it was only a plateau and the peak was still somewhere far off in the clouds. Locked in his strong embrace, when the final release came any inhibitions were long forgotten. She was in the moment, didn't want it to end, and didn't care who heard her.

"I have to ask," Penelope said as she nuzzled in closer. "What is so different about us today than three days ago?"

"You are not the same woman," Walker said as he patted down a few hair frizzies that were tickling his nose.

"What does that mean?"

Walker slowly stroked her hair, "Later," he said as he glanced at the clock on the nightstand next to the king-sized bed. "We need to get going."

"Going where?"

"To the world headquarters of Walker Telecom," Walker answered.

"Can't you clean out your desk tomorrow?" Penelope asked as she made finger curls with his chest hair. "I'm pretty comfortable right here."

"You're welcome to stay if you like," Walker said as he tried unsuccessfully to pull away but was reeled back in by Penelope, "but you'll kick yourself later."

Penelope released him and then propped herself up on an elbow and studied Michael Walker's face. His eyes twinkled with mischief. "What are you up to?"

"One way to find out."

"I need a shower first," Penelope said as she started to untangle herself from Walker and the sheets.

Michael Walker snaked his hand under her and pulled her close again. While nibbling on her ear, he whispered, "Would you like some company?"

Round three.

"THANK GOD," SALLY Winters said the moment she saw Penelope and Walker enter the control room of Walker Telecom.

"What?" Penelope demanded.

"We were all about to choke on the sexual tension between you two."

Ian Fleming nodded his agreement.

Penelope lowered her voice as her eyes grew large. "Is it that obvious?"

"Sweetie," Winters said, "if you had any more of a glow I would have to put on my sunglasses."

Penelope glanced sideways at Walker who was trying, without much success, to keep a straight face. She wasn't exactly embarrassed that her bliss was so obvious. She felt like, well, she wasn't sure what she felt like since she had never felt like this before. For the first time in her life she could be completely herself, confident that if she lowered her guard, there would be no price to pay. She was in a relationship without games, one-upmanship, or value judgments. While very different, she knew she and Walker were now like the two off-center characters of *yin* and *yang*. For the moment they had come together to form a perfect circle with endless potential and no limitations. She wasn't going to over think it. Instead she planned to simply enjoy it for as long as the moment lasted. If the past few hours were a harbinger, then she would really enjoy it.

Michael Walker, sensing what she was thinking without the need for words, gave her hand a quick squeeze. Craning his neck he found what he was looking for. He maneuvered around Sally Winters and headed toward the center of the control room. The oversized space was similar in design and function to the Boeing Long Beach command center.

Surrounded by a group of technicians, at first Penelope didn't see her. As the group parted with the approach of Michael Walker, standing in the middle, was a tall, severe woman with her back toward them. When she turned to greet Walker, Penelope's mouth fell open.

Walker kissed her on both cheeks. "Natalie, you deserve an Oscar for your performance. The tear was perfect."

"Thank you Mikhail," Natalie Seleznyov said.

"Where are we on Hermes?" Walker asked.

"Sergei, vhat is the current status of the Hermes satellite?"

Penelope was speechless when the man who had hit the "destruct" button at the Boeing facility just a few hours earlier pivoted in his seat and said, "The solar panels have fully engaged. We have run a level three diagnostic and should be online in ninety seconds."

"Excellent," Seleznyov said. "Yuri, what is the status of the communications satellite?"

The hits just kept on coming for Penelope Drayton Spence as the man who had supposedly tried to blow up the Boeing command center's backup generator answered, "We have restored power to the communication satellite and it is fully functional. We are still transmitting parallel redundant data identical to that of the leased satellites to be sure there are no errors. If we don't experience any problems we should be able to make the cut-over within a few hours."

"Whoa, whoa, whoa," Penelope said as she marched to the middle of the room to quiz Walker. "Let's back up a little. First off, what is she doing here? And second," as she pointed at the men working in front of her, "vhy aren't they in jail?" Penelope asked in a spot on impersonation of Seleznyov.

"She does not know?" Seleznyov asked. Walker shook his head. "Oh, Mikhail, you are such a bad boy," she said as she wagged a finger in his direction. "I have many things to do, so I vill leave you two."

A bemused smile covered Michael Walker's face. "To answer your first question, Natalie is now the Chief Operating Officer of Walker Telecom."

"And them?" Penelope asked as she pointed to the two men working shoulder to shoulder at a massive console.

"Sergei and Yuri are Senior Vice Presidents." Hearing their names, both looked up and waved at Penelope.

Penelope blinked a few times, closed her eyes and rubbed her forehead. "Am I to understand that the Hermes satellite was not destroyed and the telecommunication satellite, whose failure was going to bankrupt you, had merely been turned off for the past few months?"

"Correct," Walker answered.

As Penelope began to process all of this new information and its implications, she began to giggle. The giggle quickly turned into a chuckle then a full blown laugh loud enough to turn heads in the control room. "You are awful! Kursolov will be kicking himself with both feet."

Michael Walker shrugged, "I told you this was going to be fun. What we did..."

"No, no, no," Penelope said cutting across him. "Let me take a whack at this and you correct me when I miss something." Walker motioned for her to continue. "You've had the Hermes satellite finished for months, but you had to get around Robert Smith."

"We figured..." Walker started to say before Penelope held up a finger to stop him.

"I'm the one writing this story." Walker again motioned for her to continue. "Much to your surprise, Smith, with more than a little help from Viktor Kursolov, had come close to securing you a spot on a NASA launch. This caused you to go to plan 'B', your cable TV meltdown." Penelope waited for an acknowledgement, which she got in the form of a nod. "With the NASA pooch screwed your original plan was back on track. You figured having it in your building would be irresistible, and they took the bait." Penelope's eyes narrowed. "Hmm, one question."

"What would that be?" Walker asked.

"When you bought the building nearly a year ago, did you really expect it to be blown up?"

"We considered it a high probability."

"How long have you been planning this?" Penelope asked.

"You said one question."

"Bite me," Penelope answered.

"Bite me?" Walker said with a laugh. "That doesn't sound like the delicate flower I know."

"I'm releasing my inner Josephine. The days of trying to live up to the limitations put on me by my mom and grandmother are in the rearview mirror. Besides, all pretenses between us are long gone."

"Plus," Walker said with a laugh, "I've seen you naked."

"Calm down Sparky, unless you want that to be a onetime event. You said you would answer all of my questions, so go ahead and get started. How long have you been planning this?"

"We started this in motion immediately after Homeland Security had the problem with the test volunteers."

"That was six months before you even met me."

"Correct."

"So my foray with the Fourth Awakening a year ago was just one small part of this grand master plan?"

"Yes. Getting worldwide exposure for the Hermes Project with your help was phase two."

"Phase two? What was phase one?" Penelope asked. Walker waited a few seconds to let her work it out. "Ah, of course," she said, "you had to be sure Hermes would work first."

"Correct."

"Okay," Penelope said as she rubbed her hands together. "Then you turned off your cash cow satellite so Kursolov would assume the unguarded one at the Boeing facility was a replacement, but it was really Hermes."

"Correct."

"Question, do you really have a replacement satellite stashed somewhere?"

"Yes," Walker answered, "but it is not a replacement unit. It will just add capacity. We needed..."

"Yeah, yeah," Penelope said, "without a real satellite in production, you would never be able to convince Kursolov it existed." Walker nodded.

Penelope's eyes unfocused as her mind raced ahead. "So," she said to herself, "How could you be sure Kursolov would try to sink the Boeing Sea Launch *Commander*?"

Walker laughed. "Kursolov didn't try to sink the ship."

"Then who put the charges on the hull?"

"We did."

CHAPTER THIRTY-THREE

"Y OU DID WHAT!?" Penelope shouted loud enough to turn heads. "You could have gotten us all killed!"

"That's highly unlikely," Walker said with a shrug and a wave. "While they did poke a few pretty good sized holes in the hull, even with no emergency repairs, it would have taken the ship at least an hour to sink."

"That is not the least bit reassuring," Penelope answered.

"How about this," Walker said chuckling. "It was daytime, we had calm seas, there wasn't a cloud in any direction for at least 500 miles in any direction. We also had about a third of the U.S. Navy's Pacific fleet within eyeshot. For everyone who might have potentially hit the water, there were ten waiting to pull them out."

Penelope folded her arms across her chest and glared at Walker. "So what was the point?"

"We figured Kursolov likely had at least half a dozen men on board who would have been both able and willing to sabotage our launch, so we had to get control of the launch away from the Boeing command ship."

"What good did it do to transfer launch control to Long Beach? Wasn't there the same risk of sabotage..." As was usually the case when she was processing information, Penelope's eyes began to dance from side to side before finally locking on Natalie Seleznyov. Walker's smile grew larger as he watched and waited for Penelope to put the final pieces in place. "Oh My God! She transferred the launch codes to this facility and not to Boeing's back-up location. The Hermes launch was never at risk!" Walker touched the end of his nose. Penelope's eyes started moving again. "So that means everything that happened in Long Beach was just more smoke and mirrors."

"Exactly." Walker nodded in the direction of Sergei and Yuri. "They are the only two men Natalie completely trusts, and the ruse was too much for one person to pull off by herself. While everyone thought

Sergei was acting as flight commander he was actually insuring that no one else in the room figured out what was happening. The other techs at the Boeing facility were all getting the rocket telemetry in real-time but every command had to pass through here."

"But why the big production of having these men captured?" Penelope asked.

"It was a simple diversion," Walker answered. "I had let it slip at Josephine's party that not only do I speak Russian, but it was a requirement for my senior staff and security details. He couldn't be sure if we were listening in on voice communications. Plus," Walker said as he placed a hand on Yuri's shoulder, "starting about the time of Josephine's party, the Sea Launch *Commander* began experiencing communications problems. The internet and email were both offline. "

"What about ship-to-ship radio?" Penelope asked.

"Kursolov had a surveillance trawler about 300 miles from the launch site, but it had a US Navy destroyer off its bow for the past two days," Walker said. "We did everything possible to cut off all of his lines of communication. When combined with the fact that he didn't have much time to plan for this, we were pretty confident our charade would work."

"How does that help you?" Penelope asked.

"You've met Kursolov. Does he strike you as the kind of person you would want to cross?"

"Absolutely not," she answered softly.

"So," Walker said, "if you were a Kursolov operative and you had not received any direct orders to destroy this particular satellite, what would your first inclination be?"

"Sit tight and await orders."

"If while sitting there waiting for orders," Walker said, "you saw what you thought was a successful effort to blow up our satellite, what would you do?"

Penelope nodded her head that she understood. "I'd put my head down, shut my mouth and start thinking about my dinner plans."

"That was exactly the result we were looking for. We didn't need anyone feeling the need to show any initiative so we gave them a floor show to keep them occupied."

"Wait a minute," Penelope said. "Kursolov had to know he had not ordered the attack on the Boeing ship."

"True," Walker answered, "but he also knew there were other players who didn't want to see Hermes in orbit."

"Ahh," Penelope nodded. "That's why you made such a big production out of Lucas arriving with Chinese-built explosives. He wasn't showing them to you, he was showing them to everyone else in the room."

"Exactly. We figured eventually someone would let Kursolov know what had happened, and even he has to tread lightly if he thinks the Chinese are involved."

"Where exactly do you get Chinese contact mines?" Penelope asked.

"*eBay.*"

"Is it within you to be serious for more than ten seconds at a time?"

"Probably not."

"I can believe that," Penelope said with a sigh, "but why go through the Kabuki dance of pretending to blow up your satellite?"

"After a satellite reaches the proper orbit, it still has to deploy. This means it has to jettison all of the packaging material and extend its solar panels. This takes about four hours and during that time it is a sitting duck for an anti-satellite attack."

A puzzled expression covered Penelope's face. "Hold on. If the satellite didn't explode, what did they see on the *USS Ronald Reagan*?"

"Natalie rigged a charge in the second stage booster, and once it had separated from the positioning booster and had fallen far enough away to not impact the satellite, we detonated it. We figured Kursolov had ships monitoring the launch, and the clear visual indication of a massive failure would muddy the water further and give us more time to deploy."

Penelope rubbed her chin as she tried to think of any more questions she needed to ask. Her mind retraced the past few days and ended up on her balcony with Kent Lazlo. "Is the new CEO of Walker Industries going to be pleased when he discovers the backbone of Walker Telecom had not malfunctioned but had been intentionally disabled?"

"Kent knows me pretty well," Walker said with a wry smile. "When he heard it was a one hundred percent certainty that the communication satellite would not be an issue, he knew everything was under control."

Penelope laughed. "Like your one hundred percent certainty that the Boeing command ship was going to be attacked since you were the one arranging it?

"Exactly," Walker answered with a laugh. "Timothy gave him an update a few hours ago, and Sally will have a press release out before the markets open in New York. Everyone who dumped Walker Industries in the past few weeks is going to be kicking themselves after the opening bell."

Penelope nodded that she understood, then her eyes flew open. "Wait a minute! That means you're not broke!"

"Nope," he said with a laugh, "I'm still stinking rich."

"And charming," Penelope said with a wry smile as she ran her hand up his chest.

Natalie Seleznyov approached with a sterner than usual expression on her face. "Excuse me. Mikhail, Viktor Kursolov is on the secure com line and vants to talk to you."

CHAPTER THIRTY-FOUR

Penelope and Walker headed down the corridor a half stride behind Natalie Seleznyov, and two strides ahead of Timothy Ellison and Ian Fleming. "Pretty heavy duty security," Penelope noted as they approached a door which required both a palm and iris scan for entry.

Michael Walker seemed as pensive as he had been the night of Josephine's party. "We do a great deal of top secret work for a variety of agencies," Walker said absently as he waited for Natalie to open the door.

Penelope was incredulous. "Viktor Kursolov was able to just dial you up on a secured communications network?"

"He's resourceful," Walker said as he shifted his weight back and forth. In the first attempt the iris scanner failed to recognize Seleznyov and she had to try again.

"How much of this is on the record?" Penelope asked.

"As far as I'm concerned, from this point forward everything is on the record."

"Really?"

"Yep," Walker said as the thick door finally swished open and they entered a room nearly identical to the one where Penelope had watched the terrorist take-down. It was dimly lit with a large screen in the front. The only major difference was the higher ceiling which allowed for three rows of eight theater-style tiered seats. "No more games, we're out of moves."

Before Penelope could respond the screen in front of them came to life. Sitting behind a desk, about three times his normal size was Viktor Kursolov. "Michael."

Walker moved to the middle of the area in front of the seats and stood on an "x" painted on the floor. "Viktor."

"I just received a report that you have managed to overcome the problem with your primary communications satellite, Michael. That must be a comfort after the loss earlier today."

"What loss would that be Viktor?"

"I have heard there was an incident in Long Beach and there were reports of an explosion over the launch site."

"Fortunately," Walker said with a rare edge to his voice, "the incident had no impact on the launch and the explosion was merely some extra fuel in the second stage booster igniting in the atmosphere."

"So I am to understand your launch was a success?"

"Yes," Walker answered. "The Hermes Project satellite is in orbit and fully functional."

"That is very good news indeed," Kursolov said in a dull monotone. "It is hard to imagine that I could have been so badly misinformed, especially since this information came from eyewitnesses."

"Perhaps I could clarify that for you," Walker said evenly. "Do you have access to the major financial wire services where you are?" Walker asked.

"Of course," was Kursolov's guarded answer. "Why do you ask?"

"There should be an announcement coming across about the new Chief Operations Officer for Walker Telecom." Walker motioned for Natalie Seleznyov to join him at the front of the room and within view of the camera. "We have also acquired the services of Yuri Ivanski and Sergei Turov."

"I see," said Kursolov without flinching, "that explains many things. Congratulations Natalie." Walker nodded, and she moved back out of camera range.

"Walker Telecom was fortunate to get her and her associates, having lost a senior person this weekend. How is Robert Smith?"

"Settling in nicely," Kursolov said as he forced himself to control his anger. "I'll give him your regards."

"I must apologize, Viktor. I know you are a major shareholder in Boeing Sea Launch. I'm afraid some of my men did some rather extensive damage to the Sea Launch *Commander.* Please be assured they will be dealt with accordingly. Send me the repair bill."

"I will do that, Michael." Viktor Kursolov squirmed slightly. "I believe you also owe me a bottle of Macallan"

"Really?" A flicker of a smile broke on Walker's face but quickly vanished. "So with the satellite in position you have abandoned your efforts?"

"As I told you the other evening I have never tried to duplicate your Hermes project, Michael." Viktor Kursolov's eyes narrowed and a knowing grin covered his face. "While you were developing your little novelty, I was working on something much more interesting."

"What would that be, Viktor?"

"Are you aware that over one third of the world's population lives within 3,000 miles of my villa here in Kazakhstan?"

"What is your point, Viktor?"

"Why should I bother with a play toy when I have nearly limitless human assets? I'll have one of my assistants arrange for delivery of the whiskey. You will be hearing from me again soon."

The screen went dark.

Walker was scratching his chin while still staring at the now blank screen. "That certainly took an ugly turn," Walker said.

"How so?" Penelope asked.

"It appears I wasn't toying with Kursolov; he was toying with me."

EPILOGUE

"THE MAN IS insatiable," Penelope said with a sigh.
"You say that like it's a bad thing," Josephine answered with a laugh as she took a sip of wine. "It sounds like us before our first marriages."

"Us? What's this 'us' nonsense?" Penelope said while shaking her head. "I was the good girl, remember?"

Josephine crinkled her nose as a cool, fresh breeze swept in off the Ashley River. "I keep forgetting I had much more fun in high school and college than you did."

"That's the understatement of the year," Penelope said with a sideways glance.

"Be nice." Josephine nodded toward the path leading back in the direction of a massive white tent that had been erected between Drayton Hall and the Ashley River. "We'd better be getting back. It wouldn't do for the mother of the bride to be gone too long." Josephine hooked her arm under Penelope's as they headed back toward the tent. "Nice turn-out."

"I really owe Sally one for this. To pull this off in a month was incredible."

Josephine nodded. "Having Prince 'What's His Name' was a nice touch. Even with the future queen being a Middleton, I didn't have British Royalty for my wedding."

Penelope patted Josephine's hand. "Don't worry, your first wedding is still the gold standard for Charleston."

"Hmm," Josephine said as she made a face.

"Hmm what?"

"Now I'm worried," Josephine said as she finished her wine and looked for a place to jettison the glass. "You still have an unmarried daughter."

"As do you," Penelope answered. "Is there a point somewhere in my future?"

"If Sally could pull something like this off on such short notice, what if she had had more time?" Josephine asked.

Penelope shook her head and muttered, "Demented."

"Enough of that," Josephine said, "let's get back to the important stuff. Has lover boy given you a pet name yet?"

"What in the world are you talking about?" Penelope asked.

"You know," Josephine said, "the kind of name that would mortify you if your children ever heard it."

"Are you twelve years old?" Penelope pulled her lifelong friend closer. They walked a few paces in silence before Penelope said softly, "Miss Scarlett."

"Oh fiddle-dee-dee," Josephine said as she nodded her approval and began fanning herself. "That is nice on so many levels. And what do you call him?"

"None of your business."

"It must be good," Josephine said as she pulled Penelope to a stop. "Give."

"No," Penelope said flatly.

"Okay," Josephine said as she started walking again.

"Wait a minute," Penelope said as she pulled her lifelong friend to a stop. "What are you going to do?"

"If you won't tell me," Josephine said as she tilted her head and smiled, "I'll just make one up and spread it around to all of our friends."

"You wouldn't." Penelope closed her eyes and rubbed her forehead. "What am I saying? Of course you would." Penelope leaned in close. "If you tell a living soul..."

Josephine made a sweeping "X" over her chest. "Cross my heart."

"Rocket Man," Penelope whispered.

Josephine burst out laughing wagged a finger in Penelope's direction. "We are definitely going to need to hear more about this."

"Maybe later," Penelope said as she nodded up the path. Approaching from the opposite direction were Ian Fleming and a woman he had introduced as his mother when they'd made their way past Penelope in the receiving line. In their brief time together Ian had not given the impression of being much of a lady's man. But, Penelope had sensed, when he introduced his mother, that there was more going on than Ian's inability to find a date. The woman was roughly the same age as Penelope and Josephine and had the most remarkable pale blue eyes. They met halfway between the spectacular river overview of Drayton Hall and the billowing white wedding tent.

Penelope nodded at the woman on Ian's arm before turning her attention on him. "You vanished right after the launch. Where in the world have you been?"

Fleming glanced at his mother, a look that didn't escape either Penelope or Josephine. "Here and there," he said as he gave Penelope a hug. "We're leaving soon," Fleming said as he pulled away from the embrace, "but Mom insisted on talking to you first."

Penelope turned and faced Ms. Fleming. The two mothers' eyes locked. "I don't know how to thank you," said Mrs. Fleming.

Penelope smiled. It had taken her awhile but she had finally figured how Ian could have been involved with the Hermes Project for so long without her ever meeting him. While she was at Jackson Hole, he had been confined to a mental ward. "I really didn't have much to do with it," Penelope answered. "It was mostly Dr. Altman and Mr. Walker."

Ian Fleming's mother touched Penelope gently on the cheek as tears welled up in her eyes. Her hand was warm and soft. "All I know is my son spent nearly a year in the hospital before you arrived, and a week later he was home again." Her pale blue eyes began to overflow with tears that ran down both cheeks. "If there is any way to thank you..."

"She has another daughter," Josephine offered. Penelope shot her a look that would stop an unruly two year old dead in her tracks. "What? I'm just saying."

"For everything your son has given me, Mrs. Fleming, I would have to say the books are balanced." Penelope gave her a hug and then wagged a warning finger in Ian's direction."

"You stay in touch, young man."

A broad smile broke across his face. "Yes ma'am."

The four headed back in the direction of the tent together. "So," Penelope asked, "what was Ian like when he was a child? Was he always this laid back?"

"Lord no. He was a nightmare."

"Mom," Ian protested, "Ms. Spence doesn't need to hear about my misspent youth."

"Maybe not," Josephine said as she released her grip on Penelope's arm and exchanged it for Mrs. Fleming's, "but I'm certainly interested." As Josephine and her new friend started walking away, Penelope heard Josephine say, "If things don't work out with Penelope's little darling, I happen to have a daughter, too."

Alone on the path, Penelope turned to Ian and asked, "What have you been up to for the past month?"

"Mr. Walker has me traveling around the world trying to build alliances."

"What kind of alliance and with whom?" Fleming shook his head. "I should have known," Penelope said with a sigh. "Michael just seems so preoccupied with Viktor Kursolov."

"As well he should be," Fleming answered.

"Has Kursolov developed something to compete with the Hermes technology?"

"If it were only that simple," Fleming said with a sigh. "I'm really not the one to be talking to about this. I've probably said too much already."

"Fair enough," Penelope said as she hooked her arm under Ian's and started heading back toward the tent. "Come on. I'll introduce you to my daughter." They both laughed.

THE CROWD HAD thinned out to just the hard core of close friends and family. All of the dignitaries and celebrities were long gone. The Secret Service had packed up their airport style metal detectors, and the parking lot was now nearly empty. The band was playing softly, but no one was dancing. This party was running out of steam.

Penelope, sitting alone on a white folding chair, was exhausted but it had been a remarkable day. For the past month Michael had helped her to release any residual anger she held toward her family, and it had worked like a charm. Even being in close proximity for the past three days with the trio of her mother, brother and ex-husband hadn't been able to rattle her.

She had thought since she was seven that her brother Rob was 'poopy head' and her mother was a 'big meany'. While her vocabulary had improved over the years the sentiment hadn't, until recently. Now, with a lifetime of personal baggage in the cosmic landfill, for the first time she was actually enjoying their company. The things she had found so annoying previously only made her laugh. Like everyone else they had been molded and shaped by the world and the people around them and were still a work in progress. The past was gone and the future had not arrived. In the moment they were pretty nice people that she shared a common history with.

Even her ex-husband Bill had been a pleasant surprise. While the parents' dance had the potential to be awkward, it was anything but. The few years since their divorce had been enough time for old wounds on both sides to heal and memories of the good times to take their place. And in the nearly three decades in which they had raised three wonderful kids together, there had been plenty of good times. Watching Bill and Carrie both bawling like babies while they danced to "Daddy's Little Girl" was a highlight of the evening.

A smile covered Penelope's face when she saw Michael Walker on the other side of the room talking to her son William. Walker had changed into the Speakeasy style tuxedo he had worn the night they'd danced the tango in Jackson Hole. Flanking William were Penelope's daughters, Kelly and the bride, Carrie Drayton Ellison. They were all listening intently to Walker with smiles on their faces. William shook Walker's hand, and Penelope watched as both of her girls gave him a hug and a kiss on the cheek. What was that man up to now?

Michael Walker turned and left her children and walked straight toward Penelope. When he arrived, he held out his hand. "Ms. Spence."

Penelope accepted his hand. "Mr. Walker."

"A tango?"

"Argentine?"

"Is there any other kind?" With a flourish, Penelope flipped out of her shawl and rose to her feet. To her surprise, all of the remaining guests were already on their feet and jockeying for position around the edge of the dance floor. "Maestro, if you please. A tango!" A ripple of applause filled the nearly empty tent. When they reached the center of the floor, Walker spun Penelope away, but instead of immediately pulling her back in he released her hand and the band stopped playing.

Confused, Penelope glanced first at Michael Walker and then caught the eye of all of her children. The trio had tears running down their cheeks. "What in the world is going on?" Penelope thought to herself. She turned her attention back to Walker and immediately got her answer.

Michael James Walker was on one knee in front of her. He had an oversized blue Tiffany box in his hand.

"Penelope Drayton Spence. Here in front of our wonderful friends and family, I ask you this question. Would you to do me the great honor of becoming my wife?"

Read the First Book in the Series, available on Kindle:

The Fourth Awakening

AMAZON REVIEWS FOR
THE FOURTH AWAKENING

"I read some of the other reviews, which warned that once started it is impossible to put down this book. "Pshaw, nonsense!" said I, that is until the sun rose this morning as I was finishing the last page."

S. L. OREILLY

"Wow! This book totally caught me from the first page till the last!"

SHERRON THOMPSON

"This book was just flat out fun. Well written with lots of twists. The only complaint is that the next one in the series is not out."

S. D. FORD

"Wow this book kept me up late at night. What a book!"

N. DROUIN "TELL me about books"

"Once I started the book, couldn't put it down."

MATRIXTRAVELER

"This is a must read no matter your taste. Fast paced page turner with a plot that makes you think. I can't recommend this book highly enough on a scale of 1 - 10 I give it a 20."

STUCK IN LA

"Reading this book was the most fun I've had in quite awhile! It is definitely hard to put down! I read it in one day by starting it during my lunch break and finishing it in one late evening. Hoo boy!"

DIANA L. ENDRESEN

"What else do I need to say? I couldn't put it down. It was a perfect Sunday spent with a good book."

DANMILLER

"I couldn't put this one down! Half way thru the first Chapter I knew I wouldn't be able to stop reading until I was finished."

CAROL

"Plain and simple, this book is 5 stars."

JAMESQ

"I've tried to sell my friends on reading this book by telling them that it's like a Dan Brown novel. And it is. Except it's better."

TANA SCHOTT

"I don't remember when I enjoyed reading a book more than this one."

MIKE

"Wow! This book totally caught me from the first page till the last!"

SHEBIE

Visit Us on FaceBook as:

The Fourth Awakening
Rod Pennington
and Jeffery A. Martin

If you have any questions or comments
AskRod@RodPennington.net

Rod Pennington will personally answer every email

THE GOD FORMULA

*A simple scientifically proven blueprint that
has transformed millions of lives*

By
Dr. Jeffery A. Martin

O VER THE LAST decade a revolutionary scientific research project
has been taking place that's led to major advances in how to produce
what seem like miraculous results in your life, and extraordinary levels
of meaning and happiness. The research (conducted by the Center for
the Study of Intent) uncovered a new dimension of human development
and has revolutionized the way personal growth, meaning, happiness,
and ultimately advanced spiritual topics such as 'enlightenment' are
understood. The results, if you let them, will transform the quality of
your life in ways you currently cannot even imagine as possible.

During the research a formula was uncovered that is so effective at
producing what seems like miracles in people's lives it began to be referred
to as the "God Formula" among participants and researchers. This book
outlines that formula and is the final version of the highly successful
training material that was used with research participants. The result
has been the discovery of a series of techniques that lead from everyday
consciousness to increased daily happiness and satisfaction, and finally to
enlightenment and beyond (yes, there is a beyond!).

It's important that you not take the information this book contains
lightly. Unlike other personal growth and self-help books, this one is

driven by a vast amount of actual research into what works. It was revised continually based on research participant feedback so it's very simple and easy to understand and use. Don't let this simplicity fool you. Every line is there for a reason. This material has changed a lot of lives, if you'll let it...yours can be next.

If you like fast-paced dark political comedy fiction

A FAMILY REUNION

(A Charon Family Adventure)

By
Rod Pennington

Decades earlier Michael Charon was the head of a division of the CIA that fulfilled so many "wet" hit contracts it was code named "Water Works." Blindsided by a media leak after a covert mission gone bad, Charon found himself in the political crosshairs. The ensuing scandal created a firestorm in Washington which required a high profile scapegoat. To protect his team, Charon cut a deal. Instead of embarrassing The Company by pointing fingers or naming names, he fell on his own sword.

After a seven-year self-imposed exile, when he traveled throughout the Far East, Charon resurfaced in Washington. With unexplained but seemingly unlimited funding, he set up an ultra-high-end boutique security firm. With a knack for getting results in impossible situations and a history of keeping his mouth shut, the services of Sariel International were soon much in demand by the rich and the powerful of the world.

Charon's life is turned upside down when a beautiful but mysterious young woman appears unannounced at his office. He soon learns that members of his old Water Works team have come out of retirement and for unknown reasons are killing each other.

When he follows the trail, he discovers the identity of the person who had leaked the story years earlier and the startling reason why.

CPSIA information can be obtained
at www.ICGtesting.com
Printed in the USA
BVHW031306240619
551819BV00001B/26/P

9 781572 420021